Inside the pages of this stunning cookbook, you'll find:

- **Nutrient-dense recipes that can be adapted to any diet:** Simple, whole-food, plant-forward, and gluten-free recipes offer maximum nutrition without compromising flavor. Recipes are clearly labeled when they are vegan, dairy-free, or grain-free.

- **Health benefits to match your unique needs:** Nutritional icons on every recipe highlight those that are high in fiber or protein or low in carbohydrates, and a health benefit classification system shows those that are supportive of gut health, beauty and anti-aging, detoxification, and more.

- **Recipes for every day, all day:** Mikaela's accessible and easy-to-follow recipes are meant to mix and match, and she shares countless suggestions for how to combine them into delicious, balanced meals.

eat to love

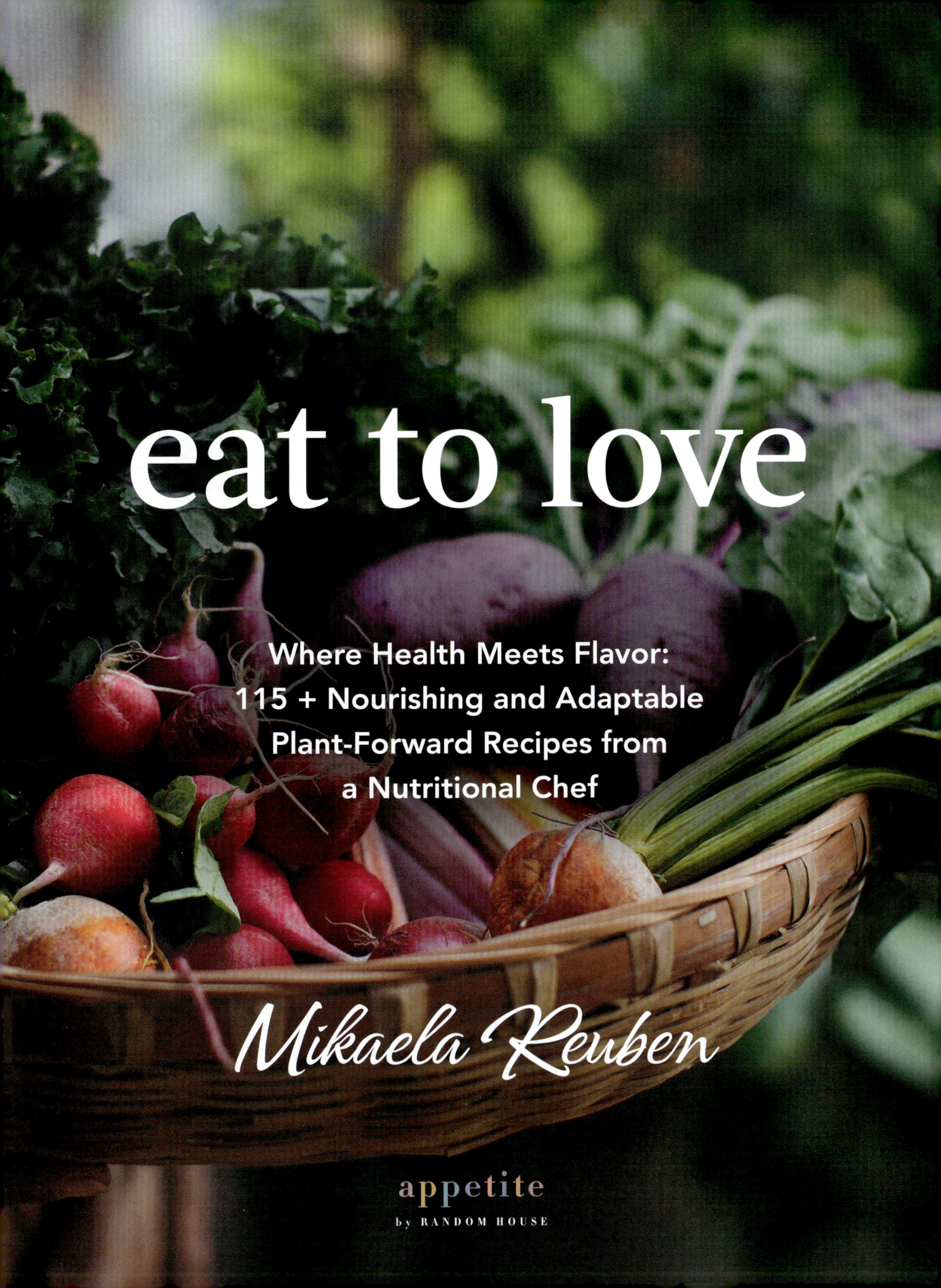

eat to love

Where Health Meets Flavor:
115 + Nourishing and Adaptable
Plant-Forward Recipes from
a Nutritional Chef

Mikaela Reuben

appetite
by RANDOM HOUSE

Appetite by Random House® and colophon are registered trademarks of Penguin Random House LLC.

The content of this book is for informational purposes only. It is not intended to serve as a diagnostic tool or prescription manual, or to replace the advice and care of your medical doctor. Please be certain to consult with your doctor or other healthcare professional for recommendations that are specific to your health needs, before making any decisions that could affect your health.

Library and Archives of Canada Cataloguing in Publication is available upon request.

ISBN: 978-0-525-61214-8
eBook ISBN: 978-0-525-61215-5

Photography by Robyn Penn
Food styling and additional photography by Sophie MacKenzie on pages 51, 53, 77, 92 (bottom right), 94, 117, 149, 167, 185, 193, 197, 207, 209, 210 (bottom left), 213, 215, 230 (top right and bottom left), 235, 238–39, 249, 261, 265
Photo on pages 33–34 by Callum Gunn
Cover and book design by Erin Cooper and Kelly Hill
Typeset by Erin Cooper and Kianna Mkhonza

Printed in China

The authorized representative in the EU for product safety and compliance is Penguin Random House Ireland, Morrison Chambers, 32 Nassau Street, Dublin D02 YH68, Ireland, https://eu-contact.penguin.ie

Published in Canada by Appetite by Random House®,
a division of Penguin Random House Canada Limited.
320 Front Street West, Suite 1400
Toronto Ontario, M5V 3B6, Canada
penguinrandomhouse.ca

10 9 8 7 6 5 4 3 2 1

appetite
by RANDOM HOUSE

Penguin
Random House
Canada

For my two resilient
grandmothers,
for all you endured so
I could be here today.

And for Wayno,
the chef who died
before his time.
You took a chance
on me and changed
my life forever.

Contents

Introduction

Before I became a chef, and before I knew anything about nutrition, I just knew I loved food. Food is like magic to me on so many levels: food is dynamic and delicious, it fuels our bodies, and it is at the center of our survival. Food connects us with ourselves and other people, and food can tell a story.

My story is that food has always represented love. I come from a family who expressed their love through food. My paternal grandparents were concentration camp survivors; they knew and felt starvation. Mealtimes became very important to them; feeding their family was their ultimate show of love, and my father passed down this appreciation for food to my sister and me. In my grade 9 writing class, when we were asked to define love, I said, "Love is a warm mango in the palm of my mother's hand." I've thought about that sentence so many times since then, and it still holds true.

From a young age, I had a natural curiosity about cooking. I loved to explore the magic of ingredients, concocting potions out of brightly colored flower petals and oils, then trying to sell them on the street for a dollar. I would sneak up to the kitchen in the middle of the night, mixing all kinds of flours and berries in bowls and baking the result in the oven. Nothing ever worked, and I almost set the house on fire, but I was enthralled by the experiments.

When we took family trips through the Pacific Northwest in our Westfalia van, I would build little "cooking" areas in the forest with stumps and a campfire, slowly bringing things to temperature on warm coals or rocks and finding makeshift surfaces to work on (something I still do!). Fallen branches as brooms, shells to hold desserts; creating make-believe kitchens was how I liked to play. The way food transformed during cooking really fueled my imagination–I was in awe watching what each ingredient could become. What happens when I apply heat to a vegetable, or pickle it, or mix it with lemon? There was, and always has been, an infinite potential of something more, depending on how I dreamt it to be.

There was, and always has been, an infinite potential of something more, depending on how I dreamt it to be.

I've always loved food, but my true curiosity about *healthy* food began when my dad had a heart attack when I was 17. Instead of going the surgical route to turn his health around, he committed

to using food as his medicine. For two years, he tried every diet out there, and eventually found a unique combination that really worked for him. His skin improved, his mood improved, he lost 65 pounds, and he began running marathons again, healthier than he had ever been. Witnessing his food-based transformation started me on a path that shaped my life and has literally taken me around the world.

While my dad was on his journey back to health, I was doing my undergraduate degree in kinesiology. Growing up, I had been an athlete, and I loved learning about the extraordinary machinery of our bodies, how there are many cause-and-effect systems that elicit a certain physical response. For example, every time I walk up a hill, my endurance and strength grow. The natural next question for me was, what happens when I eat? I became wildly interested in how food impacts our bodies. I was studying basic nutrition as part of my undergrad, but it left me wanting more. I started to study on my own, reading every nutrition book I could find.

I also started traveling a lot—I was dating a pilot at the time, and I made the most of it! We would fly off to these amazing places around the world whenever I had a school break. I began exploring the different food cultures, health rituals, and customs in each country. I loved taking cooking classes wherever I landed, attending them in at least 10 countries before I was 21! I was so fascinated and inspired by the way you can learn about a culture through the lens of food: what grows locally and how it builds community; how people share their stories and recipes by passing them down through generations. I saw human connections form around a fire, a table, or a stove. It wasn't just eating to survive, it was eating to love.

After I graduated (and broke up with the pilot), I went to Maui and crashed on my friend Robyn's couch for a while. I was in major debt from school and really questioning what would

come next. I had a degree that interested me but was not what made my heart come to life. I wanted to understand the *whole* body and felt there was still a piece missing, and I knew it had to do with understanding food. I thought I should go back to school and applied to a physio-therapy master's program. Or maybe I could look into studying nutrition? What about cooking school? What I really wanted was something that combined nutrition and cooking, but none of the programs I looked at encompassed both.

When I was talking to Robyn one day, she said, "Why don't we try making a cookbook?" It would be a heart-healthy cookbook that would give back, inspired by my dad's health journey–I would do the cooking, and she would do the photographs. I didn't think I could make a cookbook–I wasn't a chef yet (and she wasn't a photographer yet either)–but we decided to be open to dreaming for the day. Spoiler alert: that cookbook didn't happen! But it did start my career as a nutritional chef.

Robyn suggested we shoot some of my recipes at her friend and neighbor's house. He happened to be a famous actor and was supposed to be out of town. We set everything up for our shoot, and I started cooking, making a giant mess as usual (doing the dishes has never been my strength!). We had just started taking the pictures when, suddenly, the owner showed up with a bunch of friends and his professional chef. The chef freaked out! He was meant to be cooking lunch, and we had just trashed his kitchen. He tried to kick us out, but I was so scared that I could hardly move. I just stood there, cleaning my dishes–then I sneakily started helping him with his so

I could ask him questions about his work. He began to soften and told me about himself and his career. His name was Wayno, and he was not just a chef but a nutritional chef, a job I had never even heard of. I couldn't believe it! His career sounded so exciting–the challenge to be creative and adapt to new clients in diverse settings, all while making fresh and vibrant food–it was literally everything I had dreamt of.

I asked if I could accompany him to the market the next day, and he agreed. There, we talked about how to pick the best tomato and the ripest avocado, then we carried everything we'd gathered back to the kitchen to cook. We spent two weeks like this, visiting markets every day and then cooking together, and he opened my mind to so many healthy and nutritious ways of preparing food.

Then I found out, two days before it started, that I had gotten into the physiotherapy master's program I had applied for back in Canada. Although I felt like I had finally found my passion, a career in nutritional cooking, and I was learning so much from my mentor, I also felt I couldn't give up on school just yet. My grandmother was the first woman accepted into pre-med in Warsaw, at the age of 17, just before the Second World War began. She survived the Holocaust, and migrated to Canada, but had to forgo her dreams of medical school in the process. Her greatest life tenet was that education meant freedom. So even though this new path was calling my name, I held the words of my grandmother in my heart. I left Maui and went back to school in Vancouver.

I was miserable in the master's program, and I never once stopped dreaming about a life as a traveling nutritional chef. So about a year in, when Wayno called out of the blue and asked if I would like to cook for the actor I'd met on Maui, I *immediately* said yes. I dropped out of school, packed my bags, scraped up enough money for a one-way ticket to Paris (where Wayno was working on the actor's movie set), and never looked back.

♥

For many years, I trained under Wayno: he was my mentor, a chef at the cutting edge of his profession, and I learned so much from him. He would call me to help him with jobs in celebrities' homes and on movie sets–once, we even toured the world with a rock band, sleeping in buses and waking up in new cities every day, where I'd have to run around frantically looking for ingredients! He believed in me, trusted me, and loved my food. And most importantly, he never dismissed me as being "just" a young woman. To supplement his training, I signed up for any kind of nutrition course and certification I could find, even doing online classes while chopping a client's vegetables in their kitchen! In the process, I became certified as a holistic nutritionist, sports nutritionist, and raw food chef.

My career as a nutritional chef began to take shape, and I was suddenly being recommended from one client to the next. I decided early on to say YES to every invitation I received–even the most unlikely ones. As a result, I've spent the last 15 years working for clients all over the world, in the private homes of actors, athletes, and supermodels, creating health and nutrition plans and cooking up a storm. I've contributed to magazines, consulted for large companies, and been hired to create meal plans for naturopaths and recipes for the cookbooks of some leading functional medicine doctors. I've cooked in a jungle on a wellness retreat, I've curated local menus for Olympic athletes at the Brazilian Summer Games, and I've toured Europe with a breakdance team. I've catered and hauled a picnic up a giant cliff face to watch the sunrise in Jackson Hole, Colorado, and I've slow-cooked tomato sauce with an 80-year-old grandmother in a candlelit cave in the south of Italy (using her family recipe, which preserves history in every mouthful). I even got to cook for the Dalai Lama's 80th birthday.

My path to becoming a nutritional chef has been anything but traditional. Pursuing this career meant reimagining my life's path, and it took me over a decade of questioning myself to fully appreciate that my choice to not complete my studies was valid too. I now know education comes in many forms, including lived experiences and learning from knowledge in practice. It's not been an easy course, and I've failed as many times as I've succeeded. There have been many challenges, and emotional and physically stressful times, but I don't regret jumping in and trusting my dream of traveling and cooking, because it landed me where I am today.

For me, food was, and still is, creativity and magic, nourishment and love. Food has brought me opportunities and friendships, and allowed me the privilege of travel. I have been so fortunate to have explored different cultures through their cuisines, inspired by and witness to how people around the world express love through food. It has been my tool for connection and has always given me a path forward.

Over the years, I've also seen the power food has to heal and the amazing impact it can have on our health. I've learned how to listen to and nourish the senses and the body. I've learned that nourishing others is an amazing act. But I think the most important thing I've learned is how to nourish myself. Cooking for yourself truly is one of the most beautiful forms of self-love, and even the smallest effort makes a difference. Can we eat to love ourselves? It's a wonderful idea, and one I believe is the key to our health and happiness.

I wrote this cookbook to capture all the things I have learned about nourishing myself and others. Treat it as a guide, and just do what you can–even if you can only make one sauce tonight, or roast a rainbow of vegetables on the weekend, it will be worth it. I also hope it inspires you to get creative with food–in all its joyful, messy alchemy–and to see for yourself that healthy food really can taste good.

I owe a lot to that encounter on Maui, getting in trouble in someone else's kitchen. This cookbook is kind of a full-circle moment. Robyn joined me for this one too, taking all the beautiful photographs you'll find in these pages. This is a different book than the one I imagined all those years ago. It's a better one, and a more complete one, filled with the knowledge I've gained over the years–it's the one I wish I had for myself at the beginning of my career, and it's the one I am proud to have finally made.

I hope this book can be your inspiration to explore the potential of food. Consider this an invitation to be informed, empowered, and excited in the kitchen. And a reminder to always look for the magic.

Behind the Scenes
The Story of the Photographs

The photographs in this book were taken over one summer in various locations on the west coast of British Columbia, Canada, with the help of three good friends: Robyn, Sophie, and Tara. I thought it would be easy and fun . . . until the execution! I'm not sure if you've ever tried packing and unpacking a kitchen in an Airbnb along with hundreds of pounds of groceries, but doing that on repeat wasn't a well-thought-out plan. It did make for excellent pictures, though.

The goal was to shoot at five locations: Galiano Island, Salt Spring Island, Squamish, Hornby Island, and Jordan River, stopping at home in Vancouver in between. We stayed at rentals or friends' homes, often not knowing what the property would look like until we pulled in. We shot photos on fireplaces, outdoor tables, and staircases. We used the concrete in a driveway or the stump in a backyard as our set, or cafés where friendly locals chimed in and helped direct the scene. There were times when I didn't have a recipe in its final state, so we cooked dishes on the fly and I wrote the details down as we went (a very backwards way to write a cookbook!). We had power outages, storms, broken ovens, ferry waits, hangovers, and four grumpy, sleep-deprived girls sharing beds and bathrooms. But in the end, all things considered, the experience was pretty amazing.

I would like to acknowledge that these photos were taken on the unceded territories of the Coast Salish Peoples, specifically the lands of the K'ómoks (Comox), Quw'utsun (Cowichan), səlilwətaɬ (Tsleil-Waututh), Sḵwx̱wú7mesh (Squamish), Spune'luxutth (Penelakut), Stz'uminus, W̱SÁNEĆ (Saanich), xʷməθkʷəy̓əm (Musqueam), and also the Pacheedaht First Nation. I want to give thanks for the opportunity to live and learn, eat and create on these beautiful lands.

Ethos

I like to think that my job as a nutritional chef encompasses equal parts science and art. The science is the multifaceted way that food interacts with, supports, and builds our bodies, and the art is the pure magic of food–the colors, the flavors, the deliciousness!

My approach is rooted in bio-individuality, the understanding that each body has unique needs, and that we must follow our own personal path toward optimal health. I don't believe there is a one-size-fits-all diet out there. So many lifestyle and health variables–including stress, genetics, medical history, digestive health, food quality, allergies, sleep quality, where you live, and more–will all affect what suits your body best. Your journey to discover the ideal way to nourish *your* body will be your own. But where do you start? Knowledge is the key. We need to educate ourselves about how we are nourishing our bodies (the science). Understanding the basics of nutrition is a great first step. We also need to listen to our senses (the art). What tastes good? What makes you *feel* good? Be curious. Experiment. Trust your intuition: it will help you discover your own path forward.

BUILDING BLOCKS FOR HEALTHY EATING

My goal is to provide all my clients with the ultimate nutrition to support them every day, including during periods of stress, rest, and recovery. I help athletes keep their energy high before competitions, and nourish them when they are pushing their bodies physically. I work with actors as they prepare for roles, and keep them healthy during long production hours. To do this, I develop a unique plan for each person, fine-tuned according to their individual needs. That said, here are some core fundamentals that have become my building blocks for healthy eating, for all my clients.

Eat More Vegetables

The first thing I tell anyone looking to be healthier is to eat a more plant-forward diet–and a large part of my career has been helping my clients eat more vegetables. It doesn't matter if you are vegan, keto, raw, pescatarian, or omnivore: the more vegetables, the better, especially non-starchy ones. Vegetables contain a diverse spectrum of nourishment that our bodies need, from fiber to essential vitamins, minerals, and phytonutrients. In this book, I highlight the amazing benefits vegetables offer, so you can see how adding something like a few cups of purple cabbage can change how your body experiences a meal and the nutritional benefits it receives.

Choose Whole Foods

So much of our health is based on the quality and type of ingredients we put in our bodies. Try to consume as little processed food as possible. A great way to think about this is to choose whole foods that are as close as possible to the original form in which they grew. I've purposefully included a ton of whole-food recipes in this book so you can start to incorporate more of these foods into your diet and try to avoid the excess oils and refined sugars, preservatives, stabilizers, and dyes that are present in much processed food.

Find Local Foods

Try to eat what is fresh, local, and seasonal in your area. This is much more important than getting stuck on the exact ingredients a recipe calls for. Make zucchini ribbons in the summer, when you can't keep up with the zucchini crop! Make a purple cabbage and beet slaw in the winter. Eat asparagus in the spring and green beans in the summer. If you live in North America and are looking for a healthy fat, choose locally grown hemp hearts over imported cashews. Eat with the seasons (substituting as needed) and support regenerative agriculture when you can. Whenever possible, aim for organic. All this will help you gain the full potential of nutritional benefits I mention in each recipe. A recipe's nutrient content will depend on the quality of ingredients you use, for example, produce quality can vary based on how something is grown, the health of the soil, how far it has traveled, and how it is stored and prepared. Of course, it's not always easy or affordable to access local, seasonal, organic foods, so be gentle with yourself and make adaptations where you can.

Explore the Diversity of Food

Our bodies love variation, and a diverse and balanced eating approach means we are giving ourselves access to a wider range of minerals and vitamins. One of the reasons I believe there is no single "best" diet is that our bodies are constantly changing. Don't get too caught up in a particular diet; an overly restrictive diet can mean you get stuck in the same eating pattern, consuming the same foods over and over, and can potentially lead to food sensitivities while you miss out on vital nutrients. Instead, listen to how your body feels and adapt to what is right for you (like my recipes: make them work for you and your unique preferences). Rotate your menu—eating with the seasons when possible—to incorporate different veggies, nuts, seeds, beans, tempeh, and fish and meat (if you eat those). Try new greens in your smoothie or make bright, vibrant salads with different kinds of lettuce. Diversity keeps our microbiome (the trillions of microorganisms and bacteria that live in our gut) alive and well! My advice to my clients is to always stay curious and be open to change. Our bodies change, the world changes, our knowledge of nutrition changes, the supply chain changes, our food sensitivities change, the quality of the soil changes, and our dietary needs change. Eat in a way that is uniquely you, and try lots of different ingredients to see which work.

Eat for Nutrient Density

You'll see me writing a lot about nutrient-dense foods, and by that I mean foods that are rich in protein, vitamins, minerals, healthy fats, and antioxidants in relation to the calories they provide. A high nutrient-to-calorie ratio is the definition of nutrient density in food. I design my recipes to include as many nutrient-dense foods as possible, adding finely chopped veggies to sautés, or a handful of greens to soups and frittatas, or antioxidant-rich herbs to build out sauces. I'm always sneaking in extra health for my clients where I can. (Sometimes I think I am a professional vegetable hider!) Read more about nutrition and calories on p. 17.

Consume Healthy Fats

For optimal functioning, we have to eat healthy fats. They feed your skin, aid hormonal activity, protect your organs, keep your brain healthy, and keep you full for longer by slowing digestion. In my cooking, I emphasize incorporating healthy fats into dishes through the inclusion of whole foods–like olives in a salad, nuts on steamed greens, or tahini in a dressing–because you get all sorts of incredible nutrients, vitamins, and minerals alongside the fat from these foods. Enjoy your healthy fats (both saturated and unsaturated) from a variety of vegetables, nuts, seeds, fish, and unprocessed meats. I also like to focus on foods high in omega-3 fats, for their anti-inflammatory properties.

Focus on Fiber!

I think fiber is the key to good health. It is one of the most important things for our blood-sugar management and detoxification systems, preventing toxic buildup and keeping our microbiome healthy. There are two kinds of fiber: soluble and insoluble. It's important to include both in your diet, as they do different things for your body. Insoluble fiber moves through the body undigested, while soluble fiber can absorb water and contributes to the form, flow, and consistency of bowel movements.

Because foods high in fiber take longer for the body to digest, they manage the impact of carbohydrates by moderating your blood sugar from rising too much after you eat. The more fiber in your meal, the more stable your blood sugar will be. Mitigating blood-sugar spikes helps us manage stress and energy, and reduces the effects of aging, inflammation, and damage to our bodies. I maximize fiber whenever I can, which is why I include lots of fiber-rich foods, such as vegetables, seeds, berries, and legumes, in my recipes. Throughout the book, I've highlighted recipes that are high in fiber, so you can celebrate one more thing when you eat them (read more about that on p. 30)!

10 Healthy Eating Habits

1. Eat Smaller Portions (and Use Small Plates): Eat a variety of smaller portions for more flavor, more nutrients, and more fun!

2. Add More Vegetables: Including more veggies in your diet allows for a greater diversity of minerals, vitamins, and fiber.

3. There's Always Time for Tea! Sip on antioxidant-infused tea (or warm lemon water) to stay hydrated all day long!

4. *When* You Eat Is as Important as What You Eat: Space your meals and snacks throughout the day, and try not to eat large amounts close to bedtime.

5. Start the Day Right: Avoid refined carbohydrates and processed sugars in the morning. Focus on foods that are high in protein, healthy fats, and complex carbohydrates.

6. Celebrate as You Prepare: Listen to music or make food with friends! Enjoying the cooking process makes the meal all the sweeter.

7. Fresh Is Best: Find a local farmers market to see what seasonal ingredients you can buy there.

8. Slow and Steady: Take your time to chew each bite. This helps regulate calorie consumption, supports optimal digestion, and allows you to be more present.

9. Choose Spices for More Than Their Taste: Be amazed and intrigued by the ways in which spices add not only flavor but many unbelievable health benefits.

10. An Attitude of Gratitude: Appreciate the meal in front of you. Being grateful for your food enriches the experience of eating.

Protein builds the structural and functional components of our bodies and helps energize us. In North America, we've been conditioned to believe that we can only get protein from animal sources, but by looking to plants to supplement at least some of our protein needs, we receive a multitude of benefits that lead to longevity and healing for our bodies, as well as for the earth. If we strictly consume animal protein without looking for plant-based sources too, we can potentially miss out on health-promoting fiber and phytonutrients at each meal. If you're new to the idea of eating more plant protein, it means reimagining your plate so that meat or other animal products are no longer the star but rather a side dish or add-on.

If you don't eat any meat or other animal products, you'll want to be intentional around your menu planning and eat creatively to ensure you're incorporating a diverse array of plant-based protein sources, like legumes, seeds, nuts, and cruciferous vegetables. In my recipes, I emphasize where we can build layers of plant protein in and with salads, soups, spreads, and even breads. I also provide a protein breakdown on every recipe page.

Manage Carbohydrates

Carbohydrates are a source of energy for the body and contain fiber and minerals that we need in order to thrive, but they have developed a bit of a bad reputation over the years. The problem is not carbohydrates themselves, but the type and amount of carbohydrate you consume, the timing of when you consume it, and the impact it can have on your body's blood sugar. Blood-sugar levels rise and fall in the body naturally, but we want to mitigate large blood-sugar swings (for the reasons explained in the fiber section on p. 13). We can do so by ensuring more fiber is present in our meals by choosing complex carbohydrates over refined carbohydrates, balancing starchy vegetables with non-starchy vegetables, adding fat and protein to each meal, and exercising. Exercise can lower blood sugar when it is too high, which is why going for a short walk after eating is recommended and why staying active is important if you're eating a high-carb diet.

My approach to carbohydrates is one of balance and optimal energy management. Some people find an overall lower-carbohydrate diet offers better focus and energy, while others (especially athletes) find just the opposite! I design many of my recipes to combine complex carbohydrates with healthy fats, and protein. Manage your carbohydrate intake with awareness and flexibility, as your needs will change with your stress, fatigue, hormone, and activity levels. I have identified my low-carb recipes throughout the book with an icon (see p. 31), and the per-serving net carbohydrate value is noted on each recipe as a guide to help you find your best balance.

Remember the Antioxidant Rainbow

The phrase "Eat the rainbow" refers to the fact that the color of a food is often indicative of the antioxidants it is rich in. Eating a rainbow of different-colored fruits, veggies, herbs, and seeds will ensure that you consume a range of antioxidants to protect and support the body. Each anti-oxidant serves a unique function, working together in an elaborate synergy. They bind to and neutralize our bodies' free radicals (unstable molecules that can damage other molecules). By disarming free radicals before they do harm, antioxidants can help combat everything from aging and loss of skin elasticity to cognitive decline, cancer, chronic disease, and joint deterioration. I refer to antioxidants many times throughout the book because they are so important!

Understand Calories

Calories are units of energy contained in the food we consume. The calories are released during digestion when the body breaks down the food. The calories we receive from the food will vary based on our enzymes and digestive capabilities, and be utilized differently from person to person. People often focus only on "calories in versus calories out," but it's important to consider the package in which those calories are contained. In general, you can be less concerned about calories when you eat a lot of beautiful veggies, healthy fats, and whole ingredients, because you receive the calories alongside other valuable nutrients and fiber. The calories from healthier foods are much more nutrient-dense and do more for your long-term health than those found in less nutritious or processed options. A bag of chips, for example, may contain the same number of calories as hummus with fresh vegetables, but the effects they have on the body will not be the same because of the difference in nutrients they provide.

The number of calories needed varies from person to person. Some factors that affect it are exercise, weight, muscle mass, age, and hormones, just to name a few. Depending on your personal health goals, calorie intake may be an important consideration for you. Although I am mindful to not include extra calories when they aren't necessary for either health of flavor, my main focus is on the nutrient-to-calorie ratio of the dish rather than on the number of calories themselves. To help you combine recipes and build meals that balance each other calorically over the course of the day, the calorie breakdown is given for each recipe in this book, along with its nutritional benefits. Please note that the calorie calculations for the recipes do not include the ingredients marked as "optional" in the ingredients list (read more about this on p. 31).

Maintain Hydration

Without water, our bodies cannot detoxify and get rid of waste. Water plays a critical role in supporting our bowels in waste elimination, and is required for our kidneys to function properly. Water is necessary for the production of hydrochloric acid to break down protein in the stomach. Without adequate water, we can end up with symptoms ranging from low energy to poor digestion to stiff joints. My recipes incorporate foods with a higher water content, to increase hydration in the body. Some of the most hydrating foods include cucumber, celery, lettuce, tomatoes, watermelon, peaches, and oranges.

Recognize That Food Is Only Part of the Picture

It is important to remember that on our journey to self-nourishment, food is just one piece of the puzzle. The thing I've come back to over and over again is that all the green juice, all the kale, and all the salads in the world won't save you if you're really stressed. Over the years, I've come to ask myself what self-nourishment *really* looks like. For me, it isn't going on a juice cleanse for five days. Instead, I've created systems of accountability so that I put myself first, prioritizing my nourishment, mental health, pleasure, physical activity, and sleep above all else. And although I don't succeed with this every day (by any means!), when I fall short, I take a breath, make a plan, and commit to trying again tomorrow. Self-compassion is one of the strongest forms of self-nourishment there is!

Find out what feeds your body and work to understand what self-nourishment means for you, whether it's in the form of food, routine, relationships, or experiences. How we nourish ourselves affects who we are and who we will become.

How we nourish ourselves affects who we are and who we will become.

Health Benefit Categories

I have always been deeply curious about how food impacts the body. The more I learn, the more intrigued I become. Understanding food's nutritional impact has been key when cooking for my clients, as they all have different needs—like being energized for competition, or eating for an on-set glow, or being supported while recovering from an injury. When I am with my clients, I always explain to them *how* the food I serve is beneficial. For this book, I've designed specific categories to explain the overall health benefits of the recipes for you!

Each recipe has a unique combination of vitamins, minerals, and nutrients that will support the body's systems. The health benefit categories summarize the effects of each recipe so you don't have to decipher all the specific nutrition details each time, or remember what vitamin C does or why magnesium is good for you! (Although, for those of you who are nutrition nerds like me, I have included a full vitamin and mineral breakdown at the back of the book, on p. 292.) Everyone has different health goals, and I want you to be able to tell at a glance if a recipe will help with yours, whether it's to nourish beauty, support the immune system, or aid with detoxification. You will see that I have assigned each recipe two or three of these health benefits, because the truth is, there is a lot of crossover when you look at the body as a whole. Here, I have summarized each category. I am so proud of this system, and I hope you get as excited about it as I do!

Anti-Inflammatory

These recipes include foods with nutrients that help reduce inflammation in the body. Many diseases are accompanied by an overactive or underactive inflammation response—we either can't respond to infection or our response is overactive and we damage healthy tissues. If left unaddressed over time, inflammation can cause more and more damage, eventually promoting chronic inflammatory diseases. Foods that reduce inflammation are high in omega-3s, quercetin, vitamins C and E, and antioxidants. Some examples are ginger, berries (especially blueberries and raspberries), tomatoes, oregano, and cold-water fish.

Beauty + Anti-Aging

These recipes include foods that emphasize dietary compounds supporting healthy collagen, skin, and hair. They are full of antioxidants, which protect our cells at the metabolic level and help remove the free radicals that cause accelerated aging, and are high in vitamins C, E, and A, which are magic for our skin health. These recipes also contain healthy protein to build tissues, and healthy fats and fiber to stabilize our energy systems, helping reduce stress, which can lead to aging. Foods in this category include colorful fruits and vegetables (especially those with blue, purple, red, and orange pigments), flaxseeds, fish, avocados, pumpkin seeds, and tahini.

Cellular Building + Healing

These recipes include foods high in the nutrients that support us at a deep cellular level. They help build the structure and systems of the body—tissue, hair, nails, blood, bones, and brain—and help us recover from injury and repair damage. Foods high in vitamins B, D, and K, folate, iron, potassium, selenium, omega-3s, and protein are all protective, preventive, and supportive, and they provide strength and longevity. Some examples are kale, Swiss chard, and other dark, leafy greens, as well as cruciferous vegetables, mushrooms, seaweed, eggs, and turmeric.

Detoxifying

These recipes include foods that help our bodies process and eliminate the toxins we create internally and those we are exposed to externally. We can modify our diets to remove potentially problematic ingredients, like dangerous food additives and unhealthy oils, and add detoxifying ingredients, such as herbs, spices, and fiber-rich vegetables. It's important to include foods that support the liver and bowels, as they remove toxins to keep our whole system running optimally. Look for foods that contain antioxidants, vitamins C and E, and, of course, fiber. Examples are high-fiber vegetables (including but not limited to broccoli, cabbage, brussels sprouts, beets, garlic, and onions) and turmeric (many other spices and herbs also stimulate detoxification).

Energy + Focus

These recipes include energy-stabilizing foods that slow the release of sugar into the bloodstream, to keep you energized and satiated, and help with weight management, stress, and focus. On a macro level, the addition of healthy fats, fiber, and protein contributes to energy stabilization and cognitive function. The intake of micronutrients and foods high in iron and vitamin B will support energy and focus at the neural level. Some examples of energy-stabilizing foods are nuts, seeds, avocados, tahini, legumes, coconut milk and oil, mushrooms, cinnamon, and high-fiber foods.

Gut Health

These recipes include foods that nurture a healthy gut microbiome, which can profoundly impact our metabolism and immune and detoxification systems. A healthy gut will help us digest and absorb nutrients more efficiently, promote energy production, balance hormones, reduce unwanted inflammation, and keep our skin healthy. Foods that promote a healthy gut are high in fiber, prebiotics, probiotics, and supportive minerals and vitamins like zinc and the B spectrum. They include those with probiotic fiber (such as yogurt, sauerkraut, and other ferments) and those with prebiotic fiber (such as garlic, leeks, legumes, ginger, and mint).

Immune Support

These recipes include foods that strengthen and support the body's ability to protect itself from potentially harmful microbes. The immune system is one of the most complex systems in the human body, a complicated network of cells, tissues, and organs that help protect us from infection and other diseases. Your immune system can be compromised in many different ways: if your diet is deficient in certain vitamins, if you experience high stress, or if you consume too much sugar or alcohol, just to name a few. Immune-supportive foods are high in essential fatty acids, antioxidants, minerals like zinc and selenium, and vitamins A, C, and E. Some examples are garlic, shiitake and maitake mushrooms, whole oranges (including the pith and peel), cayenne, dried chilies, and all foods rich in beta-carotene.

Mood Balancing

These recipes include foods that help with cognitive support, mood balancing, and stress reduction. They are high in essential fatty acids and choline, which help protect the health of the nervous system, and magnesium and B vitamins (especially folate and B12), which are known to fight depression and uplift the nervous system. Some mood-balancing foods that are rich in minerals, like iron, calcium, and copper, also support energy production. Mood-balancing foods include flaxseeds, walnuts, eggs, and cacao.

Where Health Meets Flavor

The recipes in this book reflect how I cook for myself, my clients, and my loved ones. It's not fancy, gourmet cooking; it's a style rooted in my work as a plant-forward nutritional chef at the intersection where health meets flavor. My goal is to create food that is exceptionally tasty and nutritionally dense.

My cooking has never been about perfection. My philosophy is this: Work with what you've got, and don't get too attached to the outcome. Over the last 15 years, I've encountered every different diet under the sun, so I'm used to cooking on the fly and constantly changing and adapting my recipes as I go. The result is a set of super-flexible recipes that I use slightly differently for every client and that you should consider as guides to mold and make your own. Adaptability is at the heart of my cooking philosophy, and I want to encourage you to embrace it in yours.

Part of my approach also comes from being a *traveling* chef, and learning to create and cook from what I have on hand. The sauce from a Sunday dinner becomes a dressing for lunch on Monday. Roasted vegetable leftovers turn into a frittata. A cashew spread is first used as a dip on a charcuterie board, then served on toast with soup for lunch. It's about flavor and health, yes, but it's also about versatility and using what I have to create ever-evolving, satisfying food. I've given you tons of ideas on how to adapt these recipes to suit your taste, your body, your season, and your locale. And don't stress about exact measurements or perfect chopping–because this is a formal cookbook and I decided to give nutritional breakdowns, there are precise measurements, but please don't let that make the recipes harder for you. Use them as inspiration! There is room for improvisation–this isn't baking. We put far too much pressure on ourselves in our daily life, and we *do not* need to bring that energy into the kitchen!

> *My goal is to create food that is exceptionally tasty and nutritionally dense.*

HOW TO USE THIS BOOK

I like to compose meals from multiple dishes, always layering, mixing and matching different elements–sauces, spreads, salads, sides, and more–to build nutritionally complete meals. Within these pages, there are countless options of meals to make (it's a bit of a choose-your-own-adventure style). To get you started, I've given suggestions with each recipe on how you might combine it with other recipes in the book. Dive in and choose a single recipe or a combination of a few that will be just right for *you*. Pick a sauce for tonight's meal or make a batch of staples on the weekend. Play with salads and sides, build beautiful plates, and discover what helps you thrive!
On pp. 22 to 23, I describe what you can expect from each chapter of the book.

How-Tos (pp. 274–281)

As you work your way through these recipes, you'll see I refer to some commonly used cooking methods. These are the basic skills I use every day in the kitchen when creating healthy food for my clients: I roast root vegetables and toast seeds, I blend up plant-based milks and make veggie rices and noodles. I usually do all of this before I know what's on the menu! I've provided these how-to techniques at the back of the book to help you gain confidence in the kitchen.

Start the Day (pp. 32–79)

In the book's first chapter, Tonics, Plant Milks & Smoothies (p. 34), I introduce some of the ways I like to add extra nutrition to drinks. My recipes in Breakfast & Brunch (p. 58) have been designed with an emphasis on healthy fats, fiber, protein, and complex carbohydrates. Starting the morning with nutritionally dense, less-refined foods allows for more sustained energy levels. Whether for a new morning coffee or a beautiful brunch spread to share with friends, these recipes are my favorite way to start the day.

Staples (pp. 80–117)

I always have a bunch of versatile staples on hand, prepped and ready, to help me compose meals throughout the week. My Breads & Crackers (p. 82) are gluten-free options that are packed with vegetables, fiber, and protein. Rarely do we look at bread as a source of health benefits, but these recipes have all been created to deliver just that. I've given you many ideas throughout this book on how to include protein in creative places but the Protein Add-Ons (p. 92) are my protein-packed go-tos to add to many of the other recipes in this book–they're key for building up salads and bowls–or enjoy as snacks on their own. In Other Essentials (p. 108) you'll find simple recipes I make in larger quantities and always keep on hand to enhance the texture, flavor, and sparkle of any plate.

Sauces & Spreads (pp. 118–143)

My sauces and spreads are where I shine as a chef, and are my key to making healthy food taste amazing! Sauces are built from healthy fats and vitamin-rich ingredients, and showcase the magical potential of herbs and spices. A great sauce is truly a meal maker, harmonizing all the elements of a plate. Spreads are the thicker, denser, vegetable-rich cousins of sauces, and are an important part of the puzzle when you're building healthy meals. All of my spreads are designed for maximum flavor and nutrition, and are often high in plant-based protein. Sauces and spreads are so versatile, I always keep one or two in my clients' fridges, ready to layer into an existing recipe or to build into a meal or snack.

Soups, Salads & Sides (pp. 144–199)

The soups, salads, and sides recipes celebrate the diversity and versatility of vegetables. All of the recipes are layered with fiber, vitamins, minerals, antioxidants, and healthy fats. Purée vegetables into a creamy, warm soup, chop them up for a crunchy, enzyme-rich salad, or put the spotlight on single jewel-toned vegetables in the sides to showcase their unique nutritional profile and what they do for the body–because each vegetable offers something special! With these recipes in my (and now your) repertoire, the possibilities for creating beautiful, nourishing meals are endless.

Large Plates (pp. 200–253)

Large plates are "center-of-the-meal" dishes that satiate and satisfy. In this section, you'll find some of my favorite foods, like noodles of all kinds, wraps stuffed with beautiful veggies, and fragrant, saucy plates of fish and vegetables. There may be a bit more prep involved in these recipes, but they are some of the most nutrient-diverse and filling recipes in the book. They don't need much more than a light salad or side to make them a complete meal.

Sweets (pp. 254–273)

In my experience, people don't lose their sweet tooth just because they want to eat healthy! I've done my best to design these recipes to satiate a craving for something sweet while sticking to my goal of always using highly nutritious ingredients. Wherever I can, I've reduced sweeteners and added healthy fats, fiber, and protein so you can celebrate your indulgences in a healthier way. Like most special things, enjoying sweets in moderation keeps them sacred and leads to a deeper appreciation.

Flavor Makers ✳

As a nutritional chef, I am committed to creating meals at the intersection of health and flavor, so I want you to meet my flavor makers, the ingredients I return to time and time again to create taste and depth in my cooking. I think of my flavor makers as the primary colors I would use to start a painting, layering and building from my palette as I go. You'll see them in most of my recipes as stand-alone flavors or complex seasoning combos, as a way to boost creaminess or give a pop of spice. They have an incredible ability to make things taste good, and most of them also pack a nutritional punch! Read more about their health benefits in the Glossary of Ingredients on pp. 283–290.

I think of my flavor makers as the primary colors I would use to start a painting, layering and building from my palette as I go.

Almond butter is a great source of healthy fat and protein, and also gives a boost of nutty flavor and creamy depth. I love it in a smoothie, where it balances out the sweetness and adds nutrition, or in a savory sauce, where I can build endlessly on its rich flavor.

Apple cider vinegar offers a wonderful tanginess to pickled veg and a perfect sharpness to a dressing, sauce, or soup. It adds a sweet-tart acid that balances out other flavors and has been shown to support digestion too!

Capers are little punches of salt and brine. These tiny pickled flower buds are one of my favorite ways to add saltiness to dressings, sauces, and spreads. I use them in many recipes to season and add a savory layer of salted depth—so much more flavorful than just adding sea salt!

Cilantro is definitely the most used herb in my repertoire. Full of antioxidants, fresh cilantro adds brightness to any salad or sauce. When cooked in something like a frittata or a soup, it gives a beautiful, subtle, savory taste.

Coconut milk is a great dairy-free food with which to create a subtle, creamy base. It has a lovely light taste on its own, and can also act as a blank canvas for flavor creation, as it's neutral enough to be taken in either a savory or a sweet direction. Spiced up, it becomes a curry or soup base. Blended with fruit, it makes a great smoothie or chia pudding.

Dijon mustard is, in my opinion, incredibly underutilized—it is so much more than just a spread. I love exploring ways to use its sharp, spicy, unique taste in everything from sauces and dressings to soups and savory baking. It adds a ton of flavor without adding calories, and it has healing properties too!

Fish sauce is an umami-packed seasoning that I love to use with sauces, soups, and roasted or steamed veg. It is salty, tangy, and sharp, and adds a unique flavor experience to any savory dish. If you haven't tried a fermented fish product like this before, it's worth exploring!

Garlic is one of my favorite savory flavors. When cooking, I like to start with garlic, usually as a base with oil and onions, then go on a flavor adventure with what I add next. I use raw garlic often in my dressings and spreads, as it has more of a spicy kick when uncooked. It is another flavor maker that has outrageous health-boosting properties.

Ginger is a beautiful, warming spice with amazing healing power. I could find ways to add fresh ginger to almost everything I make! It can go in either a sweet or a savory direction, and is perfectly at home in everything from smoothies and sweets to sautés, sauces, and soups. Grated ginger will transform your steamed veggies, and even just a few drops of ginger juice will enhance a dressing.

Jalapeño gives a little pop of spice and crunch to whatever you add it to. I love its fresh, peppery notes and often use it to build layers of flavor and texture alongside other vegetables. Leave the seeds and pith in if you love spice, or take them out for a milder flavor.

Lemons and limes are a great way to add acid to a dish, along with vitamin C and immune support. The juice of these fruits heightens other flavors—sweet or savory—and brings everything into balance. The zests can also be used to build a uniquely sharp and citrusy flavor profile.

Miso is a beautiful ingredient for building flavor and texture. This salty, protein-rich paste will thicken and season a broth, soup, or sauce. Different types of miso vary in their sweetness and saltiness, but all of them will give a boost of umami richness to a dish!

Onions, green onions, leeks, and shallots are all from the same family, and all four boast many health-supportive properties. They each offer their own flavor profile, and different qualities when raw or cooked, changing from powerful and spicy to subtle and sweet. You'll find one of these in the majority of my savory recipes.

Smoked paprika can enhance so many different dishes, from roasted vegetables to soups, sauces, and marinades. I love the smokiness it provides. Just a dash will lend a rich flavor to any dish.

Tahini is such a beautiful base to create from. Commonly used in the Middle East to create spreads, dips, and dressings, it is nutty and earthy, with a slightly bitter flavor and smooth finish. Plus, it's a source of healthy fat, protein, and minerals. I add it to anything I want to make richer and creamy in texture, like a soup or dressing.

Tamari is one of my favorite ways to add saltiness to a meal. Because it is in liquid form, it infuses its seasoning evenly throughout, coating vegetables and building umami depth in sauces and dressings.

Thyme can provide the entire flavor profile of a dish on its own, or it can help elevate the other flavors it's combined with. Whether subtle or strong, this antioxidant-rich herb has the loveliest flavor, earthy and savory, with a slight hint of citrus.

Toasted sesame oil has an unmistakable rich, nutty, aromatic flavor. I love the unique way it accentuates any dish. It can be lightly drizzled to finish a stir-fry or added to sauces and dressings for a deep, toasty richness.

Turmeric gives both sweet and savory dishes a beautiful complexity of flavor and a brilliant color—not to mention an anti-inflammatory boost. I like to use the fresh root in sweeter items, like smoothies, teas, and tonics. The ground spice compliments more savory dishes.

Ume plum vinegar, the brine left over from pickling umeboshi plums, is an intriguing combo of taste sensations: a sour vinegar that is also very salty. There is nothing else quite like it! It's a beautiful ingredient to get to know. A drizzle of this potent pink liquid goes a long way. Add it to dressings or marinades, or sprinkle it over vegetables instead of salt.

NOTES ON INGREDIENTS AND SUBSTITUTIONS

I've included a comprehensive glossary of the most common ingredients I use throughout the book on pp. 283–290, and there you'll find all the information you need to understand the health benefits and flavor profiles of many familiar ingredients, and maybe some that are new to you! However, everyone is unique in which foods their bodies tolerate and which their taste buds prefer (and I've worked with every diet, preference, limitation, and allergy under the sun!), so I wanted to mention here a few ingredients often used in the book, and the possibilities for substitutions and adaptations if you would rather avoid them or if they are not available because of the season or your location.

DAIRY I generally limit the use of dairy when developing my recipes, because it's easier to add later if I want to than it is to take it out, and many choose not to eat it or can't tolerate it. For those recipes that do include dairy, always feel free to substitute your favorite dairy-free or vegan alternative, or omit completely. If you *are* eating dairy, choose organic, full-fat, and grass-fed whenever possible. For dairy cheese, I have suggestions! I prefer goat or sheep cheese in my cooking; they add great flavor and, for many, can be more easily digestible than cow's cheese. I also love using hard cheeses, as a little provides a lot of flavor. Some of the common cheeses I use are feta (goat or sheep), Manchego (sheep), pecorino (sheep), and parmesan (cow). I love to use butter to add a salty creaminess, but you can substitute ghee or virgin coconut oil. I also choose locally produced dairy whenever I can.

EGGS Eggs offer a great amount of nutrition for such a small package! If they're available, try to buy fresh, pasture-raised, organic eggs, ideally from local farmers or farmers markets. For those of you who've chosen not to eat eggs, I offer some egg substitutes throughout the book, such as tofu, flax meal, and chickpea flour. In many of the baking recipes, a flax egg can be used as a substitute. If you want to try this yourself, a flax egg is generally made by mixing 1 tablespoon flax meal with 3 tablespoons water and resting for 10 minutes before adding to the recipe.

GARLIC AND ONIONS I am a big lover of all things garlic and onion. But if they cause you digestive upset or you have an aversion to them, they can be omitted or replaced in most recipes. When a recipe calls for raw garlic or onions, start with less than is called for if you aren't used to them. If you choose to omit them altogether, just know that the flavor of the recipe might be different without them, so taste and adjust with other spices and herbs–and when removing larger amounts of onion, try substituting a different veggie to maintain the recipe's bulk. Try replacing raw onion and garlic with their cooked or powdered versions, as this does seem to work for some people, or try garlic-infused oil instead. Or, rather than regular onions and the whites of green onions, use green onion tops and chives, as these can be less intense.

GLUTEN AND GRAINS Many people do not eat gluten due to intolerance or preference, and more and more often, people want grain-free or legume-free options for similar reasons. All of my recipes are gluten-free (GF), and I have noted which are also grain-free (GRF). I like to use vegetables where we usually find grains–for example, cauliflower rice, zucchini noodles, and collard wraps. However, if your diet is not gluten- or grain-free, you can easily substitute grains or pseudograins, such as rice or quinoa, for a recipe's cauliflower rice (I tested every recipe with both rice and cauliflower rice), or your favorite GF, GRF, or regular noodles or pasta in place of veggie noodles–some great noodle varieties are rice, mung bean, vermicelli, shirataki (aka Miracle Noodles), edamame, sweet potato, and even kelp. Where I suggest collard wraps or buckwheat crepes, you can substitute your favorite flour, corn, or cassava tortillas.

NUTS I use a lot of nuts and nut butters in my cooking as sources of plant-based protein, healthy fats, vitamins, and minerals. When I call for nuts (or seeds) in a recipe, they are always raw unless I specify toasted (see p. 276 for how to toast nuts and seeds). I like to use almond meal in my baking, for moisture and density. However, if you or someone in your family has a nut allergy, you can substitute seeds, seed butters (like tahini), or flour alternatives like cassava, chickpea, oat, or sunflower seed meal.

OILS One of the benefits of cooking for yourself is that you can control the quality of oil in your food. Overall, if I use oil, I prefer one that has been minimally processed, like organic extra virgin olive oil. Different oils have different ideal uses, but please feel free to substitute your favorite oil for any I call for. My personal preference is to use organic extra virgin olive oil or avocado oil for sautéing or roasting. For dressings, I like to use organic extra virgin olive oil or toasted sesame oil. In sweet baking, I most often use organic cold-pressed virgin coconut oil, although sometimes I use extra virgin olive oil. For those who would like to avoid oil, there are some oil-free (OF) recipes in the book that make creative use of fats from whole foods. Store-bought items, like milks and nut butters, may contain hidden oils. I highly recommend checking the label if you are trying to avoid added or unhealthy oils.

10 Noteworthy High-Protein Plant-Based Recipes

Here, I have highlighted some of my favorite recipes in the book that are full of plant-based protein (and healthy fat, which helps absorb the nutrients from the plants). For me, this is one of the most exciting parts of my job: creating amazing high-protein breads, sauces, small plates, and spreads! Whether you are trying to reduce or remove animal protein, or introduce more vegetables into your diet, these recipes are for you!

1. Bean-Free Butternut Chili, made with tempeh (22 g protein), p. 228

2. Lentil Lettuce Cups with Tahini Ginger Sauce (22 g protein), p. 208

3. Lentil Bolognese over Zucchini Noodles (18 g protein), p. 214

4. Raw Walnut Lettuce Tacos (17 g protein), p. 206

5. Marinated Mediterranean Tofu (15 g protein), p. 93

6. Red Lentil Dal (15 g protein), p. 226

7. Wilted Swiss Chard with White Beans & Capers (13 g protein), p. 196

8. Spiced Tofu Scramble (12 g protein), p. 72

9. Sesame Gomae (11 g protein), p. 169

10. Edamame Cilantro Hummus (10 g protein), p. 142

POULTRY AND FISH Although I specialize in veggies and sauces, in this book I offer some recipes for fish and poultry, as these are the animal proteins most requested by my clients. Try to buy meat from your local butcher or farmers market and, if possible, choose organic, sustainably raised options without added antibiotics. For seafood, I shop at seafood markets, farmers markets, or fisher-direct options whenever possible. In my recipes, I call for salmon, halibut, cod, and scallops, but they can be used interchangeably with other fish that may be more sustainable or local to you. Keep an eye out for Ocean Wise or other ocean-friendly options; these are updated regularly. I tend to go for cold-water varieties, which often contain more omega-3s, and I avoid farmed fish. I also like to keep canned salmon, sardines, and mackerel in my pantry so I can easily add protein to sauces, wraps, and salads.

SALT AND PEPPER My preference is to use Himalayan or sea salt in my cooking, but you can also use kosher salt. Anytime I call for pepper, freshly ground pepper is best.

SOY Throughout the book, I occasionally call for soy products, including edamame, tempeh, tofu, miso, and tamari. I highly recommend seeking out organic soy products. Soy has indisputable health benefits, but it acts as an allergen for some people. Fermented soy products, like miso, tempeh, and tamari, are thought to be more digestible than non-fermented ones, like soy milk or tofu. If you don't want to use tofu, try edamame or crumbled tempeh as a protein source instead. If you are trying to stay away from gluten, be mindful when buying tempeh, miso, or tamari to look for those labeled "gluten-free," as sometimes a gluten-based grain is added to the product. The soy product you will see most often in this book is organic gluten-free tamari. If you are trying to avoid soy, coconut aminos is a great substitute at a $1:1\frac{1}{2}$ ratio of tamari to coconut aminos. You can also use fish sauce, but start with a $\frac{1}{2}:1$ ratio of fish sauce to tamari and add more to taste, as fish sauce is saltier. If you are trying to avoid fermented foods, substitute Bragg liquid aminos at a 1:1 ratio. If none of these options is right for you, try seasoning to taste with sea salt, but know that the recipe's depth of flavor, umami, and consistency may not be as designed.

SWEETENERS I try not to use refined sugar in my cooking. When I am sweetening, I generally use maple syrup or honey, but in the smallest amount possible, as they still impact blood sugar. For those avoiding all sweeteners, I have noted where you can omit them and still get good results.

4 Simple Health-Changing Habits

Besides stress management, sleep, and exercise, here are four tips that can improve your health!

1. Water When You Wake: Within the first hour of waking, try to drink 2 to 3 cups of room temperature or warm water. We become dehydrated through the night, and it's important to rehydrate upon rising. You will notice a huge difference in your skin, energy, hunger levels, and digestion. To make it more interesting and mineral-rich, add some lemon or orange juice and a pinch of sea salt or a little apple cider vinegar, chlorophyll, or oregano oil. Or make one of my favorite drinks: either the warming Lemon Ginger Tonic (p. 35) or my own take on a replenishing electrolyte drink (p. 36).

2. Chew Before You Brew: Delay your morning coffee until after you've hydrated and eaten breakfast, to help manage your blood-sugar levels and mitigate an afternoon crash. Ideally, you'll incorporate protein, fat, and a little fiber-rich complex carb into your first morning meal—even if it is just something small. This morning routine has been one of the most transformative things I have done for my energy levels, stress, and anxiety.

3. Green Routine: Enjoy some form of dark-green leafy vegetables or a salad with a light vinaigrette (like olive oil with lemon juice or apple cider vinegar) before your meals. This simple addition is a game-changer, as it helps control blood sugar, aids digestion, supports portion control, and gives you more nutrients!

4. Light at Night: Try not to eat within three hours of your bedtime. If you are hungry, choose warm tea, broth, a small handful of nuts, or a super-light soup. I struggle with this one, but I make a concerted effort because I know how important it is to give the body a break from digesting so it can focus on other important things. This adjustment not only will help you sleep better but will allow your body to restore, recover, and repair through the night.

Recipe Icons

At the top of each recipe you will see a set of icons that represent its nutritional classifications and the dietary preferences it's inclusive of. Below are more details about what each icon means.

NUTRITIONAL ICONS

Protein and carbohydrate: Everyone's requirements for protein and carbohydrate differ based on several factors, including age, hormonal balance, the amount of sleep and exercise you get, and your personal health goals. For the purposes of this book, I have assumed an average intake of 2,000 calories per day and analyzed each recipe as a whole to determine whether it could be considered high in protein or low in carbohydrate based on grams of protein or carbohydrates *per 200 calories*. I did this to show you the amount of protein or carbohydrate *in relation* to the total calories of the serving, which is a truer reflection of a recipe's specific macronutrient density than the isolated amount in grams alone (which is also given). For example, a smoothie that has 20 grams of protein may sound like a good serving of protein, but if the smoothie is 1,500 calories, the number of calories you need to consume to benefit from the protein is also very high, so the resulting macronutrient-to-calorie ratio is low and the recipe would be considered low-protein.

Fiber: For fiber, I use a standard grams-per-serving approach to measure if a recipe serving is a good, high, or super source of fiber.

Fat: You may notice that I chose not to include an icon for the fat-to-calorie ratio. I try to balance the healthy fats in my recipes and don't want to define them as high- or low-fat. If you are curious, you can look at the grams of fat per serving listed along with the total calories, carbs, protein, and fiber per serving at the bottom of each recipe.

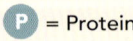

P = Protein

HP = High-protein

Based on an average of 2,000 calories per day, consuming between 50 and 175 grams of protein is recommended, where the lower end represents the required minimum to prevent deficiency. I consider recipes with about 5 to 10 grams of protein *per 200 calories* to be a good source of protein; these are labeled with a "P." Recipes with more than 10 grams of protein *per 200 calories* are high protein and are labeled with "HP." If you ate 2,000 calories' worth of P recipes, you would be getting 50 to 100 grams of protein; if you ate 2,000 calories' worth of HP recipes, you would be getting 100 grams of protein or more. The exact amount of protein you get will vary based on how well a protein can be utilized (absorbed) by the body and how digestible the protein source is; eating a wide variety of protein sources is the best way to ensure protein needs are met. Read more about protein on p. 14.

F = Fiber
HF = High-fiber
SF = Super-fiber

The ideal daily intake of fiber is 25 to 35 grams, regardless of calories consumed in a day. I consider recipes with 2.5 to 5 grams of fiber *per serving* a good source of fiber and mark those with a "F"; recipes with 6 to 10 grams of fiber *per serving* are a high source of fiber and are labeled with "HF"; recipes with more than 10 grams *per serving* are a super source of fiber and are labeled with "SF." Read more about the importance of fiber on p. 13.

LC = Low-carbohydrate

Based on an average of 2,000 calories per day, a daily intake of carbohydrates of 100 to 150 grams or less is generally considered low (although some diets, like keto, set "low" as less than 50 grams per day). In this book, recipes with about 12 grams of carbohydrates or less *per 200 calories* are marked with "LC." All of the recipes are balanced with protein and fat to optimize how your body responds to carbohydrates. Read more about balancing carbohydrate intake on p. 14.

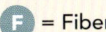 = Recommended recipe

Ultimately, my goal is to create recipes that are nutritionally dense, considering not just single ingredients but how these ingredients *combined* will impact you. When you see a recipe with a love heart, it means it has an exceptional balance of nutrients—healthy fats, protein, carbohydrates, vitamins, and minerals. These recipes are excellent choices to include in your repertoire.

DIETARY PREFERENCES

DF/DFO = Dairy-free / Dairy-free option

Dairy is more often a suggested addition rather than a base ingredient in my cooking, but this icon indicates which recipes are completely dairy-free. Those labeled with "DFO" have an easy dairy-free variation.

GF = Gluten-free

All of the recipes in this book are gluten-free. I eat gluten-free, and many of my clients do too, whether by choice or necessity. I've added this icon to every recipe so it is clear at a glance.

GRF = Grain-free

Recipes with this icon are suitable for people on a grain-free diet, whether for health or personal preference.

OF = Oil-free

I have noted when a recipe is or can be oil-free for those who would like to eliminate added oils and get more of their healthy fats from whole-food sources.

V/VO = Vegan / Vegan option

Recipes marked with "V" are completely free of animal products, and recipes marked with "VO" include an easy vegan variation.

NUTRITIONAL BREAKDOWNS

At the bottom of each recipe, you will see a per-serving nutritional breakdown for calories, carbohydrate, protein, fat, and fiber. Please note that the calculations for these do not include the ingredients marked as "optional" in the ingredients list or the garnishes. Where there is a choice of ingredients, the calculations are based on the first option listed, unless otherwise noted. Calculations for nutritional breakdowns are based on accepted averages and have not been verified in a lab; please use these numbers for general guidance only.

Start the Day

tonics, plant milks
& smoothies

Lemon Ginger Tonic

DF/GF/GRF/OF/V

Beauty + Anti-Aging, Gut Health, Immune Support

Makes about 4 cups (1 serving)

Juice + rind of 1 large lemon

2 inches fresh ginger (unpeeled), washed well and chopped

4 cups water

Pinch of sea salt (optional)

I consider this my everyday tonic. If you're feeling a little run-down, have an upset stomach, or are looking to stimulate digestion in the morning or nourish your body at night, look no further. This tonic is high in vitamin C, which does so many great things for our bodies, from promoting cellular health to aiding with stress management to supporting the immune system. The combination of ginger and lemon further encourages absorption, digestion, and detoxification—all of which promote healthy and hydrated skin.

Serving Note: I like to sip this throughout the day at room temperature, or over a few ice cubes, but it is equally lovely served warm after a meal. You can also freeze it in an ice cube tray and add it to your water for an infusion of health and flavor whenever you want!

In a medium pot, heat the lemon juice and rind, ginger, and water over medium heat for 5 minutes or before it begins to boil. Remove from the heat, sprinkle in the salt, if using, and let cool slightly. Strain through a fine-mesh sieve into a heatproof jar.

Note: This is a perfect use for all those little nubs of ginger and lemon rinds you don't know what to do with after cooking. Add a drizzle of honey while the tonic is cooling for a little sweetness.

Calories/serving: 30
Carbs/serving: 7 g
Protein/serving: 0 g
Fat/serving: 0 g
Fiber/serving: 0 g

Turmeric Tonic

DF/GF/GRF/V

Anti-Inflammatory, Beauty + Anti-Aging, Immune Support

Makes about 2 cups (1 serving)

1 navel orange, peeled
4 inches fresh turmeric, peeled
2 inches fresh ginger, peeled
1 to 1½ cups water
1 tsp MCT oil
1 tsp honey (optional)
Pinch of sea salt
Pinch of fresh ground pepper

Variation: Try adding aloe vera for gut support and a squeeze of fresh lemon juice for an extra pop of citrus.

I love experimenting with different ways to infuse beverages with vitamins and minerals so that they both nurture and nourish the body. This hydrating, skin-brightening, and antioxidant-rich tonic is high in vitamin C and full of beautifying minerals for your skin and nails. It is a subtly sweet and spiced tonic that derives its brilliant orange color from anti-inflammatory turmeric.

Serving Note: Serve in a glass over a handful of ice, or top with sparkling water to make it a spritzer! You could also heat it gently in a small pot on the stove if you want a warm version.

In a high-powered blender, combine all the ingredients (starting with 1 cup of water and adding more as needed). Blend until smooth, starting on low and increasing to high after a few seconds. Strain through a fine-mesh sieve into a glass or jar.

Calories/serving: 100
Carbs/serving: 12 g
Protein/serving: 1 g
Fat/serving: 5 g
Fiber/serving: 0 g

Electrolyte Chlorophyll Drink

DF/GF/GRF/OF/V

Beauty + Anti-Aging, Cellular Building + Healing, Mood Balancing

Makes about 3 cups (1 serving)

3 cups filtered water
¼ cup fresh orange juice
1 tbsp fresh lemon juice
1 tbsp fresh lime juice
½ tsp chlorophyll (unflavored)
⅛ tsp sea salt

Variation: For a chia fresca, add 1 tsp chia seeds and more lemon juice to taste!

I have been working with athletes for a long time and really wanted to develop an alternative to the artificially colored and flavored electrolyte drinks they were using to rehydrate. This is a simple solution made with sea salt, antioxidant-packed citrus juice, and mineral-rich chlorophyll to help oxygenate the blood. Drink it whenever you need to bring your body back to balance–after a lot of sweating, a sauna, or a workout. Whether or not you are an athlete, this is a replenishing beverage that will help you hydrate and recover.

In a large jar, combine all the ingredients and stir until well mixed.

Calories/serving: 42
Carbs/serving: 10 g
Protein/serving: 0 g
Fat/serving: 0 g
Fiber/serving: 0 g

Blended Morning Coffee

DF/GF/GRF/V

Energy + Focus, Mood Balancing

Makes about 2 cups (1 serving)

1½ cups hot coffee + more as needed

¼ cup milk of choice (see p. 275 or use store-bought) (optional)

1 tbsp hemp hearts

2 tsp maple syrup + more if desired

2 tsp Udo's or MCT oil

1 tsp pure vanilla extract

1 tsp cacao powder

1 tsp reishi or maca powder

¼ tsp ground cinnamon

Pinch of sea salt

Here is a simple yet elevated morning coffee recipe that helps sustain your energy levels and optimize your mood. To achieve this, I add a little protein in the form of hemp hearts, some healthy fat, antioxidants, and some adaptogens from the reishi (or maca) to help the body adapt to stress; I also add cinnamon because it is thought to stimulate the circulatory system and help balance blood-sugar levels. I absolutely love starting my day with this delicious, frothy coffee!

In a high-powered blender, combine all the ingredients. Blend until smooth and frothy, starting on low and increasing to high after a few seconds.

Add a little more hot coffee (or hot water) as needed to taste and to warm it up. If you like it really hot, heat in a small pot over low heat; if you like it cold, refrigerate or serve over ice.

Note: If you like a creamy latte-style coffee, be sure to add the optional milk.

Calories/serving: 202
Carbs/serving: 12 g
Protein/serving: 5 g
Fat/serving: 14 g
Fiber/serving: 5 g

Plant-Based Milk: 3 Ways

Brazil Nut Ginger Milk
Almond Lavender Cardamom Milk
Pumpkin Seed Coconut Milk

For me, plant-based milks are a special treat–they are refreshing and delicious–plus you get to drink in all the beautiful, nourishing vitamins and minerals from the nuts and seeds! You'll find the basic method for how to make plant-based milks on p. 275, as well as some mix-and-match options to build your own creations. The recipes below are three of my personal favorites, and the ones most requested by my clients.

Brazil Nut Ginger Milk

DF/GF/GRF/OF/V

Makes about 4 cups (4 servings)

1¼ cups raw Brazil nuts

4 cups filtered water

2 large Medjool dates, pitted
(see variation)

3 inches fresh turmeric, peeled,
+ more if desired

1 inch fresh ginger, peeled,
+ more if desired

½ tbsp pure vanilla extract

¼ tsp ground nutmeg

¼ tsp sea salt + more if desired

Variation: Add 1 to 2 tsp of adaptogens, such as ashwagandha or mushroom powder (like lion's mane), after you strain the milk! It's a great way to add more health benefits. Two dates work great; 3 will give you a nice, much sweeter milk.

This golden-hued ginger and turmeric-infused nut milk is a beautiful thing to drink on its own, or it can be mixed with anything from tea to granola to a smoothie. Spicy, smooth, and delicious, it is brimming with antioxidants, which support the immune system, reduce inflammation, and build beauty from the inside out. This one is very special.

In a bowl of water, soak the Brazil nuts overnight in the fridge. The following day, drain and rinse.

In a separate bowl of ½ cup of the filtered water, soak the dates for 20 minutes at room temperature.

Place the dates with their soaking water and all other ingredients, including the remaining 3½ cups filtered water, in a high-powered blender. Blend on high until smooth.

Turn to p. 275 and follow the steps for straining the milk. Transfer to an airtight container and store in the fridge for up to 3 days. Shake well before serving.

Calories/serving: 140
Carbs/serving: 6 g
Protein/serving: 3 g
Fat/serving: 11 g
Fiber/serving: 1 g

Almond Lavender Cardamom Milk

DF/GF/GRF/OF/V

Makes about 4 cups (4 servings)

1 cup raw almonds

4¼ cups filtered water

1½ tbsp dried lavender

2 tsp pure vanilla extract

2 tsp maple syrup or honey
(optional but highly
recommended)

½ tsp sea salt

½ tsp ground cardamom

¼ tsp ground cinnamon

This floral stress-reducing drink will put you in a good mood. Lavender, cardamom, vanilla, and cinnamon are all known to lift the spirits, while almonds provide calming minerals that support the nervous system, such as magnesium. Enjoy this one cold during the day or warm before bed, to help you relax.

In a bowl of water, soak the almonds overnight in the fridge. The following day, drain and rinse.

In a medium pot, heat the filtered water until just boiling. Turn off the heat and add the lavender (in a tea ball or loose). Cover and let steep for about 10 minutes (taste at 5 minutes, as the strength of the lavender will vary based on its freshness; you can leave it for 15 minutes if you want it stronger). Strain the lavender from the water and discard.

Put the lavender-infused water in a high-powered blender with the remaining ingredients and blend on high until creamy and smooth.

Turn to p. 275 and follow the steps for straining the milk. Transfer to an airtight container and store in the fridge for up to 3 days. Shake well before serving.

Calories/serving: 82
Carbs/serving: 4 g
Protein/serving: 3 g
Fat/serving: 6 g
Fiber/serving: 1 g

Pumpkin Seed Coconut Milk

DF/GF/GRF/OF/V

Beauty + Anti-Aging, Immune Support, Mood Balancing

Makes about 4 cups (4 servings)

1 cup raw pumpkin seeds

1 cup unsweetened shredded coconut

2 large Medjool dates, pitted

4 cups boiled filtered water + more if needed

1 tsp pure vanilla extract (optional)

½ tsp sea salt

Variation: For a golden milk option, add 1½ inches peeled fresh turmeric to the blender. It tastes so good and will give you a boost of anti-inflammatory support!

This velvety-green-tinted, coconutty milk is sweet, satisfying, and full of health benefits. Pumpkin seeds are high in immune-supporting zinc and stress-reducing magnesium, and are packed with antioxidants to protect the skin against aging! Drink this delightful beverage over ice or use it as the base for a chai latte.

In a bowl of water, soak the pumpkin seeds overnight in the fridge. The following day, drain and rinse.

In a separate bowl, soak the coconut and dates in the boiled filtered water for 10 minutes.

Place the coconut, dates, and their soaking water in a high-powered blender. Blend on high until well blended. Add the pumpkin seeds and remaining ingredients and blend on high until smooth, adding more water if needed.

Turn to p. 275 and follow the steps for straining the milk. Transfer to an airtight container and store in the fridge for up to 3 days. Shake well before serving.

Calories/serving: 130

Carbs/serving: 6 g

Protein/serving: 2 g

Fat/serving: 11 g

Fiber/serving: 1 g

Strawberry Hemp Milk

DF/GF/GRF/V

Anti-Inflammatory, Beauty + Anti-Aging, Energy + Focus

Makes about 1½ cups (1 serving)

1 cup filtered water

10 medium-to-large fresh or frozen strawberries (see note)

½ inch fresh ginger, peeled

2 tbsp hemp hearts

½ tbsp oil of choice (see note)

½ tsp pure vanilla extract

½ tsp ground cinnamon

⅛ tsp sea salt

2 ice cubes (if you don't use frozen strawberries)

1 to 2 tsp maple syrup or honey to taste (optional)

I love using hemp hearts as a milk base because they thicken up so nicely when blended, plus they don't take as much time or effort as other milk alternatives (because there's no need to soak and strain them first), *and* they have incredible health benefits. I designed this milk to be delicate, refreshing, and beautifying for your skin. Antioxidant-rich strawberries protect against sun damage from the inside out. Meanwhile, the warming spices of ginger and cinnamon are great for fighting inflammation. With a good dose of fiber and protein from the hemp, this drink will keep your energy levels stable. It's a great way to start the day, or enjoy it as a snack in the afternoon.

In a high-powered blender, combine the water, strawberries, ginger, hemp hearts, oil, vanilla, cinnamon, and sea salt. If using fresh strawberries, add the ice. Blend until smooth, starting on low and increasing to high after a few seconds. Add the sweetener to taste (the natural sweetness of strawberries varies, so you may or may not want it). Enjoy right away.

Note: Only use fresh strawberries when they're in season; out-of-season ones aren't very sweet. Use hemp, MCT, or Udo's oil for an energizing and sustaining drink. The oil also makes the hemp milk a bit creamier, which I love.

Calories/serving: 237
Carbs/serving: 8 g
Protein/serving: 7 g
Fat/serving: 17 g
Fiber/serving: 4 g

Cacao Cold Brew Smoothie

DF/GF/GRF/OF/V

Cellular Building + Healing, Energy + Focus, Mood Balancing

Makes about 1½ cups (1 serving)

1 cup cold brew coffee

1 cup chopped frozen banana (see note)

2 tbsp almond butter

1 tbsp cacao powder

1 tbsp chia seeds

1 tsp ashwagandha (optional)

1 tsp mushroom powder, like reishi or lion's mane (optional)

½ tsp pure vanilla extract

¼ tsp ground cinnamon

⅛ tsp sea salt

3 ice cubes

1 tbsp cacao nibs

1 to 2 tsp maple syrup (optional)

I love cold brew coffee, and when it's blended into a smoothie with cacao, banana, chia, and almond butter, you have the perfect morning pick-me-up. Full of supportive antioxidants and minerals like zinc, copper, and magnesium for your body's tissues, this smoothie also contains a balanced amount of protein, fat, and fiber for sustained energy. If you add the mushrooms and ashwagandha, it has amazing benefits for brain health and stress management too.

In a high-powered blender, combine all the ingredients except the cacao nibs and maple syrup. Blend until smooth, starting on low and increasing to high after a few seconds. Add the cacao nibs and maple syrup (if desired for more sweetness) and pulse for 10 seconds.

Note: Any chilled coffee will do. If you don't drink coffee, you can replace the cold brew with 1 cup of your favorite milk, to make a chocolate almond banana milk instead. Don't worry if you don't have a frozen banana; a room temperature one will work just fine, it just makes the milk a little thinner. Don't let this sit for too long, or the chia will begin to gel.

Calories/serving: 558

Carbs/serving: 54 g

Protein/serving: 16 g

Fat/serving: 26 g

Fiber/serving: 20 g

Turmeric Orange Strawberry Smoothie

DF/GF/GRF/OF/V

Beauty + Anti-Aging, Detoxifying, Immune Support

Makes about 1½ cups (1 serving)

1 navel orange, peeled

1 cup packed baby spinach

1 cup frozen strawberries

½ cup chopped frozen banana
    (optional, if more sweetness
    is desired, but delicious)

¼ cup filtered water + more
    if needed

2 tbsp hemp hearts

1 tbsp dulse flakes

3 inches fresh turmeric, peeled

1 inch fresh ginger, peeled

½ tbsp fresh lemon juice

½ tsp pure vanilla extract

3 ice cubes

I could drink this smoothie every day. It has everything I love: citrus, berries, vegetables, spices, even seaweed, all blended up into a beautiful, brilliant-emerald-green smoothie. The antioxidants, vitamins, and minerals here are high across the board, especially beauty-boosting vitamins A, C, and E; you get a healthy dose of protein and fiber, as well as anti-inflammatory support; and all these amazing ingredients together will help to detoxify and strengthen your immune system. Drink this smoothie in the morning to start your day, or if you are feeling sick, or when you need a reset from a night out.

In a high-powered blender, combine all the ingredients. Blend until smooth, starting on low and increasing to high after a few seconds. Add up to ¼ cup more water if needed (especially if not using the banana).

Calories/serving: 335
Carbs/serving: 37 g
Protein/serving: 12 g
Fat/serving: 13 g
Fiber/serving: 12 g

Mixed Berry Antioxidant Smoothie

DF/GF/GRF/V

Anti-Inflammatory, Beauty + Anti-Aging, Cellular Building + Healing

Makes about 2½ cups (1 serving)

1 tbsp chia seeds

1¼ cups filtered water

1 tsp pure vanilla extract

2 tbsp hemp hearts

⅛ tsp sea salt

1 cup frozen or fresh blueberries

1 cup frozen strawberries
(or a mix of raspberries and
strawberries)

½ cup chopped frozen banana
(optional, if more sweetness is
desired, but delicious)

1 tbsp spirulina

1 tbsp Udo's oil (or hemp oil
or MCT oil)

2 tbsp cacao nibs (optional)

I designed this smoothie for a client who didn't have time to eat on a film set. I had to figure out how to pack as much nutrition as possible–lots of protein, fiber, minerals, and vitamins–into just one smoothie, and still make it taste good! It is high in antioxidants from the berries and cacao, and lots of naturally occurring protein from the hemp hearts, chia, and spirulina. The oil adds a special blend of healthy fats to support optimal cellular functioning. This smoothie is highly energizing and filling–it's an exceptional example of how a smoothie can become a meal–and my client loved it!

In a small bowl, mix the chia seeds, ¼ cup of the filtered water, and the vanilla together. Soak for 20 minutes.

In a high-powered blender, combine the hemp hearts, remaining 1 cup filtered water, sea salt, berries, banana (if using), spirulina, oil, and soaked chia mixture. Blend until smooth, starting on low and increasing to high after a few seconds. Add 1½ tablespoons of the cacao nibs and pulse until smooth. Serve topped with the remaining ½ tablespoon of cacao nibs, if desired.

Calories/serving: 594
Carbs/serving: 39 g
Protein/serving: 19 g
Fat/serving: 35 g
Fiber/serving: 16 g

Mint Chocolate Smoothie

DF/GF/GRF/OF/V

Cellular Building + Healing, Gut Health, Mood Balancing

Makes about 2 cups (1 serving)

2 large Medjool dates, pitted

⅔ cup filtered water

2 tsp flax meal

2 cups packed baby spinach

2 tbsp creamy almond butter

2 tbsp cacao powder

2 tsp spirulina or greens powder of choice

½ tsp pure vanilla extract

½ tsp chlorophyll (optional)

¼ tsp mint extract

6 large ice cubes

1 tbsp cacao nibs

Variation: You can add a third large date, or some maple syrup, for a sweeter taste.

I like to think that the chocolaty cacao and the bright mint extract in this smoothie distract you from how healthy it is! I've added in a bunch of beautifying and anti-aging green superfoods, like spinach, spirulina, and chlorophyll, and it also has a ton of protein, B vitamins, iron, magnesium, fiber, and omega-3s. This smoothie will support your body, help repair and protect cells, and give you a nice boost of energy.

In a small bowl, soak the dates in ½ cup of the filtered water for 20 minutes. Meanwhile, in another small bowl, soak the flax meal in the remaining 2 tbsp of filtered water.

In a high-powered blender, combine the dates with their soaking water, the soaked flax mixture, and all other ingredients, except the cacao nibs. Blend until smooth, starting on low and increasing to high after a few seconds. Add the cacao nibs and pulse for 10 seconds.

Calories/serving: 495

Carbs/serving: 41 g

Protein/serving: 19 g

Fat/serving: 24 g

Fiber/serving: 14 g

Acai Bowl

DF/GF/GRF/OF/V

Beauty + Anti-Aging, Detoxifying

Makes 1 serving

1 (3½ oz/100 g) packet frozen unsweetened acai berries

1 cup chopped frozen banana

½ cup frozen blueberries

¼ cup filtered water or plant-based milk of choice (see p. 275 or use store-bought) + more if needed

¼ cup fresh orange juice

½ to 1 tbsp spirulina powder (I like 1 tbsp for more protein)

Handful of fresh blueberries, strawberries, raspberries, or blackberries to serve

Sprinkling of unsweetened coconut flakes, hemp hearts, or granola to serve

1 tbsp almond butter to drizzle (optional)

Variation: You can add endless options right into the blender: for more protein, add 1 to 2 tbsp almond butter, protein powder, or hemp hearts; for creaminess, add a scoop of coconut or Greek yogurt; for an extra hit of fiber, add soaked flax meal or chia seeds.

The Brazilian acai bowl is a celebration of the vibrant antioxidant-packed acai berry. The antioxidants in acai berries help neutralize free radicals, defending against the effects of aging and disease—consider them a first line of defense against cellular deterioration. This beautiful bowl is built on a smooth and creamy acai berry base, then topped with an assortment of fresh fruits, coconut flakes, hemp hearts, or granola. With an impressive amount of vitamins, minerals, and fiber, this bowl is a wonderfully sweet way to nourish your body.

In a high-powered blender, combine the acai berries, banana, blueberries, water, orange juice, and spirulina powder. Blend on low until smooth, using the tamper to push the frozen fruit down so it catches the blade. Add more liquid if necessary to blend completely (but remember, this is a bowl, not a smoothie—you want it thick).

Pour into a bowl and top with your favorite toppings. Enjoy immediately!

Calories/serving: 312
Carbs/serving: 50 g
Protein/serving: 8 g
Fat/serving: 9 g
Fiber/serving: 10 g
(without toppings)

breakfast & brunch

Coconut Berry Chia Pudding

DF/GF/GRF/OF/V

Makes 4 servings

2 cups fresh or frozen blueberries

1 cup fresh or frozen strawberries
  or raspberries

1 (14 oz/400 ml) can coconut milk

½ cup water

4 tsp maple syrup

2 tsp pure vanilla extract

½ cup chia seeds

I've loaded this delicious chia pudding with antioxidant-rich berries that provide beautiful color and flavor when simmered down in creamy coconut milk, creating a nutritionally balanced base. Chia is a great source of plant-based omega-3s, making this pudding the perfect way to stock up on these healthy fats. This recipe is also packed with vitamins C and K, high in bone-building minerals like phosphorus and manganese, and especially high in fiber, to help eliminate toxins from the body and keep you full longer. I love to pack up these puddings in cute single-serving jars for my clients to grab and go. Start the recipe the night before, as the chia needs to chill for at least 30 minutes, and ideally overnight.

Serving Note: Top this pudding with some unsweetened coconut flakes or more fresh berries to enjoy alongside your morning coffee or tea.

In a small saucepan, combine the blueberries, strawberries, coconut milk, water, maple syrup, and vanilla. Bring to a simmer over medium heat. Keep at a low simmer until jammy, about 5 to 6 minutes. Remove from the heat and crush the berries with a fork. Add the chia seeds, mix well, and let cool slightly.

At this point, you can either transfer the pudding to a bowl and cover it, or divide it between four sealable 1-cup jars for an easy to-go breakfast. Either way, chill and thicken it in the fridge for at least 30 minutes before serving, and ideally overnight. Store in the fridge for up to 4 days. Garnish as desired before serving.

Calories/serving: 324
Carbs/serving: 20 g
Protein/serving: 5 g
Fat/serving: 21 g
Fiber/serving: 9 g

Tahini Honey Parfait

DFO/GF/GRF/OF

Beauty + Anti-Aging, Immune Support, Mood Balancing

Makes 4 servings

2 tbsp chia seeds

½ cup water

1 cup plain Greek, coconut, or cashew yogurt

4 cups sliced fruit of choice + more if desired

¼ cup tahini

3 tbsp canned coconut milk, stirred well, or another milk of choice

2 tbsp honey + more to serve

¼ tsp lemon zest + more to garnish

2 tbsp fresh lemon juice

⅛ tsp sea salt

2 tbsp toasted sunflower seeds (see p. 276) to garnish

2 tbsp toasted unsweetened shredded coconut (see p. 276) or flakes to garnish

Fresh mint leaves to garnish (optional)

Hemp hearts to garnish (optional)

Variation: The yogurt is amazing in this recipe, but the tahini honey drizzle is good with just the chia and fruit on its own too!

The combination of rich tahini and coconut milk mixed with sweet honey and tart lemon creates a tasty drizzle that easily elevates a bowl of fresh fruit into a delicious parfait. The healthy fats from the tahini honey sauce balance out the natural sweetness of the fruit, not just in flavor but also in nutrition. I love this dish with mangoes and peaches or mixed berries and sliced apple, but sub in your favorite fruits or whatever is seasonally available.

Serving Note: You can serve this in jars, like a traditional parfait: start with a layer of chia yogurt, followed by the fruit, then the tahini honey, then the garnishes. Top with an extra drizzle of honey. Eat it for breakfast, as part of a brunch spread, or even as a vibrant dessert at a dinner party on a summer eve!

In a small bowl, soak the chia seeds in the water for 20 minutes.

Mix the soaked chia into the yogurt. Spread the yogurt mixture over a serving platter and arrange the fruit on top.

In a separate small bowl, combine the tahini, coconut milk, honey, lemon zest, lemon juice, and salt, stirring until smooth, about 1 minute. Gently pour or spoon the tahini honey drizzle over the fruit. Garnish with sunflower seeds, coconut, mint, hemp hearts, more lemon zest, and a drizzle of honey, if desired. Enjoy right away. (Alternatively, store the components in separate airtight containers in the fridge for up to 4 days and assemble right before serving.)

Calories/serving: 368

Carbs/serving: 38 g

Protein/serving: 9 g

Fat/serving: 19 g

Fiber/serving: 7 g

Blueberry Vanilla Overnight Oats

DF/GF/OF/V

Energy + Focus, Gut Health, Immune Support

Makes 4 servings

1 cup gluten-free old-fashioned rolled oats

1 cup frozen blueberries + more to serve

¼ cup chia seeds

¼ cup hemp hearts

2 cups almond milk or another milk of choice

¼ cup almond butter

2 tbsp maple syrup + more to serve

2 tsp pure vanilla extract

1 tsp ground cinnamon

Pinch of sea salt

I love the flavor combination of blueberries and almond butter in these overnight oats, which are easy to prepare and sustain your energy throughout the day. Oats are high in iron and other essential minerals, like selenium and zinc, that support the immune system and metabolic functioning at a cellular level. Oats are also high in carbohydrates, so to mitigate their effect on blood sugar, I've increased the protein, fiber, and healthy fats by adding hemp hearts, chia, and almond butter. Start this recipe the night before, as the oats need to sit overnight.

Serving Note: Top your oats with a couple of spoonfuls of the blueberry compote from the Blueberry Squares (p. 272).

In a large bowl, combine the oats, blueberries, chia seeds, and hemp hearts.

In a small bowl or a blender, combine the remaining ingredients. Stir or blend on medium speed until smooth, then add to the oat mixture.

Divide the mixture into four 1-cup jars. Cover and chill in the fridge overnight, or for up to 3 days. To serve, top with a drizzle of maple syrup and more berries.

Note: If you are grain-free, the Coconut Berry Chia Pudding (p. 59) is a lovely alternative.

Calories/serving: 316
Carbs/serving: 24 g
Protein/serving: 10 g
Fat/serving: 18 g
Fiber/serving: 9 g

Tahini Orange Granola

DF/GF/V

Beauty + Anti-Aging, Energy + Focus, Mood Balancing

Makes about 7 cups (12 servings)

3 cups gluten-free old-fashioned rolled oats

½ cup raw almonds, roughly chopped

½ cup raw pumpkin seeds

½ cup raw and shelled sunflower seeds

½ cup virgin coconut oil or extra virgin olive oil

½ cup maple syrup

¼ cup tahini

Zest of 2 oranges

¼ cup fresh orange juice

2 tsp pure vanilla extract

2 tsp ground cinnamon

1 tsp sea salt

¼ tsp ground nutmeg

Variation: Make this grain-free by omitting the oats and adding 2 more cups of chopped nuts and seeds. Change things up for a new flavor profile and a different mix of nutrients by swapping in other seeds and nuts, your favorite nut butter for the tahini, or different juices and spices.

Granola is one of those things that is so much better when it's home-made because you can control the ingredients that go into it. This recipe is packed with nutrient-rich seeds and nuts, which provide a ton of minerals as well as vitamins B and E, helping to build healthy skin and hair. This granola is amazing. It's coated in a delicious citrusy paste of tahini, orange zest, and vanilla, with sweetness from the fresh orange juice and maple syrup–using much less sugar and oil than a store-bought version!

Serving Note: This granola is great sprinkled over the Acai Bowl (p. 56) or any fresh fruit parfait or smoothie bowl.

Preheat the oven to 300°F. Line a rimmed baking sheet with parchment paper.

In a large bowl, combine the oats, almonds, pumpkin seeds, and sun-flower seeds.

In a small pot, combine the oil, maple syrup, and tahini. Warm over low heat until creamy. Remove from the heat and stir in the remaining ingredients.

Pour the oil mixture over the oat mixture and stir until evenly coated. Spread evenly on the prepared pan.

Bake until light golden brown, about 30 to 45 minutes, stirring every 15 to 20 minutes and rotating the pan when you do. Let cool.

Store the cooled granola in an airtight jar in the fridge for up to 2 weeks.

Calories/serving: 320
Carbs/serving: 23 g
Protein/serving: 7 g
Fat/serving: 21 g
Fiber/serving: 4 g

Breakfast Scones

DF/GF/VO
Gut Health, Mood Balancing

Makes 4 scones

1 egg (see variation)

2 tbsp plant-based milk of choice

¾ cup almond meal

½ cup sorghum flour

1 tbsp arrowroot powder

½ tsp grain-free baking powder

½ tsp sea salt

2 tbsp melted and cooled virgin coconut oil

Savory Flavor Options

1 cup shredded sharp sheep cheese

¼ cup chopped fresh chives

¼ cup fresh thyme leaves

1 tsp fresh ground pepper

Sweet Flavor Options

½ cup chopped candied ginger

½ cup fresh blueberries

½ cup freeze-dried raspberries or chopped dried strawberries

2 tbsp dried lavender

Variation: To make vegan scones, omit the egg and milk. Instead, mix ½ cup almond milk and ½ tbsp psyllium husks in a small bowl. Set aside to thicken for 20 minutes, then add to the dry ingredients and continue as directed.

With this recipe, I've created a lower-carb version of a classic scone, which I adore. My scones are decadent, delicious, and gluten-free! They are also endlessly adaptable. I've given you some suggestions for how to flavor them, with both savory and sweet options–they take well to just about anything. My vegan variation, which is still low in carbs and high in protein, is equally fantastic! So enjoy, knowing you are getting a more nutritious version of this baked treat, however you choose to make them.

Serving Note: Serve with jam or butter, or stuff them with eggs, tomato, and basil. Or try eating them plain, warm from the oven, with a slice of goat cheddar and a cup of tea. Adding all the savory flavor options is my favorite way to make these!

Preheat the oven to 375°F. Line a baking sheet with parchment paper.

In a small bowl, beat the egg and milk together.

In a large bowl, mix the almond meal, sorghum flour, arrowroot powder, baking powder, and salt. Stir in the coconut oil. Add the egg mixture and, using a spoon or your hands, combine until the dough holds together. Fold in any of the desired sweet or (even all!) savory flavorings until combined.

Shape the dough into a 6-inch disk, then cut into four wedges. Place on the prepared pan.

Bake for 20 minutes, until golden. Serve warm.

Store in an airtight container in the fridge for up to 3 days.

Calories/scone: 264
Carbs/scone: 15 g
Protein/scone: 7 g
Fat/scone: 19 g
Fiber/scone: 3 g
(without flavor options)

Buckwheat Crepes

DFO/GF/GRF

Cellular Building + Healing, Energy + Focus, Gut Health

(P)

Makes 12 crepes

1¼ cups buckwheat flour

1 cup milk of choice

1 cup water

3 eggs

3 tbsp ghee, melted, or avocado
 oil + more for cooking

1 tsp pure vanilla extract

¼ tsp sea salt

Fillings or toppings of choice

I fell in love with crepes when I was working in France in my early 20s. I'm always looking for a way to wrap nutritious ingredients into one perfect mouthful, and crepes do just that–see the serving note for some delicious filling suggestions. This version is made with buckwheat flour, an incredible ingredient that works well for grain-free and gluten-free preferences because buckwheat is actually a seed. It makes a high-protein, high-fiber flour that has tons of minerals and a nutty flavor. These crepes are wonderfully versatile, tasty, and fun–and they pair excellently with light French café music.

Serving Note: These crepes can be taken in any direction–sweet or savory, rolled up or open-faced. For a savory option, try serving with a fried egg, chopped tomato, basil, and grated goat cheddar. For a sweet option, try almond butter, sliced banana, cacao nibs, cinnamon, and a drizzle of maple syrup.

In a large bowl, whisk together all the ingredients except the toppings.

Heat a 10- to 12-inch nonstick sauté pan over medium heat and add a touch of ghee. Add ¼ cup of batter and, moving quickly, gently tip the pan to spread the batter around. Cook the crepe until golden on the bottom, about 50 seconds, then flip and cook on the other side for 30 to 40 seconds, until golden. Remove from the pan and keep warm. Repeat with the remaining batter.

Serve warm with the fillings or toppings of your choice. Store any leftover crepes in the fridge for up to 3 days. Before storing, let the crepes cool, layer parchment paper between them, then seal in a bag or airtight container. Before serving, reheat gently in a sauté pan over low heat.

Calories/crepe: 98
Carbs/crepe: 8 g
Protein/crepe: 4 g
Fat/crepe: 6 g
Fiber/crepe: 1 g

Zucchini Parmesan Egg Muffins

GF/GRF/OF

Energy + Focus, Mood Balancing

Makes 12 muffins or
24 mini muffins (6 servings)

6 cups grated unpeeled zucchini

1 tbsp sea salt

3 cups finely grated parmesan cheese (see note)

1 cup almond meal

¼ cup chopped fresh thyme leaves

¼ cup finely chopped green onions

1 tsp fresh ground pepper

½ tsp onion powder

5 eggs, beaten

Variation: You can replace the parmesan with either pecorino or Manchego if you would rather use a sheep cheese, for either health or flavor.

Soft, chewy, and cheesy, these decadent egg muffins are not to be missed. They are deliciously indulgent, full of zucchini, low in carbs, and have no added oil or sugar. They are also really good if you are looking for a high-protein treat. The only thing wrong with them? They are hard to stop eating! I love making the mini versions for brunch get-togethers or as hors d'oeuvres when I want to impress at a dinner party. I recommend buying pre-grated cheese for this, or using the fine grater on your food processor. If you only have a regular grater, get ready for a workout–this is a lot of cheese!

Serving Note: Serve these with *Kale Pine Nut Caesar (p. 168), Cauliflower Leek Soup (p. 148), or Arugula & Roasted Squash Salad (p. 172).*

Preheat the oven to 375°F. Line a 12-cup muffin tin or 24-cup mini muffin tin with muffin cup liners or parchment paper, or use a silicon muffin tray.

Place the grated zucchini and salt in a colander and massage the salt into the zucchini for 15 seconds. Let sit for 20 minutes, then gather the zucchini in a dish towel or a fine-mesh sieve and squeeze until dry.

In a large bowl, combine the zucchini, parmesan, almond meal, thyme, green onions, pepper, and onion powder, mixing thoroughly. Add the eggs and stir well to combine.

Add about ⅓ cup of the mixture to each muffin cup if making standard muffins, or 2 tablespoons if making mini muffins.

Bake regular muffins for 30 minutes or mini muffins for 20 minutes, until golden brown on top. Serve warm.

Store leftover muffins in an airtight container in the fridge for up to 3 days. Reheat in the oven before serving.

Calories/serving: 394
Carbs/serving: 7 g
Protein/serving: 30 g
Fat/serving: 27 g
Fiber/serving: 3 g

Spiced Tofu Scramble

DF/GF/GRF/V

Anti-Inflammatory, Immune Support, Mood Balancing

Makes 4 servings

Tofu

1 lb (454 g) medium-firm tofu

2 tbsp gluten-free tamari

1 tsp dried oregano

¼ tsp fresh ground pepper

Scramble

4 tbsp extra virgin olive oil

2 cups finely diced red onions

2 cups finely diced red peppers

1 jalapeño, finely diced (leave some seeds for heat if desired)

¼ cup chopped fresh cilantro + more to garnish

½ tbsp pressed garlic

1 tsp sea salt

½ tsp smoked paprika

¼ tsp cayenne

½ cup finely chopped tomato

¼ cup tomato paste

Variation: To switch things up, you can replace the tofu with 8 eggs; just whisk the eggs with the oregano and pepper, and omit the tamari.

Drawing inspiration from Turkish scrambled eggs, this delicious tofu scramble is slow-cooked with a wonderful blend of herbs and spices. It is full of antioxidant-rich peppers, tomatoes, and red onions—all packed with immune system-supporting vitamin C, and lycopene, which protects the skin. The sweet and savory umami of the tomato seasons the tofu beautifully, making this one of my favorite dishes to start the day with. This scramble keeps nicely in the fridge and can be quickly reheated, so it's a great option for easy eating.

Serving Note: Enjoy this with Rosemary Onion Skillet Bread (p. 90) or your favorite toasted bread with a drizzle of olive oil. Or try it with a side of avocado or some Rainbow Escabeche (p. 114), or even a scoop of Edamame Cilantro Hummus (p. 142). I also love it alongside a green salad with Dijon Vinaigrette (p. 128).

In a large bowl, roughly crumble the tofu, then toss with the tamari, oregano, and pepper.

In a large nonstick sauté pan, heat the oil over medium heat. Add the onions, red peppers, and jalapeños and sauté for 8 minutes, until they begin to soften. Add the cilantro, garlic, salt, paprika, and cayenne and cook, stirring, until fragrant, about 2 minutes. Add the chopped tomato and tomato paste, and cook, stirring often, for 5 minutes, until the tomatoes are soft. Remove 1 cup of the mixture and set aside.

Reduce the heat to medium-low and add the tofu mixture, stirring well. Cook, stirring often, for 4 to 5 minutes, until the tofu is hot and well mixed with the flavors.

Serve warm, topped with the reserved tomato mixture and garnished with cilantro.

Leftovers store well in an airtight container in the fridge for up to 4 days. Reheat in a sauté pan over low to medium heat before serving.

Calories/serving: 292

Carbs/serving: 17 g

Protein/serving: 12 g

Fat/serving: 20 g

Fiber/serving: 4 g

Spring Vegetable Frittata

DFO/GF/GRF

Beauty + Anti-Aging, Cellular Building + Healing, Energy + Focus

Makes 4 servings

1½ cups chopped peeled white potatoes

3 tbsp extra virgin olive oil, butter, or ghee

2 cups finely chopped leeks, white parts only

1 tsp onion powder

½ to 1 tsp smoked paprika

¾ tsp fresh ground pepper

1 tsp sea salt

2 cups finely chopped asparagus

1 cup finely sliced snap peas (or frozen peas)

1 cup very thinly sliced zucchini

1 tbsp pressed garlic

3 heaping cups baby spinach

10 eggs

⅓ cup finely chopped fresh dill + more to garnish

⅓ cup goat chèvre + more to garnish (optional)

Variation: You can whip up a frittata with almost any type of veggie: the basic formula is about 10 eggs to 3 to 4 cups of veg.

I've probably made more frittatas in my life than any other dish. This recipe showcases one of my favorite frittata flavor combinations, featuring crunchy snap peas, tender asparagus, fragrant dill, slow-cooked leeks, and aromatic garlic–an ode to the flavors of spring. With the basic building blocks for beauty (protein and vitamins A, C, and E), loaded with healthy fiber for the gut, and rich with the nutrients that support cellular healing and repair, this frittata satisfies my goal as a nutritional chef: to make delicious meals that maximize health.

Serving Note: Serve next to a simple side salad with Dijon Vinaigrette (p. 128), or with Lemon Garlic Spinach (p. 184). Top with some Caramelized Balsamic Onions (p. 110) for sweetness or Chipotle Cashew Aioli (p. 141) to add some smokiness to each bite!

Preheat the oven to 350°F.

Place the potatoes in a pot and cover with cold water. Bring to a boil, and once the potatoes are tender, drain, and set aside to cool.

In a 12-inch ovenproof sauté pan (see note), warm the oil over medium-low heat. Add the leeks and cook, stirring, for about 10 minutes, until golden brown and tender. Stir in the onion powder, ½ teaspoon of the paprika, and ½ teaspoon each of the pepper and salt. Add the asparagus and peas and sauté for 3 to 4 minutes, until cooked through. Add the zucchini and garlic and cook, stirring well, for 2 minutes. Add the cooled potatoes, then fold in the spinach and allow it to wilt, about 1 to 2 minutes. Taste and add the remaining ½ teaspoon of paprika, if desired.

Meanwhile, in a large bowl, beat the eggs. Season with the remaining salt and pepper, and stir in the dill. Add to the sauté pan and stir thoroughly to combine. Reduce the heat to low and cook for 1 minute, stirring very well.

Place the pan in the oven and bake for 20 to 25 minutes, until a knife poked into the center comes out clean. If adding chèvre, crumble on top and return the pan to the oven for 1 minute, or until the cheese softens. Let rest for 5 minutes.

Recipe continues

Serve warm, garnished with more dill and more crumbled cheese on top, if desired.

Store leftovers in an airtight container in the fridge for up to 3 days. Reheat before serving: wrap in aluminum foil and bake in the oven at 350°F until heated through, about 10 to 12 minutes. Or reheat in a sauté pan over medium-high heat with a few tablespoons of water, covered so that they steam until warm all the way through.

Note: If you don't have an ovenproof sauté pan, wrap aluminum foil around the handle before placing the pan in the oven.

Calories/serving: 399
Carbs/serving: 20 g
Protein/serving: 22 g
Fat/serving: 24 g
Fiber/serving: 6 g

Cauliflower Benny
with Spinach & Pesto

DF/GF/GRF
Anti-Inflammatory, Beauty + Anti-Aging, Gut Health

Makes 4 servings

1 large head cauliflower

½ tsp smoked paprika

½ tsp sea salt + more to serve

½ tsp fresh ground pepper + more to serve

½ tsp onion powder

3 tbsp extra virgin olive oil

4 to 8 eggs

1 recipe Lemon Garlic Spinach (p. 184)

½ recipe Caramelized Balsamic Onions (p. 110) (optional)

1 recipe Cilantro Sunflower Pesto (p. 123)

Chili flakes and/or fresh herbs to garnish

Variation: Instead of eggs, try topping these bennies with a scoop of warmed Marinated Mediterranean Tofu (p. 93). Instead of spinach and pesto, try roasted tomatoes and Chermoula (p. 125): Drizzle four ¾-inch-thick tomato slices with olive oil and season with salt and pepper. Add to the baking sheet with the cauliflower for the last 7 minutes of roasting. Build the benny, then top with chermoula. Or try swapping the pesto for the warmed Pine Nut Cream sauce from the Wild Mushrooms recipe (p. 234).

This recipe offers a delightful twist on the classic eggs benny and is a versatile choice for brunch, lunch, or dinner. Instead of hollandaise, I opt for a bright cilantro pesto, served over roasted cauliflower steaks and sautéed garlicky spinach, then topped with a perfectly poached egg. The result is a truly delicious plate that's high in healthy fats, fiber, and protein. Feel free to experiment with different combinations of vegetables and sauces–for a little inspiration, check out the variation below.

Serving Note: Try this with Wilted Swiss Chard (p. 196), a salad with Dijon Vinaigrette (p. 128), or Thyme Oyster Mushrooms (p. 187).

Preheat the oven to 425°F. Line a rimmed baking sheet with parchment paper.

Cut the cauliflower in half, from the top down, then cut each half in half again–you are aiming for four even 3/4-inch-thick cross-section cuts, but don't worry if some of them crumble into bits. These extra florets will work as a base too (I have yet to make four perfect cuts). Arrange the cauliflower on the prepared pan.

In a small bowl, mix the paprika, salt, pepper, and onion powder. Stir in the oil to combine. Brush the spiced oil over both sides of the cauliflower slices.

Roast the cauliflower for 7 minutes, then flip to the other side and roast for another 7 minutes, until golden.

Meanwhile, poach the eggs and, in a small pan, warm the spinach and balsamic onions (if using) over low heat.

To assemble, place one cauliflower slice on each plate, then top each with one-quarter of the spinach, onions (if using), and a ¼ cup of the pesto. Top with 1 to 2 eggs, depending on your appetite, and sprinkle with salt, pepper, and chili flakes.

Calories/serving: 591
Carbs/serving: 13 g
Protein/serving: 17 g
Fat/serving: 52 g
Fiber/serving: 10 g
(with 1 egg per serving)

Eggplant Shakshuka

DFO/GF/GRF

Anti-Inflammatory, Beauty + Anti-Aging, Mood Balancing

Makes 4 servings

¼ cup extra virgin olive oil

1 cup finely diced red onions

1½ tbsp pressed garlic

1½ tsp ground cumin
+ more to taste

1 tsp smoked paprika
+ more to taste

1½ tsp ground coriander
+ more to taste

4 cups diced peeled eggplant

1 (28 oz/796 ml) can whole
peeled tomatoes

1 tsp onion powder

1 tsp sea salt + more to serve

2 cups thinly sliced quartered
zucchinis

8 eggs

¾ cup crumbled goat, sheep,
or vegan feta

¼ cup roughly chopped fresh
flat-leaf parsley or cilantro
to serve

Chili flakes to serve

Fresh ground pepper to serve

There are many iterations of shakshuka–the North African egg and tomato sauce dish–all flavored differently and deliciously. This version is exquisitely seasoned and bursting with nutrient-rich vegetables. The eggplant and tomato meld into the sauce perfectly, while the zucchini adds a touch of texture and color. The veggies in this dish provide vitamins A, C, E, and K, which have amazing anti-aging properties and promote healthy skin. Eggs give us iron, which, in the presence of the vitamin C from the veggies, gets absorbed into our bodies much more efficiently. If you are hosting a brunch, look no further!

Serving Note: I love to serve this dish with toasted Seed Bread (p. 88) or with some Lemon Garlic Spinach (p. 184)!

Preheat the oven to 375°F.

In a large ovenproof sauté pan (at least 10 inches), heat the oil over medium heat. Add the onions and sauté for 5 minutes, until soft. Add the garlic, cumin, paprika, and coriander, stirring well. Add the eggplant and cook, stirring occasionally, for 5 minutes, until the eggplant has started to soften.

Add the tomatoes, onion powder, and salt. Cook, stirring often and crushing the tomatoes with a wooden spoon, for 10 to 12 minutes, until the eggplant is fully tender and the tomatoes are simmering. Add more spice here if you like! Reduce the heat to medium-low if it starts to spit. Add the zucchinis and cook, stirring, for 5 minutes, until al dente; you want them heated through, but not collapsed.

Using a spoon, make eight small "nests" in the sauce. Crack 1 egg into each nest (I like to crack each egg into a bowl first, then tip it gently into the nest). Cover and cook over medium-low heat for 5 to 6 minutes, until the eggs are set but not completely cooked.

Remove the lid and sprinkle the feta over top. Place the pan in the oven and bake for 3 to 5 minutes, until the eggs are cooked to your liking. The eggs will continue to cook a little after they come out of the oven, so bring them out a minute earlier than you think!

Serve the eggs with a big spoonful of sauce. Finish with parsley, chili flakes, and salt and pepper to taste.

Calories/serving: 448
Carbs/serving: 17 g
Protein/serving: 23 g
Fat/serving: 32 g
Fiber/serving: 8 g

Staples

breads & crackers

Broccoli Parmesan Mini Flatbreads

GF/GRF/OF
Cellular Building + Healing, Energy + Focus

Makes 8 mini flatbreads

2½ cups riced broccoli (see p. 277)

1 cup finely grated parmesan or hard sheep cheese

2 eggs

1 tbsp Dijon mustard

1 tsp dried oregano or basil

1 tsp onion powder

1 tsp sea salt

½ tsp fresh ground pepper

1 cup almond meal

Variation: If broccoli's not your favorite, you can substitute the same amount of riced cauliflower to make cauliflower flatbread!

These quick and flavorful flatbreads are a great example of how to get more fiber and protein into something that tends to be less nutrient-dense. Broccoli not only gives this recipe a green tint, but also provides some vitamin C. These flatbreads have 10 grams of protein each and are low in carbs, with a flavor combination I love!

Serving Note: These flatbreads are the most delicious served with Tzatziki (p. 240). Another great way to serve these flatbreads is with Lemon Garlic Spinach (p. 184) and a sprinkling of goat feta on top. Or keep it simple with just a drizzle of olive oil next to my Herby Greek Salad (p. 164) or Everyday Detox Salad (p. 166).

Preheat the oven to 425°F. Line a large baking sheet with parchment paper.

In a large bowl, combine the broccoli rice, cheese, eggs, Dijon, oregano, onion powder, salt, and pepper. Mix well, then add the almond meal and stir to combine.

Divide the broccoli mixture into 8 equal portions and shape them into 3-inch circles to create individual flatbreads. Arrange the flatbreads on the prepared pan.

Bake for 15 minutes, rotating the pan midway through and flipping the flatbreads, for a golden-brown toast on both sides. These are best served warm.

Store in the fridge for up to 3 days. To reheat, simply sear in a warm pan over medium heat.

Calories/flatbread: 172
Carbs/flatbread: 3 g
Protein/flatbread: 10 g
Fat/flatbread: 13 g
Fiber/flatbread: 3 g

Sesame Flax Crackers

DF/GF/GRF/V

Makes 40 to 50 crackers
(8 servings)

½ cup raw sunflower seeds

1 cup flax meal

¼ cup raw black or white
    sesame seeds

3 tbsp chia seeds

½ tbsp onion powder

½ tbsp garlic powder

½ tbsp dried thyme

½ tbsp dried basil

1¼ tsp sea salt

½ cup water

2 tbsp extra virgin olive oil

Fiber is one of the most fundamentally important parts of a healthy diet, and it's always a goal of mine to find little ways to add more. Simple, tasty, and perfect to snack on, these savory sesame crackers provide a wonderful serving of fiber and plant-based protein. They are great for your digestion, help regulate blood-sugar levels, and are high in vitamin E, a powerful antioxidant that helps support the immune system.

Serving Note: Serve these crackers alongside any of my soups or salads! They are perfect paired with the Chunky Guacamole (p. 137), cheese slices or the Beet Thyme Cashew Dip (p. 138). They are great topped with sliced cucumber and a sprinkle of salt and pepper, the Edamame Cilantro Hummus (p. 142) or goat chèvre, smoked salmon, and capers!

Preheat the oven to 300°F.

In a food processor, pulse the sunflower seeds to a coarse flour.

In a large bowl, combine the ground sunflower seeds, flax meal, sesame seeds, chia seeds, onion powder, garlic powder, thyme, basil and salt. Mix very well, then add the water and oil, stirring well. Let sit for 10 minutes.

Cut two 12 × 16-inch squares of parchment paper. Place the dough between the squares and roll it out to about ⅛ inch thick. Try to roughly cover the whole bottom square with the dough, if you can get it that thin! Thicker crackers work too; just make sure the dough is as evenly spread as possible, all the way across. Don't make the area smaller than 10 × 12 inches.

Lift the parchment paper onto a large baking sheet. Remove the top piece of parchment and score the dough with a knife or a pizza cutter if you have one. Aim for 1½ × 2-inch crackers by making even vertical and horizontal scores.

Bake for 20 minutes, then rotate the pan and continue baking for 15 minutes, until toasted and a touch golden (thicker crackers may need an extra 10 minutes). Let sit for 5 minutes before breaking the crackers apart along the score lines. Let cool completely.

Store in an airtight container at room temperature for up to 1 week, or in the fridge for up to 2 weeks.

Calories/serving: 197
Carbs/serving: 3 g
Protein/serving: 6 g
Fat/serving: 16 g
Fiber/serving: 6 g

Curried Socca

DF/GF/GRF/V
Anti-Inflammatory, Energy + Focus

Makes 1 (10-inch) flatbread
(4 servings)

1 cup chickpea flour (see note)

1 cup water

4 tbsp extra virgin olive oil

1 tsp sea salt + more to serve

1 tsp coriander seeds

½ tsp black mustard seeds

½ tsp cumin seeds

½ small red onion, finely sliced

2 tsp pressed garlic

1 tsp onion powder

½ tsp curry powder

½ cup finely chopped fresh cilantro

Note: If you can't find chickpea flour, you can make your own in a high-speed blender or food processor; 1 cup of dried chickpeas makes about 1¼ cups of flour. Blend on high until finely ground, then sift.

Found often in French and Italian cuisine, socca is a flatbread made from chickpea flour, a versatile flour that is naturally high in plant protein. This flatbread is vegan and gluten-free, with a dense chew that can satisfy a starchy craving. I loved the idea of marrying socca with the flavors (and nutritional support) of Indian-inspired spices for this recipe!

Serving Note: Best served hot and fresh from the oven! Try it next to the Cucumber Herb Salad (p. 159) with some Quick Pickled Jalapeños (p. 112). Or serve with some smashed avocado or Edamame Cilantro Hummus (p. 142), a drizzle of olive oil, and some flaky sea salt! It's also great with scrambled eggs or the Butternut Squash Soup (p. 152).

In a medium bowl, whisk the chickpea flour with the water, 1 tablespoon of the oil, and ½ teaspoon of the salt, blending until smooth. Set aside covered at room temperature for 2 hours. The batter will be thin at first, but will thicken to a cream-like consistency as it sits.

Meanwhile, in a dry pan, combine the coriander, mustard, and cumin seeds. Toast over medium heat until fragrant. Transfer the seeds to a plate and set aside.

Preheat the oven to 450°F.

In a 10-inch cast-iron pan (if you don't have one, use an ovenproof sauté pan, see note, p. 74), heat 2 tablespoons of the oil over medium-low heat. Add the red onions and sauté for 5 to 6 minutes, until soft. Add the garlic, onion powder, curry powder, reserved toasted spices, and remaining ½ teaspoon salt, stirring well. Add the cilantro and sauté for 2 minutes. Transfer to a small bowl and let cool slightly.

Stir the cooled onion mixture into the chickpea batter.

Wipe out the sauté pan and heat over high heat until very hot. Add the remaining tablespoon of oil, swirling the pan to coat, then add the chickpea batter. Bake for 20 minutes, until set and starting to get brown and crispy at the edges. If you'd like the top toasted too, broil for 1 minute.

Transfer the socca to a cutting board and cut into four pieces. Serve hot, with a sprinkle of salt. Store leftovers in an airtight container in the fridge for up to 5 days. Toast to serve.

Calories/serving: 220
Protein/serving: 6 g
Carbs/serving: 12 g
Fat/serving: 15 g
Fiber/serving: 3 g

Seed Bread

DF/GF/GRF/OF/V

Makes 1 loaf (15 slices)

1 cup raw sunflower seeds

¾ cup raw pumpkin seeds

⅓ cup raw almonds, chopped

⅓ cup flax meal

⅓ cup psyllium husk

¼ cup chia seeds

2 tsp chopped fresh or dried thyme (optional)

1 tsp sea salt

1⅓ cups hot water

¼ cup tahini

This bread was inspired by the famous Life-Changing Loaf of Bread from Sarah Britton of *My New Roots*. I wanted to play around with a totally grain-free version and put further emphasis on the mighty magic of tiny seeds. Each slice of this nutrient-dense bread is an incredible source of minerals, protein, healthy fats, and fiber, and is a great low-carb option too. Since it's a touch more crumbly than regular bread, it doesn't work well for closed sandwiches; instead, toast it as a base for open-face sandwiches.

Serving Note: Make this bread the star of your meal. All it needs is something simple, like the Beet Thyme Cashew Dip (p. 138) topped with sliced avocado or one of my pestos (p. 123) and some fresh tomato. Or just drizzle it with olive oil, sprinkle with salt and pepper, and serve with scrambled eggs.

Line a 5 × 9-inch or 4½ × 8½-inch loaf pan with parchment paper, with a couple of inches of paper hanging over the sides.

In a large bowl, combine the sunflower seeds, pumpkin seeds, almonds, flax meal, psyllium husk, chia seeds, thyme (if using), and salt. In a separate bowl, mix the hot water and tahini together, then add to the bowl with the dry ingredients and mix everything together. Transfer to the prepared pan and pack the top down well.

Meanwhile, preheat the oven to 375°F.

Bake for 30 minutes. Remove the loaf from the pan by lifting it up with the parchment overhang. Turn the loaf upside down onto the same parchment paper and transfer directly onto the oven rack. Bake for 20 to 25 minutes, until the seeds on the bottom are golden and a slight crust forms. Let cool completely on a wire rack, for at least 2 hours and up to 3 hours before slicing.

Store in an airtight container in the fridge for up to 5 days. This bread is best served toasted.

Calories/slice: 160
Carbs/slice: 3 g
Protein/slice: 6 g
Fat/slice: 13 g
Fiber/slice: 5 g

Rosemary Onion Skillet Bread

DF/GF/GRF

Makes 1 (10-inch) bread (8 slices)

2 cups fine almond meal

¼ cup tapioca starch

2 tbsp flax meal

1 tsp onion powder

1 tsp sea salt

¾ tsp baking soda

4 eggs

1 cup Caramelized Balsamic
    Onions, cooled (p. 110)
    (see note)

¼ cup extra virgin olive oil

2 tsp apple cider vinegar

1 tbsp chopped fresh rosemary
    + more for garnish

A favorite among my friends and clients, this is a simple, incredibly satisfying, and nutritious gluten-free bread. With characteristics similar to focaccia (the best bread, in my opinion), it is dense and full of flavor, with a crispy exterior. The almond meal adds a light, chewy texture, protein, and an assortment of vitamins, while balsamic onions lend their sweetness. I guarantee this is one recipe you'll keep coming back to!

Serving Note: Make this bread on the weekend as part of a brunch spread, or as a side for dinner with friends. It goes great with soups, like the Butternut Squash Soup (p. 152), Creamy Cashew Mushroom Soup (p. 154), or Lemon Lentil Soup (p. 147), or toasted and enjoyed with the Kale Pine Nut Caesar (p. 168).

Preheat the oven to 350°F. Grease a 10-inch cast-iron skillet.

In a large bowl, whisk together the almond meal, tapioca starch, flax meal, onion powder, salt, and baking soda.

In a separate bowl, whisk together the eggs, onions, oil, vinegar, and rosemary.

Add the egg mixture to the flour mixture and stir until combined.

Pour the batter into the prepared skillet and press some more rosemary into the top.

Bake for 25 to 30 minutes, until soft and golden. Let cool for at least 5 minutes. Slice it and eat straight out of the skillet.

Once cool, leftover slices can be stored in an airtight container in the fridge for up to 3 days, but they probably won't last that long! Reheat in a toaster or a 350°F oven.

Note: If you don't have time to make Caramelized Balsamic Onions, swap them out for 1 cup of chopped sautéed red onions—just make sure they are cooled before using.

Calories/slice: 311
Carbs/slice: 10 g
Protein/slice: 10 g
Fat/slice: 25 g
Fiber/slice: 4 g

protein add-ons

Marinated Mediterranean Tofu

DF/GF/V

Beauty + Anti-Aging, Cellular Building + Healing, Mood Balancing

Makes 4 servings

3 cups water

1 lb (454 g) firm tofu, cut into ½-inch cubes

3 tbsp extra virgin olive oil + more to serve

2 tbsp apple cider vinegar

2 tbsp fresh lemon juice

1 tbsp shiro or aka miso

1 tbsp nutritional yeast

1 tbsp onion powder

2 tsp dried oregano

1½ tsp sea salt + more to serve

Fresh ground pepper to serve

This is such a wonderful way of preparing tofu, the Mediterranean marinade infusing the tofu with a balanced salty, herbed flavor. I love that it can be enjoyed either hot or cold and how versatile it is as a quick add-on or snack. Easy to make and keep stocked in the fridge, it's a perfect way to add a delicious protein-rich topping to any plate, salad, or bowl.

Serving Note: My favorite way to enjoy this tofu, besides eating it solo, is to add it to roasted spaghetti squash (p. 211) with some Savory Tomato Sauce (p. 134). You could also try a little scoop on the Summer Pesto Quinoa Bowl (p. 224) or over the Herby Greek Salad (p. 164). Or use it as a sub for feta in the Caper Feta Broccoli (p. 192) or even alongside the feta as an added protein boost! It's wonderful on a simple avocado toast with olive oil and chili flakes.

In a medium pot, bring the water to a boil. Add the tofu and cook for 4 minutes; the water will come to a boil again. Drain the tofu and let it cool in the colander.

In a large bowl, combine all the remaining ingredients, mixing until smooth.

Add the cooled tofu to the marinade and mix with a spoon, smashing some of the cubes into smaller pieces. Cover and marinate in the fridge, stirring a few times, for at least 1 hour, and ideally overnight, as the tofu will only continue to get better. Stir well before serving.

Eat cold or heat in a warm pan, and serve with a drizzle of oil and a sprinkle of salt and pepper. Store in the fridge for up to 4 days.

Calories/serving: 242
Carbs/serving: 2 g
Protein/serving: 15 g
Fat/serving: 18 g
Fiber/serving: 1 g

Smoky Maple Tempeh

DF/GF/GRF/V

Cellular Building + Healing, Gut Health

Makes 4 servings

3 tbsp maple syrup

2 tbsp gluten-free tamari

2 tbsp extra virgin olive oil

1 tsp smoked paprika (add ½ tsp more if you love it smoky)

1 tsp garlic powder

½ tsp ground cumin

¼ tsp chipotle powder

8 oz (227 g) grain-free tempeh, cut into ¼-inch-thick strips

Tempeh is a live-cultured soy product that is a great source of highly digestible plant-based protein. Make this tempeh for easy snacking when you need a hit of protein; it is a super mineral-rich addition to almost anything, from wraps and rolls to noodles and bowls. The marinade has a sweet and subtle smokiness and is easy to prepare ahead of time. You may want to double the recipe, as it goes fast!

Serving Note: These strips can go in a breakfast wrap with Sweet Potato Fries (p. 178) and Chunky Guacamole (p. 137), or can be crumbled or cubed to use as croutons on any salad or charcuterie platter. They're also great in a sandwich with tomato, red onion, and lettuce, or in any noodle bowl, nori roll, or salad roll.

In a small bowl, whisk together all the ingredients except the tempeh.

Arrange the tempeh in a shallow dish or container, or a sealable plastic bag (this option works best). Pour the marinade over top, making sure each piece is well coated. Cover or seal and let marinate at room temperature for 60 minutes, turning the pieces halfway through to ensure they're marinated evenly. (Or marinate in the fridge overnight; they only get better!)

Preheat the oven to 350°F. Line a rimmed baking sheet with parchment paper.

Arrange the tempeh on the prepared pan, setting any remaining marinade aside. Bake for 10 minutes, then flip each piece and brush any remaining marinade over top. Bake for 10 minutes, until browned.

Store the cooled tempeh in an airtight container in the fridge for up to 3 days.

Calories/serving: 217

Carbs/serving: 13 g

Protein/serving: 13 g

Fat/serving: 13 g

Fiber/serving: 2 g

Salmon Bites: 2 Ways

Dill Dijon Salmon Bites
Miso Maple Salmon Bites

I make these little flavor-packed bites for myself all the time. I love having them in my fridge, ready to go. I eat them straight, hot or cold, and add them to salads and bowls for a quick protein boost with a healthy dose of omega-3s, fatty acids, and vitamins.

Dill Dijon Salmon Bites

DF/GF/GRF

Anti-Inflammatory, Cellular Building + Healing

Makes 4 servings

1 lb (454 g) wild salmon or steelhead trout fillet, deboned and skin removed

1 tbsp maple syrup or honey

1 tbsp Dijon mustard

1 tbsp gluten-free tamari

Zest of 1 lemon

1 tbsp fresh lemon juice

1 tbsp extra virgin olive oil

1 tsp pressed garlic (optional)

¼ tsp fresh ground pepper

¼ cup chopped fresh dill to serve

Variation: For a crispier finish, broil the bites for the last minute of the baking time.

These delicately flavored lemon and dill bites have a lovely sweetness and a fresh taste.

Serving Note: These bites are perfect as a protein-forward side at a big brunch! They also go beautifully with the Buttered Sweet Potato Ribbons (p. 179).

Pat the salmon dry and cut it into 1-inch-wide strips, about 3 inches long.

In a medium bowl, combine all the remaining ingredients except the dill. Add the salmon and mix well. Cover and marinate in the fridge for 25 minutes.

Meanwhile, preheat the oven to 400°F. Line a rimmed baking sheet with parchment paper.

Arrange the salmon on the prepared pan. Use a spatula to scrape any remaining marinade over top.

Bake for 7 minutes, until the fish flakes easily with a fork. Let rest for 2 minutes. Serve garnished with dill.

Store cooled salmon bites in an airtight container in the fridge for up to 3 days. Leftovers are delicious eaten cold or can be wrapped in aluminum foil and gently warmed in the oven at 350°F for 10 minutes.

Calories/serving: 226
Carbs/serving: 4 g
Protein/serving: 26 g
Fat/serving: 12 g
Fiber/serving: 0 g

Miso Maple Salmon Bites

Anti-Inflammatory, Cellular Building + Healing

Makes 4 servings

1 lb (454 g) wild salmon
or steelhead trout fillet,
deboned and skin removed

1 tbsp micrograted peeled
fresh ginger

2 tbsp aka miso

2 tbsp maple syrup

1 tbsp toasted sesame oil

1 tbsp gluten-free tamari

1 tbsp mirin

½ Thai red chili, finely chopped
(optional) (see note)

⅓ cup finely chopped green
onions

3 tbsp finely chopped fresh
cilantro

Sea salt to taste

Variation: For a crispier finish,
broil the bites for the last minute
of the baking time. You can also
leave the salmon skin on.

These gingery maple miso bites have an amazing flavor that my clients love. They satisfy a craving for sweet, spicy, and savory, all in one.

Serving Note: My clients love it when I leave some of these bites in their fridge for snacking. They are great served warm with the Cauliflower Fried Rice (p. 222), Acorn Squash (p. 182), or Sesame Gomae (p. 169). You can also mash them and wrap them in nori with avocado, sprouts, and sweet pickles.

Pat the salmon dry and cut it into 1-inch cubes.

In a medium bowl, combine the ginger, miso, maple syrup, oil, tamari, and mirin, mixing until completely smooth. Stir in the chili, green onion, and cilantro. Add the salmon, cover, and marinate in the fridge for 30 minutes, stirring occasionally.

Meanwhile, preheat the oven to 400°F. Line a rimmed baking sheet with parchment paper.

Arrange the salmon on the prepared pan and pour the marinade over top, removing as many red chilis as possible (be forewarned–they're spicy!).

Bake for 7 minutes, or until the fish flakes easily with a fork. Let rest for 2 minutes. Serve garnished with green onions and a sprinkling of salt.

Store cooled salmon bites in an airtight container in the fridge for up to 3 days. Leftovers are delicious eaten cold or can be wrapped in aluminum foil and gently warmed in the oven at 350°F for 10 minutes.

Calories/serving: 254
Carbs/serving: 11 g
Protein/serving: 26 g
Fat/serving: 11 g
Fiber/serving: 1 g

White Fish & Potato Cakes

DF/GF/GRF

Cellular Building + Healing, Immune Support, Mood Balancing

Makes 12 to 16 small fish cakes (4 servings)

2 medium russet potatoes (about 1 lb)

1¼ lb (567 g) boneless skinless halibut, cod, or other white fish

2 tbsp extra virgin olive oil

Salt and fresh ground pepper

2 eggs

¼ cup almond meal

⅓ cup minced white onions

3 tbsp minced drained capers

2 tsp micrograted peeled fresh ginger

2 tsp lemon zest

1 tsp onion powder

1 tsp garlic powder

1 tsp smoked paprika

¼ tsp cayenne (optional, if you like it spicy)

Lemon wedge to serve

Chopped fresh dill to serve

Fish cakes are a great way to incorporate fish into your meal planning; they're so versatile and can be served as a great dinner party main, a salad topping, or a solo snack. Potatoes give these a tender, fluffy texture, and I love the flavorful, immune-supporting combo of onions, garlic, ginger, and lemon. Plus, the fish contains selenium and vitamin D, which are also great for your immune system!

Serving Note: I love a fish and chips-style platter with these, Chipotle Aioli (p. 141), and Sweet Potato Fries (p. 178), or with Lemon Garlic Spinach (p. 184) and Tzatziki (p. 240), or even alongside the Green Curry (p. 216).

Preheat the oven to 350°F. Line a large rimmed baking sheet with parchment paper.

Pierce the potatoes with a fork to release steam while baking. Bake the potatoes directly on the oven rack for 70 to 90 minutes until soft. Let cool.

Meanwhile, place the fish on the prepared pan, brush with ½ tablespoon of the oil, and season with salt and pepper. Bake alongside the potatoes for 15 to 20 minutes, until the fish is opaque and flakes easily with a fork. Let cool, then flake the fish into a large bowl. Set aside.

Increase the oven temperature to 375°F. Reline the baking sheet with parchment paper and brush with ½ tablespoon of the oil.

Remove the potatoes' skins. In a separate large bowl, roughly mash the potato with a fork. Add the fish and the remaining ingredients, including the remaining 1 tablespoon of oil, and 1 teaspoon each salt and pepper; combine well.

Scoop about ¼ cup of the mixture into the palm of your hand and form into a puck roughly 2½ × 1½ inches. Place on the prepared sheet. Repeat to get 12 to 16 cakes total, spacing them evenly.

Bake for 10 minutes, flip the cakes, then bake for another 10 to 15 minutes, until lightly browned on each side. Sprinkle each cake with more salt and pepper while still hot. Serve with dill sprinkled on top and lemon wedges.

Once cooled, store the fish cakes in an airtight container in the fridge for up to 3 days or in the freezer for up to 2 months. Enjoy cold or, to reheat, wrap in aluminum foil and warm in the oven at 350°F for about 10 minutes.

Calories/serving: 365
Carbs/serving: 22 g
Protein/serving: 34 g
Fat/serving: 15 g
Fiber/serving: 3 g

Chicken Satay

DF/GF/GRF

Beauty + Anti-Aging, Mood Balancing

Makes 4 servings

Chicken Satay
½ cup canned coconut milk
2 tbsp extra virgin olive oil
2 tbsp honey
2 tbsp gluten-free tamari
2 tbsp fish sauce
2 tbsp fresh lime juice
4 tsp curry powder
2 tsp garlic powder
2 tsp micrograted peeled fresh
    ginger (optional but amazing)
1 lb (454 g) boneless skinless
    chicken breasts or thighs, cut
    into 1-inch cubes

To Serve
Sea salt to taste (optional)
¼ cup chopped fresh cilantro
Sriracha
Lime wedges

Variation: For a full veggie
option or to add to your chicken
skewers before cooking, use
2 cups bite-sized broccoli florets,
2 cups bite-sized red peppers,
½ cup cubed pineapple, and
1 small red onion, chopped into
bite-sized pieces. Marinate the
veggies in 1 tbsp extra virgin
olive oil, 1 tbsp fresh lime juice,
1 tbsp gluten-free tamari, and
½ tbsp honey or maple syrup,
mixed with 1 tsp garlic powder
and 1 tsp micrograted peeled
fresh ginger. Bake or grill as
directed in the recipe.

Simply delicious, this Southeast Asian–inspired chicken satay is one of my clients' most requested grab-and-go snacks. The chicken is beautifully seasoned with an array of fragrant spices and coconut milk, making it a perfect high-protein add-on to elevate your favorite salad or bowl. I love serving the skewers with my Coconut Almond Sauce (p. 132)—the combination is wildly delicious and makes a wonderful addition to any dinner party.

Serving Note: These are wonderful plated alongside the Sautéed Greens with Toasted Spices (p. 186), Cucumber Herb Salad (p. 159), or the Acorn Squash (p. 182). Or you can use the chicken (without sauce) to top the Shiitake Ginger Mung Bean Noodles (p. 218) or a big salad.

In a large bowl, combine all the ingredients except the chicken. Add the chicken and toss gently to coat. Cover and let marinate in the fridge overnight.

Preheat the oven to 425°F. Line a rimmed baking sheet with parchment paper. You can either bake the chicken directly on the baking sheet, or thread onto skewers. If using wooden skewers, soak 4 large or 8 small skewers in water for 30 minutes before use. Thread the chicken onto the skewers (make sure the chicken isn't falling off; you may need to thread each piece twice) and place the skewers on the prepared sheet.

Bake for 15 minutes, turning halfway through, until the chicken reaches an internal temperature of 165°F and is no longer pink inside. (Or try cooking these on the barbecue: Grill over medium-high heat for 8 to 10 minutes, rotating every couple of minutes, until nicely browned on all sides and no longer pink inside.)

Season with salt to taste, if desired. Serve garnished with cilantro, a sprinkle of sriracha, and some fresh lime wedges.

Store the cooled skewers in an airtight container in the fridge for up to 3 days. Enjoy cold or drizzle with a little olive oil, wrap in aluminum foil, and gently warm in the oven at 350°F for about 10 minutes.

Calories/serving: 281
Carbs/serving: 6 g
Protein/serving: 36 g
Fat/serving: 11 g
Fiber/serving: 1 g

Ginger Cilantro Turkey Meatballs

DF/GF/GRF

Beauty + Anti-Aging, Cellular Building + Healing, Immune Support

*Makes about 16 meatballs
(4 servings)*

1 tbsp extra virgin olive oil

1 cup finely chopped fresh cilantro + more to serve

½ cup finely chopped green onions + more to serve

1 tbsp finely grated peeled fresh ginger

2 tbsp toasted sesame oil

1 tbsp gluten-free tamari

1 tsp garlic powder

½ tsp sea salt + more to taste

¼ tsp fresh ground pepper

1 lb (454 g) ground turkey

¼ cup almond meal or chickpea flour (I prefer almond meal)

1 egg, beaten

Variation: Meatballs are also amazing when fried before baking! In a large sauté pan, heat a little olive oil over medium heat and fry the meatballs in batches, searing each side for about 2 minutes, until browned. Bake at 400°F in the sauté pan (if ovenproof) or on a parchment-lined baking sheet for about 10 to 12 minutes, until they reach an internal temperature of 165°F.

I like anything you can just grab and go, pop on a plate, or easily fold into a wrap, and meatballs fit that description perfectly. These ones are seasoned with immune-supportive ginger and my favorite detoxifying herb: cilantro. They are packed with protein, folate, iron, and a wealth of minerals and antioxidants from the herbs, which also give these meatballs their exquisite flavor.

Serving Note: These meatballs are great with Broccoli Parmesan Mini Flatbreads (p. 83) and Tzatziki (p. 240). For a dinner party or brunch, serve them on a platter with Chermoula (p. 125).

Preheat the oven to 400°F. Line a rimmed baking sheet with parchment paper and lightly brush the paper with the olive oil.

In a large bowl, thoroughly combine the cilantro, green onions, ginger, sesame oil, tamari, garlic powder, salt, and pepper. Gently fold the turkey through the mixture a few times, then add the almond meal and egg and, using your hands, mix until evenly combined, being careful not to overmix.

Scoop roughly 2 tablespoons of the mixture into your hands, shape as best you can into a ball, and place on the prepared pan. Repeat with the remaining mixture, spacing the balls evenly; you should get about 16 meatballs in total. Sprinkle the meatballs with a touch more salt.

Bake for 18 to 20 minutes, turning halfway through, until the meatballs reach an internal temperature of 165°F. Serve garnished with green onions and cilantro.

Store the cooled meatballs in an airtight container in the fridge for up to 3 days. Enjoy cold or wrap in aluminum foil and reheat in the oven at 350°F for about 10 minutes.

Calories/serving: 333
Carbs/serving: 4 g
Protein/serving: 22 g
Fat/serving: 26 g
Fiber/serving: 1 g

Herbed Butter Beans

DF/GF/GRF/V

Cellular Building + Healing, Immune Support, Mood Balancing

Makes 4 servings

¼ cup extra virgin olive oil

2 (14 oz/398 ml) cans butter beans, drained, rinsed, and dried with a towel (or 3 cups cooked butter beans)

1¼ tsp sea salt + more to serve

½ tsp fresh ground pepper

1 cup roughly chopped fresh flat-leaf parsley

1 tbsp pressed garlic

1 tbsp fresh lemon juice + more to serve

Variation: This recipe works perfectly with chickpeas too.

I love these butter beans, which are seasoned here with garlic, fresh parsley, and zesty lemon to make delightful bursts of flavor and nutrition. Packed with essential minerals and vitamins, butter beans are a fantastic way to enhance any bowl or plate with a generous boost of protein, fiber, and texture. This recipe is delicious and can be enjoyed either hot or cold!

Serving Note: These butter beans go best with light and summery salads and soups, like the Arugula & Roasted Squash Salad (p. 172), a salad with Dijon Vinaigrette (p. 128), the Herby Greek Salad (p. 164), or the Green Detox Soup (p. 150). One of my favorite ways to serve them is with thinly sliced roasted cauliflower, feta, and lemon zest, or with poached eggs and Lemon Garlic Spinach (p. 184). Or keep them in the fridge to snack on!

In a large sauté pan, heat the oil over medium heat. Add the butter beans, salt, and pepper and sauté for 8 minutes, stirring occasionally, until the beans look a little golden and some have started to blister. Add the parsley, garlic, and lemon juice and cook, stirring, for 2 minutes. Serve with more lemon juice and salt to taste.

Store the cooled beans in an airtight container in the fridge for up to 4 days. Enjoy cold or reheat in a sauté pan with a little olive oil over low heat.

Calories/serving: 293
Carbs/serving: 22 g
Protein/serving: 12 g
Fat/serving: 14 g
Fiber/serving: 11 g

other essentials

Spiced Mixed Nuts & Seeds

DF/GF/GRF/OF/V

Cellular Building + Healing, Energy + Focus, Mood Balancing

Makes about 3½ cups (10 servings)

1½ cups raw almonds

1½ cups raw cashews

½ cup raw pumpkin seeds

2 tbsp ume plum vinegar

½ tsp smoked paprika

1 tsp fresh ground pepper

Variation: Feel free to mix up the nut combo with your favorites, or do all seeds! Try other spices too; I love adding just a hint of cayenne.

Having my own nut and seed mix while traveling is one of the nicest things I can do for myself (and those with me)–it's an amazing way to receive nutrients and calories and avoid getting hangry on the road. Making your own mix also ensures the quality of the ingredients, as you know exactly what goes into it. This recipe incorporates one of my favorite ingredients, ume plum vinegar, with its naturally salty, sour kiss. With a dry roast and no added oil or sugar, followed by a light toss to bind the spices, it's an incredibly easy and delicious snack that is sure to become one of your staples.

Serving Note: Besides always having a bag of these in my pocket, I also use them to add an amazing pop of flavor and texture to any meal! I like to put a little bowl of them on an appy platter, or chop them up to crumble over Sautéed Greens (p. 186), Cauliflower Fried Rice (p. 222), the Cucumber Herb Salad (p. 159), or a noodle bowl!

Preheat the oven to 300°F. Line a baking sheet with parchment paper.

Evenly spread out the almonds, cashews, and pumpkin seeds on the prepared pan. Roast in the oven for 10 to 12 minutes, until golden and fragrant.

Immediately transfer the roasted nuts and seeds to a medium bowl. While they are still hot, toss them with the vinegar, paprika, and pepper. Mix very well, until the nuts are generously coated.

Spread the nuts back out on the pan to cool. Store in an airtight container at room temperature or in the fridge for up to 1 week.

Calories/serving: 241

Carbs/serving: 8 g

Protein/serving: 9 g

Fat/serving: 20 g

Fiber/serving: 3 g

Caramelized Balsamic Onions

DF/GF/GRF/V

Detoxifying, Gut Health

Makes about 2 cups (8 servings)

3 tbsp extra virgin olive oil

6 cups chopped or sliced
　　red onions or sweet onions

2 tbsp maple syrup

3 tbsp balsamic vinegar

1 tsp sea salt + more to taste

1 to 2 tbsp water (if needed)

½ tsp fresh ground pepper
　　+ more to taste

I always have these around because there are endless ways to use them. They give such beautiful depth of flavor to any dish they are added to! Use this recipe as a general guide, then play around with it to find your favorite flavor profile: try adding some smoked paprika or some honey and chili flakes.

Serving Note: These are a key part of the Rosemary Onion Skillet Bread (p. 90), and you can also add a few to the Zucchini Parmesan Egg Muffins (p. 70), toss a handful into the Arugula & Roasted Squash Salad (p. 172), or blend ½ cup into the Pine Nut Caesar Dressing (p. 168). I also love them on a charcuterie plate with Rainbow Escabeche (p. 114), cheese, Roasted Carrot Tahini Dip (p. 140), and lots of veggies.

In a 12-inch sauté pan, heat the oil over medium heat. Add the onions and cook, stirring often, for 5 minutes. Reduce the heat to medium-low and cook, stirring regularly, until the onions are translucent, about 8 to 10 minutes.

Add the maple syrup and stir until absorbed, about 2 minutes. Add the vinegar and salt. Keep stirring until the liquid evaporates and the onions start to caramelize, about 12 to 15 minutes. Add 1 to 2 tablespoons of water if needed to scrape up anything stuck to the bottom of the pan, then season with pepper and stir well. Remove from the heat and let cool.

Store the cooled onions in an airtight container in the fridge for up to 1 week.

Calories/serving: 122

Carbs/serving: 16 g

Protein/serving: 2 g

Fat/serving: 5 g

Fiber/serving: 2 g

Quick Pickled Jalapeños or Onions

DF/GF/GRF/OF/V

Gut Health, Immune Support

Makes about 1 cup (4 servings)

1 cup thinly sliced jalapeños or finely sliced or diced red onions

1 cup water

1 cup rice vinegar

2 tbsp apple cider vinegar

2 cloves garlic, peeled and left whole

1 tsp sea salt

1 tsp dried oregano (optional)

I love to have these in the fridge, and find myself making them at least once a week. There's something about pickled jalapeños or onions that gives a meal that extra-special sparkle: a crunch, a tangy kick, a pop of color. These are quick and easy to make, and can go on anything. Bonus: eating something with vinegar can help stimulate digestion!

Serving Note: These sugar-free quick pickles will add flavor and texture to anything from noodle bowls to wraps to savory breakfasts. I love them alongside the Spiced Tofu Scramble (p. 72), on toast with Edamame Cilantro Hummus (p. 142), or in lettuce wraps with Chimichurri Chicken (p. 252) and avocado.

Place the jalapeños or onions in a heatproof jar or bowl (enough to hold up to 2 cups).

In a small pot, bring the remaining ingredients to a boil over high heat, then immediately remove from the heat.

Pour the hot pickling liquid over the jalapeños or onions. Let sit for at least 30 minutes or, when cool, cover and refrigerate overnight (but I usually can't wait that long!).

Store in the jar or another airtight container in the fridge for up to 2 weeks.

Note: To reduce heat, remove some of the seeds from the jalapeños.

Calories/serving: 21

Carbs/serving: 1 g

Protein/serving: 0 g

Fat/serving: 0 g

Fiber/serving: 1 g

Rainbow Escabeche

DF/GF/GRF/OF/V

Gut Health, Immune Support

Makes 2 (4-cup) mason jars (10 servings)

1 medium purple or white cauliflower

2 large carrots

1 bunch radishes

1 medium red onion

1 to 2 jalapeños

4 cloves garlic, smashed

2 bay leaves

Brine

3 cups water

1½ cups rice vinegar

1½ cups apple cider vinegar

3 tbsp sea salt

1½ tsp black peppercorns

1½ tsp coriander seeds

1½ tsp dried Mexican oregano (see note)

I fell in love with escabeche the first time I saw it on the table in Mexico City. This lightly pickled, spicy rainbow vegetable mix can garnish dishes, be served on charcuterie platters, or be used as a condiment. Crunchy and flavorful, and packed with antioxidants and fiber, it's one of my favorite things to keep on hand in my clients' kitchens (and my own)! Plus, starting a meal with some vinegar-marinated veg is a great way to aid digestion and help balance blood sugar.

Serving Note: Serve this in little bowls next to the Raw Walnut Lettuce Tacos (p. 206) or as part of a big spread with Edamame Cilantro Hummus (p. 142) and Chunky Guacamole (p. 137). Or grab some to snack on at any time!

Cut the cauliflower into bite-sized florets (you should have about 4 cups). Peel the carrots and, using a mandoline, thinly slice them into rounds (about 2 cups). Using the mandoline, thinly slice the radishes into rounds (about 2 cups). Cut the onion in half, then use the mandoline to thinly slice the halves into mini rainbows. Seed and thinly slice the jalapeños.

Layer the prepped vegetables into two 4-cup heatproof mason jars, creating a mixture of colors and textures. Divide the garlic between the jars. Add 1 bay leaf to each jar.

In a large pot, bring all the brine ingredients to a boil over high heat. Reduce the heat and simmer for 5 minutes.

Pour the hot brine over the vegetables. Let cool, then seal the jars and refrigerate for at least 1 hour before eating (but if you can wait, they get even better overnight!).

Store in the fridge for up to 3 weeks.

Note: Purple cauliflower will provide a stronger color, but regular cauliflower will still be beautiful. If you can't find Mexican oregano, substitute marjoram or Mediterranean oregano.

Calories/serving: 38
Carbs/serving: 4 g
Protein/serving: 2 g
Fat/serving: 0 g
Fiber/serving: 2 g

Pistachio Dukkah

DF/GF/GRF/OF/V

Anti-Inflammatory, Beauty + Anti-Aging, Mood Balancing

Makes about 1¼ cups (12 servings)

½ cup raw walnut halves
½ cup raw sunflower seeds
¼ cup raw shelled pistachios
2 tbsp black sesame seeds
½ tsp ground cumin
½ tsp ground coriander
½ tsp sea salt

Dukkah is a mixture of spices, nuts, and seeds that is used as a condiment in Egypt and throughout the Middle East. It is spicy, crunchy, and so versatile. This one is full of healthy fats, protective antioxidants, and supportive minerals, and adds a beautiful finishing touch to any plate, enhancing its texture, flavor, and nutrition.

Serving Note: Use dukkah to garnish Lemongrass Cauliflower & Sweet Potato (p. 198), Sautéed Greens (p. 186), or Lentil Bolognese (p. 214). For added texture and flavor, sprinkle it over the Roasted Carrots (p. 236) or Chimichurri Chicken (p. 252). It's great on any soup, like Butternut Squash Soup (p. 152), or sprinkled over sliced avocado or cucumber. It's also delicious with tomatoes and hummus on toast or over hardboiled eggs.

Heat a large sauté pan over medium heat. Add the walnuts, sunflower seeds, and pistachios and toast, stirring gently, for about 3 minutes, until fragrant. In the final minute of toasting, add the sesame seeds. Remove from the heat and let cool completely.

Transfer the nuts and seeds to a mini food processor and add the remaining ingredients. Pulse a few times, until the mixture is finely ground, but leave a few larger pieces for texture and be careful not to over-blend into a paste.

Store in an airtight container in the fridge for up to 1 week.

Calories/serving: 85
Carbs/serving: 2 g
Protein/serving: 3 g
Fat/serving: 8 g
Fiber/serving: 1 g

Sauces & Spreads

sauces

Hemp Chili Crema

DF/GF/GRF/OF/V

Beauty + Anti-Aging, Cellular Building + Healing, Immune Support

Makes about 1 cup (4 servings)

¼ cup water + more if needed

2 tbsp apple cider vinegar

2 tbsp fresh lime juice

1 tbsp tomato paste

1 clove garlic, pressed

½ cup hemp hearts

¼ cup chopped fresh cilantro

1 tbsp chopped green onions

½ tsp onion powder

½ tsp ground cumin

½ tsp chili powder

½ tsp dried oregano

½ tsp sea salt

¼ tsp cayenne (optional, if you like it spicy)

This beautifully seasoned, protein-rich crema-inspired sauce is loaded with antioxidants and skin-supportive vitamins and minerals from the herbs, spices, and tomato paste. It's an exceptionally flavorful vegan cream sauce that elevates any dish, and is a wonderful way to add more protein to a meal!

Serving Note: This crema with the Raw Walnut Lettuce Tacos (p. 206) is a match made in heaven! Or try it drizzled over the Spiced Tofu Scramble (p. 72) with Sautéed Greens (p. 186). It would also make a great sauce for a collard wrap! I love to toss roasted squash or sweet potatoes with this crema a few minutes before they come out of the oven, and drizzle more over top. So good.

Adding the liquid first, combine all the ingredients in a high-powered blender. Blend until very smooth, starting on low and increasing to high after a few seconds. Add more water, 1 tablespoon at a time, as needed to reach your desired consistency.

Store in an airtight container in the fridge for up to 3 days.

Calories/serving: 151
Carbs/serving: 3 g
Protein/serving: 7 g
Fat/serving: 13 g
Fiber/serving: 1 g

Pesto: 2 Ways

Basil Pesto
Cilantro Sunflower Pesto

Oh, how I love pesto! I've selected two of my all-time favorite versions to share with you. I begin with a classic combination of basil and pine nuts, then take this beloved staple in a new direction by incorporating some of my favorite flavor makers, like capers, cilantro, tamari, and lemon zest. Either way, the results are delicious!

Basil Pesto

DF/GF/GRF/V

Makes about 1 cup (4 servings)

⅓ cup extra virgin olive oil

Zest of ½ lemon

2 tbsp fresh lemon juice

2 cups packed fresh basil leaves

½ cup pine nuts, toasted and cooled (see p. 276)

1 tsp pressed garlic + more to taste

½ tsp sea salt + more to taste

Variation: For a slightly different flavor, try the recipe with half toasted pine nuts and half toasted walnuts.

This versatile classic helps me transform yesterday's leftover vegetables into today's beautiful meal. With plenty of basil to support and protect the cells, this pesto is rich in beautifying vitamins and minerals—not to mention flavor!

Serving Note: Pair this with zucchini ribbons (see p. 277) or dollop it on top of smashed avocado on toasted Seed Bread (p. 88).

Adding the liquids first, combine all the ingredients in a mini food processor or high-powered blender. Blend on high until smooth. Adjust the seasoning with more garlic and salt to taste.

Store in an airtight container in the fridge for up to 5 days.

Calories/serving: 274
Carbs/serving: 3 g
Protein/serving: 3 g
Fat/serving: 28 g
Fiber/serving: 2 g

Cilantro Sunflower Pesto

DF/GF/GRF/V

Makes about 1 cup (4 servings)

⅓ cup extra virgin olive oil

¼ tsp lemon zest

1 tbsp fresh lemon juice

1 tbsp gluten-free tamari

3 cloves garlic (or 1 tsp pressed, or more if you love garlic)

2 cups packed roughly chopped fresh cilantro

½ cup sunflower seeds, toasted and cooled (see p. 276)

¼ cup chopped seeded jalapeños

2 tbsp drained capers

¼ tsp fresh ground pepper (optional)

Variation: Try pine nuts instead of sunflower seeds for an even richer flavor.

This pesto might just be my favorite; it's spicy, bright, and nutrient-dense. The cilantro contributes its unique flavor and is also rich in antioxidants, creating a nutritious combo when mixed with the protein-rich sunflower seeds.

Serving Note: Try this on the Spring Vegetable Frittata (p. 73) or roasted spaghetti squash (see p. 211). It's also great with thinly sliced chicken, cucumber, and tomato in a Buckwheat Crepe (p. 68) or stuffed in a wrap with the Marinated Mediterranean Tofu (p. 93) and Quick Pickled Onions (p. 112).

Adding the liquids first, combine all the ingredients in a mini food processor or high-powered blender. Blend on high until smooth.

Store in an airtight container in the fridge for up to 3 days.

Calories/serving: 273
Carbs/serving: 4 g
Protein/serving: 5 g
Fat/serving: 27 g
Fiber/serving: 2 g

Green Sauce: 3 Ways

Chermoula
Chimichurri
Salsa Verde

I use these three parsley-based sauces *often* and over *everything*. They are all composed of three basic elements: fresh herbs, an acid such as lemon juice or vinegar, and a high-quality oil. The herbs elevate the flavor experience of a meal and give you lots of beautifying vitamins, like A, C, and K, and nourishing minerals, like iron. The acid brightens the sauce while aiding digestion, and the oil holds all the tastes together. I have an affinity for these green sauces; they're like adding multivitamins in the form of flavoring. Each one also offers unique phytonutrients and anti-inflammatory support, and can aid in detoxification. A drizzle can change the entire experience of a meal!

Chermoula

DF/GF/GRF/V

Anti-Inflammatory, Beauty + Anti-Aging, Detoxifying

Makes about 1 cup (4 servings)

½ cup extra virgin olive oil

Zest of 1 lemon

2 tbsp fresh lemon juice

1 cup packed roughly chopped fresh flat-leaf parsley

1 cup packed fresh cilantro

¼ cup roughly chopped fresh mint

2 tsp pressed garlic

2 tsp micrograted peeled fresh ginger

2 tsp coriander seeds, toasted (see p. 276)

2 tsp cumin seeds, toasted

1 tsp sea salt + more to taste

½ tsp chili flakes

This chermoula recipe, based on the beautiful sauce from North Africa, is loaded with ginger, coriander seeds, and cumin seeds, which all offer inflammation support and detoxification. Add a mix of three flavor-rich herbs, and this becomes the spiciest, brightest, and most antioxidant-packed green sauce of the bunch.

Serving Note: Drizzle this over Curried Socca (p. 86), Red Lentil Dal (p. 226), or barbecued asparagus—it adds amazing flavor to any roasted veg plate or bowl. It also works on top of Herbed Lemon White Fish (p. 243) or Roasted Beet Carpaccio (p. 160), or with roasted tofu.

Adding the liquid first, combine all the ingredients in a mini food processor or high-powered blender. Pulse until the herbs are finely chopped but not puréed. Taste and adjust the seasoning as needed.

Store in an airtight container in the fridge for up to 5 days.

Calories/serving: 263
Carbs/serving: 3 g
Protein/serving: 1 g
Fat/serving: 28 g
Fiber/serving: 2 g

Chimichurri

DF/GF/GRF/V

Beauty + Anti-Aging, Gut Health, Immune Support

Makes about 1 cup (4 servings)

½ cup extra virgin olive oil

3 tbsp red wine vinegar

1½ cups packed roughly chopped fresh flat-leaf parsley

1 tbsp finely chopped garlic

1½ tsp dried oregano

1 tsp sea salt + more to taste

½ tsp chili flakes + more to garnish

Serve this Argentinian classic over starchier dishes to elevate flavor *and* nutrition: the phytonutrient-rich blend from garlic, parsley, and oregano gives both beautifying and immune-boosting properties.

Serving Note: Chimichurri is great on toasted Seed Bread (p. 88) with tomatoes, or with a roasted starchy veg like squash or potatoes. Try it in a wrap with roasted veg and hummus, or to dress a cucumber avocado salad.

Adding the liquid first, combine all the ingredients in a mini food processor or high-powered blender. Pulse until the parsley is finely chopped but not puréed. Adjust the seasoning with salt to taste. Garnish with more chili flakes.

Calories/serving: 257
Carbs/serving: 2 g
Protein/serving: 1 g
Fat/serving: 27 g
Fiber/serving: 1 g

Store in an airtight container in the fridge for up to 5 days.

Salsa Verde

DF/GF/GRF/V

Beauty + Anti-Aging, Detoxifying, Gut Health

Makes about 1 cup (4 servings)

⅓ cup extra virgin olive oil

Zest of 1 lemon

1 tbsp fresh lemon juice

1 tbsp apple cider vinegar

3 cloves garlic, finely grated

1½ cups packed roughly
    chopped fresh flat-leaf parsley

¼ cup drained capers

2 tbsp roughly chopped fresh basil

Sea salt and fresh ground pepper
    to taste

The lemon juice and apple cider vinegar combined with the parsley's phytonutrients make this Italian-inspired salsa verde great for digestion, enhancing a dish with a refreshing and zesty flavor. Its high vitamin C content will also help your body absorb iron, so it's a perfect accompaniment for iron-rich dishes like lentils and eggs.

Serving Note: Try this over Garlicky Roasted Portobellos (p. 188), white fish, or chicken breasts, or tossed with roasted spaghetti squash or Buttered Sweet Potato Ribbons (p. 179).

Adding the liquids first, combine all the ingredients in a mini food processor or high-powered blender. Pulse until roughly chopped or blend until smooth (chef's choice). Adjust the seasoning with salt and pepper to taste.

Store in an airtight container in the fridge for up to 5 days.

Calories/serving: 263
Carbs/serving: 3 g
Protein/serving: 1 g
Fat/serving: 28 g
Fiber/serving: 2 g

LC

Dijon Vinaigrette

DF/GF/GRF/V

Beauty + Anti-Aging, Energy + Focus, Gut Health

Makes about 1 cup (4 servings)

- 1 clove garlic, micrograted
- 2 tbsp minced shallots
- ¼ cup red wine vinegar
- 1 tbsp fresh lemon juice
- 1 tbsp nutritional yeast
- 4 tsp Dijon mustard
- 1 tsp honey (optional)
- ½ tsp sea salt + more to taste
- ¼ tsp fresh ground pepper + more to taste
- ½ cup extra virgin olive oil

While working in France, I quickly fell in love with the classic green salad and Dijon vinaigrette that were part of so many meals. I've strayed a little from the classic French-style dressing to up the nutritional benefits by sprinkling in some nutritional yeast, which is rich in protein and B vitamins. It's a bright, fresh, and tangy dressing that I like to serve with a salad before a big meal to moderate the appetite and prime the body for better digestion.

Serving Note: This dressing is delicious drizzled over crisp leafy greens—just add it a tablespoon at a time, as it is tart—but can really go with just about anything, from fresh herb and cucumber salads to sliced avocado to roasted veggies. It can even dress up a Roasted Beet Carpaccio *(p. 160)**.*

In a small bowl, whisk together all the ingredients except the oil. Slowly pour in the oil, whisking constantly until smooth. (Or just combine all the ingredients in a jar and shake very well until smooth!) Adjust the salt and pepper to taste.

Store in the jar or another airtight container in the fridge for up to 1 week.

Note: For a smoother, creamier dressing, use a high-powered or immersion blender and start with 1 tablespoon shallot, adding more to taste, as the flavor is stronger when blended.

Calories/serving: 259
Carbs/serving: 2 g
Protein/serving: 1 g
Fat/serving: 27 g
Fiber/serving: 1 g

Tahini Ginger Sauce

DF/GF/GRF/V

Beauty + Anti-Aging, Cellular Building + Healing

Makes about 2 cups (8 servings)

¾ cup tahini

½ cup water + more if needed

3 tbsp gluten-free tamari + more to taste

2 tbsp apple cider vinegar

2 tbsp rice vinegar

2 tbsp chopped green onions

1 tbsp toasted sesame oil + more to taste

1 tbsp micrograted peeled fresh ginger

1 tbsp chopped jalapeños or hot sauce (optional, if you like it spicy)

2 tsp pressed garlic

This high-protein, versatile sauce is what I call a meal maker— it can turn a few veggie sides into a balanced meal, or be served as a nutrient-boosting dip. Perfectly seasoned, it will enhance any dish, not only in flavor but in nutrition too. With a creamy lusciousness, tahini is the perfect base, offering healthy, skin-nourishing fats and many supportive minerals to support the body.

Serving Note: This sauce is a key component in the Roasted Rainbow Veggie Noodle Bowl (p. 220) and the Lentil Lettuce Cups (p. 208). You can also use it as a decadent dressing for a chopped romaine salad with roasted sweet potatoes and cucumber, or as a dip for veggies tucked inside a collard wrap!

Combine all the ingredients in a food processor or high-powered blender. Blend or pulse on high until smooth. Add more water, 1 tablespoon at a time, as needed to thin the sauce to a lighter consistency. Taste and adjust the seasoning with tamari or sesame oil if desired.

Store in an airtight container in the fridge for up to 5 days.

Calories/serving: 157

Carbs/serving: 4 g

Protein/serving: 5 g

Fat/serving: 14 g

Fiber/serving: 2 g

Coconut Almond Sauce

DF/GF/GRF/OF/V

Beauty + Anti-Aging, Cellular Building + Healing

Makes about 1 cup (4 servings)

½ cup canned coconut milk

⅓ cup almond butter

2½ tbsp fresh lime juice

1 tbsp gluten-free tamari

1 tsp pressed garlic

1 tsp micrograted peeled fresh ginger

1 tsp sambal oelek or sriracha + more to taste

1 tsp maple syrup

Chopped fresh cilantro to garnish

Variation: To keep the sauce thinner and easier to pour, don't heat it at all.

This delicious and luxurious sauce will strengthen you from the inside out, as it is rich with bone-building minerals. I also love that it is high in protein *and* oil-free, getting all its healthy fats from coconut milk and almond butter, which beautifully balance the flavors of the ginger, garlic, and lime. It is simple to make, incredibly versatile, and one of my all-time favorites.

Serving Note: I serve this sauce with Chicken Satay (p. 102) or alongside Rainbow Salad Rolls (p. 205). It makes a protein-rich addition to steamed or roasted vegetables. But by far its best use is in a noodle bowl (think coconut almond pad Thai)—there is nothing better! Make a double batch; you'll find a million ways to use it.

Combine all the ingredients except the cilantro in a mini food processor or high-powered blender. Blend until smooth.

Heat the sauce in a small saucepan over medium heat, stirring constantly, until just warm, about 30-40 seconds; the sauce will thicken a touch. Serve garnished with cilantro.

Store cooled sauce in an airtight container in the fridge for up to 5 days. Before serving, add just a little water to thin the sauce out again as desired.

Calories/serving: 187

Carbs/serving: 5 g

Protein/serving: 5 g

Fat/serving: 17 g

Fiber/serving: 3 g

Savory Tomato Sauce

DF/GF/GRF/V

Beauty + Anti-Aging, Cellular Building + Healing

Makes about 4 cups (4 servings)

¼ cup extra virgin olive oil

¼ cup pressed garlic

¼ cup drained capers

2 tbsp dried oregano

2 (28 oz/796 ml) cans peeled
    whole San Marzano tomatoes

1 cup roughly chopped fresh basil
    + more to serve

1 tbsp balsamic vinegar

2 tsp sea salt

Chili flakes to serve

Grated pecorino cheese to serve
    (optional)

Variation: Drain 2 (4 oz/114 g) cans of sardines, mash the fish, and add them to the sauce in the last 10 minutes of cooking; they will add a nice dose of omega-3s and protein!

Everyone should have a simple and delicious tomato sauce in their repertoire. Tomatoes are high in essential vitamins A, C, and K, as well as powerful antioxidants that protect and support healthy cells and skin. This was one of the first sauces I fell in love with when I started cooking. I would make it weekly and use it over veggie bowls, eggs, or just about any other savory dish. The quality of the tomatoes makes all the difference in this recipe; I highly recommend using San Marzano tomatoes.

Serving Note: This sauce is used in the Almond-Crusted White Fish (p. 248). It's also amazing with roasted spaghetti squash or zucchini ribbons (see p. 277), roasted potatoes with feta, roasted broccoli, or sautéed green beans and asparagus! My favorite way to eat it is spooned hot over a breakfast bowl of baked zucchini rounds, Lemon Garlic Spinach (p. 184), and scrambled eggs.

In a large sauté pan, heat the oil over medium heat. Add the garlic, capers, and oregano and cook, stirring well, for 2 minutes. Add the tomatoes, basil, vinegar, and salt, mixing very well and smashing the tomatoes to break them down a little. Bring to a rapid simmer, stirring and smashing the tomatoes a few times. Reduce the heat to low and simmer, uncovered, for 75 minutes, stirring occasionally, until the sauce is smooth and thick.

Serve topped with basil and chili flakes, and smothered in grated cheese (if using).

Store the cooled sauce in an airtight container in the fridge for up to 5 days.

Calories/serving: 241
Carbs/serving: 17 g
Protein/serving: 4 g
Fat/serving: 14 g
Fiber/serving: 8 g

spreads

Chunky Guacamole

DF/GF/GRF/V

Beauty + Anti-Aging, Energy + Focus

Makes about 2 cups (4 servings)

½ cup minced radishes

2 tbsp gluten-free tamari

2 tbsp fresh lemon juice

2 tbsp minced drained capers

2 tbsp extra virgin olive oil

2 tsp balsamic vinegar

2 tsp minced garlic

2 tsp onion powder

¼ tsp sea salt + more to taste

Pinch of lemon zest + more to taste

1½ cups diced avocados

Pinch of cayenne (optional)

Avocados are a fabulous source of healthy fat and an easy way to make a dish both creamy and delicious! This is my take on classic guacamole, made with some of my favorite flavor makers, like lemon zest, capers, and tamari, and given more texture with minced radishes. I've experimented with numerous variations over the years, but this one remains my most liked and most requested. It's glorious.

Serving Note: I love making avocado toast with this guacamole on Seed Bread (p. 88). It's also great in a wrap with Smoky Maple Tempeh (p. 95) and Sweet Potato Fries (p. 178), or in scooped-out cucumber cups!

In a small bowl, combine the radishes, tamari, and lemon juice, mixing well. Let the radishes marinate for 5 minutes.

In a large bowl, mix the capers, oil, vinegar, garlic, onion powder, salt, and lemon zest into a paste. Gently fold in the avocados, stopping after a few stirs.

Drain the liquid from the radishes and add them to the avocado mixture, discarding the liquid. Gently fold again. Taste and adjust the seasoning with salt and lemon zest. If desired, add a pinch of cayenne for some spice!

This guac is best eaten fresh, but can be stored in an airtight container in the fridge for up to 2 days. Limit its exposure to air by pressing plastic wrap on top of the guac to "seal" it.

Calories/serving: 220
Carbs/serving: 4 g
Protein/serving: 3 g
Fat/serving: 20 g
Fiber/serving: 6 g

Beet Thyme Cashew Dip

DF/GF/GRF/V

Cellular Building + Healing, Energy + Focus

Makes about 1½ cups (4 servings)

1 cup raw cashews

¼ cup extra virgin olive oil
    + more to garnish

4 tsp balsamic vinegar

1 tbsp gluten-free tamari

1 tbsp water

½ cup roasted, peeled, chopped
    beets (see p. 277)

1½ tbsp roughly chopped fresh
    thyme + more to taste

1 tbsp nutritional yeast

1 tsp onion powder

½ tsp sea salt + more to taste

Edible flowers to garnish
    (optional)

Vibrant in color and rich in flavor, this dip is the star of any appetizer platter! It is full of vitamins and minerals thanks to the beets, which are nutrient-rich and high in antioxidants. The earthiness of the roasted beets, the creaminess of the cashews, the savory taste of thyme, and the subtle umami flavor of the nutritional yeast are beautifully balanced.

Serving Note: This dip is great served on a charcuterie board with lots of fresh vegetables and Sesame Flax Crackers (p. 84) for dipping. It is perfect spread on a piece of toast with avocado or Marinated Mediterranean Tofu (p. 93), served next to the Salt & Pepper Veggies (p. 194), or even tossed with warm zucchini ribbons for a light lunch bowl!

In a bowl, soak the cashews in water overnight. Drain and rinse well.

Adding the liquid first, combine all the ingredients in a mini food processor or high-powered blender. Blend on high until creamy. Adjust the seasoning with salt or thyme to taste. Serve with a drizzle of olive oil and a sprinkling of more thyme. Garnish with edible flowers, if you have some.

Store in an airtight container in the fridge for up to 5 days.

Calories/serving: 323

Carbs/serving: 12 g

Protein/serving: 8 g

Fat/serving: 28 g

Fiber/serving: 2 g

Roasted Carrot Tahini Dip

DF/GF/V

Beauty + Anti-Aging, Detoxifying, Immune Support

Makes about 1¼ cups (4 servings)

2 medium carrots, peeled

1 tbsp extra virgin olive oil
+ more to garnish

3 tbsp tahini

2 tbsp fresh lemon juice

2 tbsp water

2 tbsp chopped fresh cilantro
(optional)

1 tbsp shiro miso

1 tsp finely grated peeled fresh
ginger

1 tsp minced garlic

½ tsp ground cumin

½ tsp onion powder

Sea salt to taste + more to
garnish

With my clients, I really try to emphasize the importance of getting seeds into their diets. Here, I use sesame seed–based tahini to thicken and deliver healthy fats. The carrots give this spread a beautiful color, but they also offer their own nutrients, like vitamin A. The combination of garlic, ginger, cilantro, lemon, miso, and tahini creates a beautiful flavor profile while offering an array of minerals and vitamins for immune support. This dip is a perfect alternative to hummus if you don't like or are sensitive to chickpeas. It is also lower in carbohydrates while still being a good source of plant-based protein.

Serving Note: This dip is thick and spreadable, and holds its own as a filling for wraps or sandwiches. I also love it rolled in cucumber ribbons with sprouts and black sesame seeds. Try it next to Salt & Pepper Veggies (p. 194), tossed with warm rice noodles and Sesame Gomae (p. 169), or as a beautiful topping on Citrus & Sesame Cabbage (p. 190) it truly is delicious with anything!

Preheat the oven to 375°F.

In a bowl, toss the carrots with the olive oil, then transfer them to a piece of aluminum foil and wrap them into a parcel. Place them directly on the oven rack (or use a baking sheet) and roast for 45 to 60 minutes, until tender. Let cool, then chop into ½-inch rounds.

Combine all the ingredients except the salt in a mini food processor or high-powered blender. Pulse in the food processor or blend on medium-high, stopping to scrape down the sides as needed, until smooth. Season to taste with salt.

Transfer the dip to an airtight container and chill in the fridge for at least 30 minutes and up to 1 hour. Store in an airtight container in the fridge for up to 4 days. Before serving, drizzle with olive oil and sprinkle with salt, if desired.

Calories/serving: 122
Carbs/serving: 5 g
Protein/serving: 3 g
Fat/serving: 10 g
Fiber/serving: 2 g

Chipotle Cashew Aioli

P LC

DF/GF/GRF/V

Cellular Building + Healing, Energy + Focus, Immune Support

Makes about 1½ cups (6 servings)

1 cup raw cashews

½ cup water

2 tbsp fresh lime juice

2 tbsp apple cider vinegar

1 tbsp extra virgin olive oil

2 to 3 canned chipotle peppers in adobo sauce, + about 1 tsp of the sauce (depending how spicy you like it)

1 tsp pressed garlic

1 tsp sea salt + more to taste

½ tsp onion powder + more to taste

½ tsp smoked paprika + more to garnish

¼ tsp ground turmeric (optional)

This creamy aioli is a dairy-free, whole-food alternative to classic aioli that's rich in both protein and minerals. Tangy and smoky, it's one of my go-tos when I'm looking to build flavor in a wrap or bowl!

Serving Note: The spark of smoky chipotle makes this aioli the perfect companion to Sweet Potato Fries (p. 178) or dip for fresh veggies. It's also great served next to scrambled eggs. You can use it wherever you would use aioli: in a sandwich, in a wrap, or in a taco. You will always want to have it on hand!

In a bowl, soak the cashews in water overnight. Drain and rinse well.

Adding the liquid first, combine all the ingredients in a food processor or high-powered blender. Blend on high until very smooth and creamy. Adjust the seasoning with salt and onion powder to taste. Serve with a light dusting of paprika, if desired.

Store in an airtight container in the fridge for up to 1 week.

Calories/serving: 150

Carbs/serving: 7 g

Protein/serving: 4 g

Fat/serving: 12 g

Fiber/serving: 1 g

Edamame Cilantro Hummus

DF/GF/GRF/V

Cellular Building + Healing, Detoxifying, Energy + Focus

Makes about 1½ cups (4 servings)

2 cups frozen shelled edamame

½ cup packed fresh cilantro leaves

3 tbsp extra virgin olive oil + more to garnish

3 tbsp tahini

3 tbsp fresh lemon juice + more to taste

3 tbsp water

1½ tbsp gluten-free tamari

2 tsp minced garlic

1 tsp Dijon mustard

½ tsp ground cumin + more to taste

½ tsp sea salt + more to taste

Over the years, I have worked with several high-performance athletes, and this recipe arose from a need to provide them with a nutrient-dense snack to support their recovery post-training. I chose edamame because it is an amazingly rich source of plant-based nutrition, containing folate, an essential B vitamin required to support cellular regeneration, and higher protein than many other legumes (10 grams per serving!). This delicious hummus is also high in healthy fats and vitamin C, to help manage stress, and includes my favorite detoxifying herb, cilantro!

Serving Note: Use this as a bowl builder: Start with a layer of hummus, then top with Herby Greek Salad (p. 164) or roasted veggies. You can also spread it over Seed Bread (p. 88) and top with olive oil, flaky salt, and fresh herbs, or serve it as part of a crudité platter. My favorite way to use it is in collard roll-ups: Spread a blanched collard leaf (see p. 278) with 4 to 5 tablespoons of hummus, top with some Quick Pickled Onions (p. 112) or Caramelized Balsamic Onions (p. 110), ribbons of carrot and English cucumber, arugula or sunflower sprouts, and chopped fresh cilantro or green onions; season with salt, pepper, and hot sauce, and wrap up like a burrito!

Bring a small pot of water to a boil over high heat. Add the edamame and boil for 3 to 4 minutes, until tender. Drain and let cool. If desired, set aside some edamame for garnish.

Combine all the ingredients in a food processor or high-powered blender. Pulse in the food processor or blend on medium-high, stopping to scrape down the sides as needed, until very thick and smooth. Adjust the seasoning with lemon juice, cumin, and salt. Garnish with the reserved edamame and olive oil, if desired.

Store in an airtight container in the fridge for up to 4 days.

Calories/serving: 235
Carbs/serving: 6 g
Protein/serving: 10 g
Fat/serving: 19 g
Fiber/serving: 4 g

Soups, Salads & Sides

soups

Lemon Lentil Soup

DF/GF/GRF/V

Makes 4 servings

- ¼ cup extra virgin olive oil + more to garnish
- 1½ cups finely chopped leeks, white parts only
- 1 tsp sea salt + more to taste
- ½ tsp fresh ground pepper + more to taste
- 1⅓ cups finely chopped carrots
- 1 cup finely chopped celery
- 1¼ cups dry red lentils, rinsed
- 1 tbsp minced garlic
- 1 tsp ground cumin
- 1 tsp ground coriander
- 6 cups vegetable broth
- ½ cup finely chopped flat-leaf parsley + more to garnish
- 1 tsp lemon zest + more to garnish
- 3 tbsp fresh lemon juice + more to taste
- Cayenne or chili flakes to garnish (optional)

When I was a little kid, maybe six years old, I would go with my dad on hikes through the Pacific rainforest, and when we were wet and damp and chilled to the bone, we would stop at a café to warm up and eat lentil soup. I still love a savory and salty lentil soup on a rainy day. In this version, I have added delicate leeks, brightened with lemon and parsley, then spiced with cumin and coriander. I send this soup with clients who need a midday energy boost when they're shooting long hours–it's a great way to get lots of plant-based protein (15 grams per serving), plus fiber and vegetables, into a meal or snack.

Serving Note: Try this soup with different garnishes, such as sautéed leeks or bright-green Chermoula (p. 125). It's great with Caper Feta Broccoli (p. 192), Sautéed Greens (p. 186), or an Herby Greek Salad (p. 164)! Or try serving it with Seed Bread (p. 88) or Rosemary Onion Skillet Bread (p. 90) and Chunky Guacamole (p. 137). You can also serve it cold on a hot summer day topped with fresh cut avocado and herbs.

In a large pot, heat the oil over medium heat. Add the leeks and ½ teaspoon each of the salt and pepper and sauté for 5 minutes, until soft. Add the carrots and celery and sauté for about 3 minutes, until beginning to soften and take on some color. Add the lentils, garlic, cumin, and coriander, stirring well.

Stir in the broth and remaining ½ teaspoon of salt. Bring to a boil, then reduce to a simmer and cover. Simmer, stirring occasionally, for 20 minutes, until the lentils are tender. Stir in the parsley, lemon zest, and lemon juice.

Remove from the heat and adjust the seasoning with salt, pepper, and lemon juice to taste. Serve garnished with more parsley and lemon zest, a drizzle of olive oil, and, if using, a sprinkle of cayenne.

Store the cooled soup in an airtight container in the fridge for up to 4 days. Serve cold or reheat before serving.

Note: This is an unblended soup, so you can choose how chunky you want your vegetables. Cut them in half-moons, or do a fine chop for a smoother soup. I have served this soup cold on a hot summer day, and it was delicious. Top it with fresh cut avocado and herbs.

Calories/serving: 400
Carbs/serving: 43 g
Protein/serving: 16 g
Fat/serving: 15 g
Fiber/serving: 9 g

Cauliflower Leek Soup

DFO/GF/GRF/VO

Anti-Inflammatory, Detoxifying, Gut Health

Makes 4 servings

- 4 tbsp ghee, butter, or extra virgin olive oil
- 4 cups chopped leeks, white parts only
- ¼ cup chopped fresh thyme + more to garnish
- 1 tbsp pressed garlic
- 1¼ tsp sea salt + more to taste
- ½ tsp fresh ground pepper
- 5 cups cauliflower florets
- 1 tbsp Dijon mustard
- 4 cups vegetable or chicken broth
- Zest of 1 small lemon
- ¼ cup tahini
- 2 tbsp fresh lemon juice

Sautéed leeks are everything. They give this soup a sweet, flavorful depth, lots of minerals, and important prebiotics, which help promote good bacteria in the gut. Add the healthy fat from the tahini, the antioxidant-rich thyme, and the vitamins from the cauliflower, and you've got a nutritious soup with decadent flavor. To make it even more delicious, I like to use ghee to sauté the leeks, but olive oil works just as well. Either way, everyone should make this soup–it is wonderful!

Serving Note: Add a sprinkle of Pistachio Dukkah (p. 116) on top of this soup and serve with Rosemary Onion Skillet Bread (p. 90), or the Broccoli Parmesan Mini Flatbreads (p. 83) with some Lemon Garlic Spinach (p. 184) and feta cheese on top. It would also pair well with the Kale Pine Nut Caesar (p. 168) or Wilted Swiss Chard (p. 196), or with Thyme Oyster Mushrooms (p. 187) and Garden Salad (p. 174).

In a large pot, warm the ghee over medium heat. Add the leeks and sauté for 6 to 7 minutes, until soft but not browned. Add the thyme, garlic, salt, and pepper, stirring well, and sauté for 2 to 3 minutes, until the garlic is fragrant and incorporated well. Add the cauliflower and Dijon and sauté for 2 minutes.

Stir in the broth and lemon zest and bring to a simmer. Simmer for 10 to 15 minutes, stirring occasionally, until the cauliflower has softened. Reduce the heat to low and stir in the tahini and lemon juice until mixed.

Remove from the heat and blend the soup with an immersion blender until smooth, or transfer small batches to a high-powered blender and blend until smooth, starting on low and increasing to high after a few seconds, then return to the pot to keep warm. Adjust the seasoning with salt to taste. Serve garnished with more thyme.

Store the cooled soup in an airtight container in the fridge for up to 4 days. Reheat before serving.

Calories/serving: 302
Carbs/serving: 17 g
Protein/serving: 8 g
Fat/serving: 22 g
Fiber/serving: 7 g

Green Detox Soup

DF/GF/GRF/V
Detoxifying, Gut Health, Immune Support

Makes 4 servings

1 bulb garlic

2 tbsp + 2 tsp extra virgin olive oil

3 cups roughly chopped sweet onions

1¼ tsp sea salt + more to taste

½ tsp smoked paprika + more to taste

¼ tsp cayenne + more if you like it spicy (I like ½ tsp!)

3 cups broth of choice (see note)

3 cups broccoli florets

4 cups baby spinach

1 cup roughly chopped fresh cilantro

1 (14 oz/400 ml) can coconut milk

1 tsp lemon zest

1 tbsp fresh lemon juice + more to taste

Fresh ground pepper to serve

Note: I wanted this to be a thin soup that's easy to sip, but if you want it a touch thicker, remove ½ cup broth and ¼ tsp salt. You can elevate the flavor and nourishment by using a bone broth, or make it a touch creamier by using ghee or butter instead of oil.

The delicious blend of coconut milk, sweet onion, roasted garlic, and lemon creates a creamy and incredibly nourishing soup. Offering a touch of warmth from the cayenne, and packed full of broccoli, spinach, and cilantro, this soup can support the body's detox pathways. I created it for a client who didn't like cold, sweet smoothies in the morning but still wanted a large serving of sippable greens (there are over 2 cups of hidden veggies per serving here!). I love it any time of day, and my clients do too.

Serving Note: Serve this soup with a slice of Seed Bread (p. 88) topped with mashed roasted garlic, a drizzle of olive oil, and flaky sea salt. Or try it with Curried Socca (p. 86) and some scrambled eggs or Edamame Cilantro Hummus (p. 142). You could also serve it alongside some warm Herbed Butter Beans (p. 105), or the Everyday Detox Salad (p. 166).

Preheat the oven to 375°F.

Cut the top off the garlic bulb to expose the cloves. Drizzle the bulb with 2 teaspoons of the oil and wrap in aluminum foil. Roast for 40 minutes, until the garlic is golden and can be pierced easily with a knife. Let cool, then squeeze the flesh from each clove into a small bowl.

In a large pot, heat the remaining 2 tablespoons of oil over medium-high heat. Add the onions and sauté until softened and translucent, about 5 minutes. Add the salt, paprika, and cayenne, stirring to coat.

Stir in the broth and bring to a simmer, about 2 minutes. Add the broccoli and simmer for 3 to 4 minutes, until tender. Reduce the heat and stir in the spinach, cilantro, coconut milk, lemon zest, lemon juice, and roasted garlic. Stir together for about 1 minute, until the spinach is wilted.

Remove from the heat and blend the soup with an immersion blender until smooth, or transfer small batches to a high-powered blender and blend until smooth, starting on low and increasing to high after a few seconds, then return to the pot to keep warm. Adjust the seasoning with more salt, paprika, and lemon juice to taste. Finish with fresh ground pepper.

Store the cooled soup in an airtight container in the fridge for up to 4 days. Reheat before serving.

Calories/serving: 323
Carbs/serving: 20 g
Protein/serving: 6 g
Fat/serving: 22 g
Fiber/serving: 5 g

Butternut Squash Soup

DF/GF/GRF/V

Anti-Inflammatory, Beauty + Anti-Aging, Immune Support

Makes 4 servings

1 butternut squash
(about 2½ lb/1 kg)

4 tbsp virgin coconut oil
or extra virgin olive oil

1 tbsp curry powder

3 tbsp grated peeled fresh ginger

1 tbsp roughly chopped garlic

1 red onion, diced

1 tsp sea salt + more to taste

¼ tsp fresh ground pepper
+ more to taste

1 cup toasted cashews, crushed,
or ¼ cup tahini
(for a nut-free version)

2 cups water

¼ cup chopped fresh cilantro
+ lots more to garnish

1 (14 oz/400 ml) can coconut milk

Juice of 1 lime (about 1 tbsp)

Lime wedges to serve

Variation: If you're looking for a thinner, lighter soup, omit the cashews. It will taste just as great! Or, if you want an extra boost of protein, replace the water with your favorite bone broth.

There are few things I crave more on a cold winter day than a bowl of this antioxidant-rich butternut squash soup—the ultimate comfort food! Full of minerals and healthy fats from the cashews and coconut milk, it is also loaded with beta-carotene from the squash. In addition, both the curry powder and the fresh ginger have warming, anti-inflammatory properties, making this soup both wonderfully nourishing and delicious.

Serving Note: Serve this with Broccoli Parmesan Mini Flatbreads (p. 83) and Lemon Garlic Spinach (p. 184), or with a Cucumber Herb Salad (p. 159), Kale Pine Nut Caesar (p. 168), or the Garden Salad (p. 174).

Preheat the oven to 375°F. Line a rimmed baking sheet with parchment paper.

Cut the squash in half and scoop out the seeds. Rub the halves with 1 tablespoon of the oil. Place cut side down on the prepared baking sheet and roast for 35 to 45 minutes, until completely soft and the skin is easy to pierce with a fork. Let cool.

Heat a large pot over medium heat. Add the curry powder and toast for about 30 seconds, until fragrant. Add the remaining 3 tablespoons of oil. When the oil is hot, add the ginger and cook, stirring, for 1 minute. Add the garlic, onions, salt, and pepper and sauté for 6 to 7 minutes, until the onions are soft and translucent. Stir in the cashews.

Scoop out the squash from its skin and add it to the pot, stirring to combine. Add the water and bring to a boil, then reduce the heat and simmer for 5 minutes, stirring often. Stir in the cilantro, coconut milk, and lime juice and heat just to warm through.

Remove from the heat and blend the soup with an immersion blender until smooth, or transfer small batches to a high-powered blender and blend until smooth, starting on low and increasing to high after a few seconds, then return to the pot to keep warm. Adjust the seasoning with salt and pepper. Serve garnished with cilantro and lime wedges on the side.

Store the cooled soup in an airtight container in the fridge for up to 4 days. Reheat before serving.

Calories/serving: 587
Carbs/serving: 34 g
Protein/serving: 10 g
Fat/serving: 43 g
Fiber/serving: 10 g

Creamy Cashew Mushroom Soup

DF/GF/GRF/V

Cellular Building + Healing, Immune Support

Makes 4 servings

3 tbsp extra virgin olive oil + more to serve

2 cups finely chopped white onions

3 tbsp chopped fresh thyme

1½ tbsp pressed garlic

1 tsp sea salt + more to taste

1 tsp fresh ground pepper + more to taste

1 lb (454 g) mushrooms (a mix of portobello and shiitake), finely chopped

4 cups mushroom broth

⅔ cup raw cashews

1½ tbsp gluten-free tamari

Chopped fresh chives to serve (optional)

Variation: If you want an extra boost of protein, replace the mushroom broth with your favorite bone broth. You may need to adjust to taste as the mushroom broth provides an umami, savory flavor.

This is the mushroom soup of your dreams. It is hearty and nutrient-rich and features all the cellular- and immune-supporting magic that mushrooms can offer. I like to use a mix of portobello and shiitake mushrooms, but if I have access to other wild or medicinal mushrooms, like maitake or oyster, I'll use those too. Blended cashews offer up a delicate cream base for this exceptionally delicious plant-based soup.

Serving Note: I like to serve a small bowl of this soup alongside something light and green, like Everyday Detox Salad (p. 166) or some butter lettuce and cucumber slices with Dijon Vinaigrette (p. 128). Or try it next to Herbed Lemon White Fish (p. 243) or Zucchini Parmesan Egg Muffins (p. 70). It's amazing with some crudités and the Beet Thyme Cashew Dip (p. 138), or with a piece of warm Curried Socca (p. 86). To up the mushroom power, garnish with a large helping of Thyme Oyster Mushrooms (p. 187).

In a medium pot, heat the oil over medium heat. Add the onions and sauté for 3 to 4 minutes, until translucent. Add the thyme, garlic, salt, and pepper and sauté for 2 minutes. Add the mushrooms and sauté for 5 minutes, until the mushrooms have softened and reduced. Remove half of the mushroom mixture from the pot and set aside.

Add the broth, cashews, and tamari to the pot. Bring to a boil, then reduce the heat and simmer for 2 to 3 minutes to allow the flavors to release and meld.

Remove from the heat and transfer small batches of the soup to a high-powered blender and blend until smooth, starting on low and increasing to high after a few seconds, then return to the pot to keep warm.

Return the reserved mushroom mixture to the pot and warm over low heat. Adjust the seasoning with salt and pepper to taste. Serve drizzled with olive oil and garnished with chives, if desired.

Store the cooled soup in an airtight container in the fridge for up to 3 days. Reheat before serving.

Calories/serving: 279
Carbs/serving: 15 g
Protein/serving: 8 g
Fat/serving: 21 g
Fiber/serving: 4 g

Rainbow Miso Soup

DF/GF/V

Beauty + Anti-Aging, Energy + Focus, Immune Support

Makes 4 servings

2 tbsp extra virgin olive oil

2 cups very thinly sliced halved leeks, white parts only

2 tbsp micrograted peeled fresh ginger

2 cups bite-sized, peeled butternut squash, or 2 cups bite-sized, unpeeled acorn or kabocha squash (see variation)

1½ cups very thinly sliced halved carrots

3 tbsp gluten-free tamari

4 cups mushroom broth

1 cup chopped tomato

3 cups sliced stemmed shiitake mushrooms

1½ cups finely sliced, peeled, and quartered watermelon radishes or finely sliced regular radishes + more to garnish

6 tbsp shiro miso

1 cup water

½ cup finely chopped green onions + more to garnish

Sea salt and fresh ground pepper to taste

Chili flakes to taste (optional, if you like it spicy)

Variation: Try a beautiful option with roasted squash, like in the photo: instead of uncooked squash, use 2 cups sliced, unpeeled roasted acorn or kabocha squash (see p. 172). Add at the same time as the mushrooms and radishes.

I cannot speak highly enough about this soup! You cook a rainbow of veggies right into the broth, so their nutrients are infused into each bite! It is high in protein, rich in fiber, and unbelievably nourishing, and can be enjoyed all year round–just sub in your preferred local in-season veggies (as long as they're bite-sized, make them any shape you desire). One of my favorite ingredients is shiitake mushrooms. Long used in traditional Chinese medicine, they are known for their medicinal properties. With this soup, you can enjoy not only the umami flavor they provide but also their fortifying qualities.

Serving Note: This soup is rather filling so it doesn't need much alongside it! But if you're looking to serve it with something, try the Cucumber Herb Salad (p. 159), Sesame Gomae (p. 169), Salt & Pepper Veggies (p. 194), Sweet Potato & Avo Sushi (p. 203), or a bowl of cooked white rice or quinoa. You can also add a handful or two of cubed tofu right into the soup for added protein. Or add cooked noodles and make mini rainbow ramen bowls!

In a large pot, heat the oil over medium heat. Add the leeks and ginger and sauté for 3 minutes. Stir in the squash, carrots and tamari and sauté for 2 minutes.

Stir in the broth and tomatoes and bring to a low boil. Boil gently for 6 to 7 minutes, stirring occasionally, until the squash is tender. Reduce the heat to low, add the mushrooms and radishes, and simmer for 10 minutes, stirring occasionally, until the radishes are soft and the soup has thickened.

In a small bowl, mix the miso and water to make a thin paste. Add this to the pot, stirring well. Heat for 30 seconds, then remove from the heat and stir in the green onions. Season to taste with salt, pepper, and chili flakes (if using). Serve garnished with more radishes and green onions.

Store the cooled soup in an airtight container in the fridge for up to 4 days. Reheat before serving.

Calories/serving: 230
Carbs/serving: 24 g
Protein/serving: 7 g
Fat/serving: 8 g
Fiber/serving: 11 g

salads

Cucumber Herb Salad

DF/GF/GRF
Beauty + Anti-Aging, Detoxifying, Gut Health

Makes 4 small servings

Salad

6 cups sliced English cucumbers (see note)

1 tsp sea salt

½ cup finely chopped fresh cilantro + more to garnish

½ cup finely chopped fresh mint + more to garnish

⅓ cup minced shallots

1 tbsp seeded, minced jalapeños + more to taste

½ cup chopped toasted almonds or other favorite nut or seed (see p. 276), or Spiced Mixed Nuts & Seeds (p. 109)

Chili flakes to serve (optional, if you like some spice)

Dressing

3 tbsp fresh lime juice

3 tbsp avocado oil or extra virgin olive oil

2½ tbsp rice vinegar

2½ tbsp fish sauce

1½ tsp pressed garlic

This salad is salty, tangy, fresh, and crunchy, with herbs, chopped nuts, and a lime–fish sauce vinaigrette that I crave. It's ridiculously satisfying, and along with hydration from the cucumbers, its beautifying vitamins and minerals are supportive of the skin. The almonds add a surprising amount of protein, which gives it a little more substance. When combined, these nutritional elements create a high–fiber, protein–rich delight that is packed with flavor.

Serving Note: Eat this as a snack, or eat the whole bowl, like I do! You can use it as a topping or small side with almost anything: it is amazing with the Herbed Lemon White Fish (p. 243) and Sweet Potato Fries (p. 178). Or serve it next to the Chimichurri Chicken (p. 252), Roasted Rainbow Veggie Noodle Bowl (p. 220), Shiitake Ginger Mung Bean Noodles (p. 218), or Green Curry (p. 216).

Toss the cucumbers with the salt and let sit in a colander for 30 minutes to release their water. Transfer to a kitchen towel and blot dry.

In a large salad bowl, combine the cucumbers, cilantro, mint, shallots, and jalapeños.

In a small bowl, whisk together all the dressing ingredients.

Drizzle the salad evenly with the dressing, then toss to combine. Let sit for 10 minutes, then mix in the toasted almonds. Serve immediately, topped with chili flakes, if desired.

Note: The quantity of cucumbers is important here. Start with 2 large cucumbers, cut them in half lengthwise, scrape out the seeds, then slice as thinly as possible into half-moons until you reach 6 cups.

Calories/serving: 196
Carbs/serving: 8 g
Protein/serving: 6 g
Fat/serving: 15 g
Fiber/serving: 5 g

Roasted Beet Carpaccio with Herb Salad

DF/GF/GRF/V

Anti-Inflammatory, Cellular Building + Healing, Detoxifying

Makes 4 servings

2 large beets (about 2 lb/900 g), roasted and peeled (see p. 279)

2 tbsp extra virgin olive oil

1 tbsp balsamic vinegar

1 tsp onion powder

¼ tsp sea salt

¼ tsp fresh ground pepper

Herb Salad

1 cup finely chopped fresh flat-leaf parsley

¼ cup finely chopped green onions

2 tbsp extra virgin olive oil

4 tsp red wine vinegar

1 tsp pressed garlic

¾ tsp sea salt + more to taste

¼ tsp chili flakes + more to taste (optional)

Brilliantly colored, nutrient-rich beets are a beautiful vegetable to get creative with–their versatility and nutritional benefits are truly unbeetable! Adorned with a vibrant herb salad, this dish is bright, savory, and spicy, truly one of my favorite ways to eat beets.

Serving Note: For an impressive starter, top with avocado slices, Pistachio Dukkah (p. 116), and a sprinkling of flaky sea salt, or toasted walnuts and some crumbled feta! This dish also works well alongside the Roasted Carrots (p. 236).

Using a mandoline, slice the beets into very thin rounds (or simply cut them into quarters). Transfer to a shallow dish or plate.

In a small bowl, gently mix the oil, vinegar, onion powder, salt, and pepper. Pour over the beets and let marinate at room temperature for 20 minutes. (If you want to make the beets ahead of time, they can be stored in an airtight container in the fridge for up to 4 days. Let them come to room temperature before topping with the herb salad.)

In another bowl, toss the herb salad ingredients together. Adjust the seasoning with the salt and, if desired, chili flakes. Let sit for 5 minutes before serving.

Gently toss the beets once, then arrange on a platter or in bowls. Top evenly with the herb salad.

Calories/serving: 231
Protein/serving: 4 g
Carbs/serving: 17 g
Fat/serving: 14 g
Fiber/serving: 7 g

Watermelon Feta Salad

DFO/GF/GRF/VO

Beauty + Anti-Aging, Gut Health, Mood Balancing

Makes 4 small servings

4 cups cubed watermelon
(½-inch cubes)

2 cups thinly sliced halved or
coined English cucumber

2 tbsp extra virgin olive oil

2 tbsp red wine vinegar

1 tbsp fresh lime juice + more
to taste

½ tsp fresh ground pepper

½ tsp sea salt + more to taste

1½ cups goat, sheep, or vegan
feta (or see variation)

½ cup thinly sliced red onions or
Quick Pickled Onions (p. 112)

½ cup cubed avocado (optional)

A handful of halved cherry
tomatoes (optional)

A few thin slices of watermelon
radish (optional)

¼ cup roughly chopped fresh
mint to garnish (optional)

Variation: For a more protein-rich option, replace the feta with Marinated Mediterranean Tofu (p. 93) or add a few tablespoons of hemp hearts to the dish.

There is something great about eating your hydration, and watermelon and cucumber are two of the most hydrating foods out there. This salad is light and so refreshing you wouldn't guess that it also has a good amount of protein! The combo of mint and watermelon is a summer dream; add the salty feta and a burst of lime, and nothing tastes better on a warm afternoon. Plus this salad provides fiber, which supports healthy digestion, and antioxidants that support healthy skin.

Serving Note: This is a fun one to share at a summer garden party or barbecue. On a hot day, serve it with chilled Lemon Lentil Soup (p. 147). Or, for a brunch, serve it next to Zucchini Parmesan Egg Muffins (p. 70) or the Spring Vegetable Frittata (p. 73)!

In a salad bowl, toss together the watermelon and cucumbers.

In a small bowl or jar, combine the oil, vinegar, lime juice, pepper, and salt. Whisk or shake to combine. Adjust the seasoning with lime juice (up to 1 tablespoon more) and salt.

Right before serving, crumble the feta over the salad. Add the onions and, if desired, the avocado, tomatoes, and radishes. Add the dressing and toss gently to coat. Garnish with mint (if using). This salad is best eaten right away.

Calories/serving: 300
Carbs/serving: 13 g
Protein/serving: 13 g
Fat/serving: 22 g
Fiber/serving: 2 g

Herby Greek Salad

DFO/GF/GRF/VO

Makes 4 servings

4 cups cubed English cucumbers (about 2 cucumbers, cut into ½-inch cubes)

2 cups finely chopped or quartered cherry tomatoes

¾ cup finely chopped pitted green or Kalamata olives

½ cup finely diced red onions

1 clove garlic, pressed

2 tbsp dried or finely chopped fresh oregano

2 tbsp balsamic vinegar

1 tbsp fresh lemon juice

1 tbsp Dijon mustard

½ tsp sea salt

¼ cup extra virgin olive oil

¼ cup finely chopped fresh flat-leaf parsley + more to garnish

¼ cup finely chopped fresh mint, tarragon, basil, or a mix + more to garnish

2 tbsp finely chopped fresh dill + more to garnish

1 cup crumbled goat, sheep, or vegan feta

Variation: You can bump up the nutrition by adding 1 to 2 scoops of cooked quinoa. My green olives of choice are Cerignola or Castelvetrano, and I prefer them to Kalamata in this recipe.

This finely chopped, herb-heavy salad ensures well-balanced flavor with every mouthful—buttery olives, spicy red onions, hydrating cucumbers, and antioxidant-rich tomatoes. What really makes it so special though is the mix of herbs: oregano, parsley, mint, and dill not only add flavor but also increase the diversity of nutrients available. Herbs are shown to be some of the most antioxidant-rich foods we can eat, helping to protect and repair our bodies at a cellular level. Everything here combines to create a light and refreshing summer salad that will give you a big dose of detoxifying and beautifying vitamins and minerals.

Serving Note: This salad works alongside so many dishes, such as Ginger Cilantro Turkey Meatballs (p. 104) and Broccoli Parmesan Mini Flatbreads (p. 83). It also really freshens up a plate of roasted veg (see p. 280). Or serve it over a painting of Edamame Cilantro Hummus (p. 142) and top with some chopped avocado to make a refreshing, protein-rich lunch!

In a large salad bowl, combine the cucumbers, tomatoes, olives, and red onions.

In a small bowl, combine the garlic, oregano, vinegar, lemon juice, Dijon, and salt. Whisk in the oil. Stir in the parsley, mint, and dill.

Toss the salad with the dressing. Sprinkle with the feta and garnish with more herbs.

Store in an airtight container in the fridge for up to 2 days.

Calories/serving: 322
Carbs/serving: 10 g
Protein/serving: 9 g
Fat/serving: 25 g
Fiber/serving: 5 g

Everyday Detox Salad

DF/GF/GRF/V
Beauty + Anti-Aging, Detoxifying, Immune Support

Makes 4 servings

Salad

2 cups packed fresh flat-leaf parsley, roughly chopped

2 cups thinly sliced radishes (I suggest using a mandoline)

2 cups thinly sliced celery (I suggest using a mandoline)

2 cups grated carrots

Dressing

¼ cup red wine vinegar + more if desired

2 to 3 cloves garlic, micrograted

1 tsp sea salt + more to taste

½ tsp chili flakes

¼ cup extra virgin olive oil + more if desired

Variation: You can substitute apple cider vinegar for the red wine vinegar; start with 3 tbsp and taste before adding a fourth, as it can be a touch stronger in flavor. To mix things up, try adding thinly sliced fresh fennel, grated yellow beet, or small-cubed cucumber.

This salad is packed with detoxifying parsley and super crisp and colorful, fiber-rich veggies like celery, radishes, and carrots. If you love a textured crunch to your salad like I do, you'll love this! Not to mention, it is loaded with antioxidants, vitamins, and minerals. Incredibly healthy and easy to make, this salad is my go-to when cooking at home—I try to eat it every day. Incorporate this recipe into your repertoire as a simple way to elevate any meal.

Serving Note: This salad goes with so many things. Try serving it with Curried Socca (p. 86), Spiced Tofu Scramble (p. 72), or any roasted veg (see p. 280). Or try it with a piece of Rosemary Onion Skillet Bread (p. 90) and an egg, the Chard-Wrapped Miso Fish (p. 250), or Mung Bean Falafel (p. 240). It is also a perfect accompaniment to Butternut Squash Soup (p. 152), Creamy Cashew Mushroom Soup (p. 154), or Red Lentil Dal (p. 226)

In a salad bowl, combine the parsley, radishes, celery, and carrots.

In a small bowl or jar, combine the vinegar, garlic, salt, and chili flakes. Let sit for a minute or two to infuse. Add the oil and stir well or shake to emulsify.

Toss the salad with the dressing. Adjust the seasoning with salt to taste, and add more vinegar or oil, if desired. Let marinate for 5 minutes before serving.

Store in an airtight container in the fridge for up to 3 days.

Calories/serving: 174
Carbs/serving: 6 g
Protein/serving: 2 g
Fat/serving: 14 g
Fiber/serving: 4 g

Kale Pine Nut Caesar

DF/GF/GRF/V

Beauty + Anti-Aging, Cellular Building + Healing, Immune Support

Makes 4 servings

Salad

1 tbsp extra virgin olive oil

2 tbsp drained capers

8 cups finely shredded or chiffonade curly kale or dinosaur kale (about 2 bunches)

1 tbsp fresh lemon juice

Fresh ground pepper, to serve

½ lemon, cut into 4 wedges, to serve

Pine Nut Caesar Dressing

½ cup pine nuts (see variation)

¼ cup extra virgin olive oil

2 tbsp drained capers

2 tbsp fresh lemon juice

1 tbsp chopped white onions

4 tsp gluten-free tamari

2 tsp pressed garlic (or more to taste)

2 tsp Dijon mustard

¼ tsp fresh ground pepper + more to taste

Variation: Try toasting the pine nuts ahead of time for a more complex and "nutty" flavor.

This one is for garlic lovers! I like creamy, softer kale salads, and this recipe is my favorite. My clients love it too. It is super straightforward: take tons of kale, dress it with my delicious plant-based Pine Nut Caesar Dressing and finish with a few fried capers. Pine nuts are such a great ingredient to incorporate into your diet, because they are high in protein and monounsaturated fats, plus they give you a healthy dose of minerals, especially magnesium and potassium. Immune-boosting, skin-supporting, and antioxidant-rich from the garlic, lemon, and kale, this is a supercharged Caesar in both nutrition and flavor!

Serving Note: I love this salad with Herbed Lemon White Fish (p. 243), poached eggs, Smoky Maple Tempeh (p. 95), Chimichurri Chicken (p. 252), or Marinated Mediterranean Tofu (p. 93). It's also great alongside Creamy Cashew Mushroom Soup (p. 154) or Herbed Butter Beans (p. 105). Or combine it on a plate with a couple of vegetable dishes, such as Caper Feta Broccoli (p. 192) and Citrus & Sesame Cabbage (p. 190), and a Chicken Satay (p. 102).

In a sauté pan, heat the oil over medium-high heat until shimmering. Add the capers and fry for about 4 minutes, until they begin to crisp up and appear a little golden. Transfer the capers to a paper towel to absorb excess oil (you can squeeze or blot them a bit if needed).

Place the shredded kale in a large salad bowl and sprinkle with the lemon juice. Massage well, until it is starting to soften.

Combine all the dressing ingredients in a food processor or high-powered blender. Blend until smooth, starting on low and increasing to high after a few seconds. Adjust the seasoning with pepper to taste. Store in an airtight container in the fridge for up to 5 days.

Pour the dressing over the kale, then massage and toss to evenly coat. Top with the fried capers, sprinkle with more pepper, and serve with lemon wedges to squeeze over top.

This salad is best enjoyed the day it is made but can be stored in an airtight container in the fridge for up to 1 day.

Calories/serving: 293

Carbs/serving: 4 g

Protein/serving: 5 g

Fat/serving: 28 g

Fiber/serving: 4 g

Sesame Gomae

DF/GF/GRF/V

Cellular Building + Healing, Detoxifying, Gut Health

Makes 4 servings

Vegetables

2½ cups chopped asparagus
(½- to 1-inch pieces)

2 cups small broccoli florets

6 cups baby spinach

1 cup frozen shelled edamame

Toasted sesame seeds to garnish
(see p. 276)

Finely minced green onions
to garnish (optional)

Sauce

3 tbsp rice vinegar

3 tbsp tahini

3 tbsp gluten-free tamari

1½ tbsp finely grated peeled
fresh ginger

1 tbsp toasted sesame oil

The ginger-infused tahini sauce is sugar-free and perfectly complements this delicious variation on one of my favorite Japanese salads. Loaded with protein, vitamins, and minerals, this nutritious gomae can be enjoyed as a beautiful side or stand-alone salad.

Serving Note: This gomae is a perfect match for Buttered Sweet Potato Ribbons (p. 179) or Citrus & Sesame Cabbage (p. 190). Try serving it with Ginger Cilantro Turkey Meatballs (p. 104) or Chicken Satay (p. 102). For lunch, I like it with Miso Maple Salmon Bites (p. 98) and the Cucumber Herb Salad (p. 159). I also leave this salad packed in small mason jars in the fridge for my clients to grab as a snack!

Bring a medium pot of water to a boil. Blanch the asparagus and broccoli for 1 to 2 minutes, until bright green. Using a slotted spoon, transfer the vegetables to a colander (keeping the boiling water in the pot), run under cold water, then let sit to drain excess water.

In the same boiling water, blanch the spinach for 20 seconds. Transfer to a colander (keeping the boiling water in the pot), run under cold water, then gently squeeze to remove excess water.

Add the edamame to the boiling water and cook for 3 minutes. Drain in a colander, run under cold water, and set aside to cool.

Spread the blanched veggies out on a large dish towel or paper towel to soak up as much liquid as possible. Squeeze gently a few times to help remove moisture.

In a small bowl, whisk together all the sauce ingredients.

In a large bowl, toss all the cooled vegetables together. Pour the sauce over top and mix well. Serve garnished with sesame seeds and, if desired, green onions.

Store in an airtight container in the fridge for up to 4 days.

Calories/serving: 186
Carbs/serving: 8 g
Protein/serving: 11 g
Fat/serving: 11 g
Fiber/serving: 7 g

Creamy Avo Cumin Coleslaw

DF/GF/GRF/V

Beauty + Anti-Aging, Cellular Building + Healing, Immune Support

Makes 4 servings

Salad

3 cups finely shredded purple cabbage (see note)

2 cups finely shredded or chiffonade dinosaur kale

2 cups finely chopped red peppers

1½ cups grated peeled beets

2 tbsp extra virgin olive oil

1½ tsp apple cider vinegar or fresh lemon juice

¼ tsp sea salt

¼ cup lightly toasted sunflower seeds to garnish (see p. 276)

Avocado Cumin Dressing

1 cup diced tomatoes

1 cup chopped avocado

½ cup minced green onions

2 tbsp apple cider vinegar

2 tsp pressed garlic (3 tsp if you love garlic)

1 tsp ground cumin

¾ tsp sea salt + more to taste

½ tsp fresh ground pepper

¼ tsp cayenne (start with a pinch if you are sensitive to heat; add more if you love it!)

This rainbow-colored slaw is always a big hit—bring it to a dinner party and watch it disappear! Slaws became a mainstay in my salad repertoire when I worked for a raw vegan client; they're a creative way to get a lot of sturdy greens and denser veggies into a meal without cooking them, which helps to better preserve some of their enzymes. The key here is to cut the raw veggies as thin as possible, then marinate and massage them with an acid (vinegar or lemon juice) to encourage the fibrous walls to break down and become softer so we can absorb more of the nutrients. This process keeps the salad alive with enzymes and antioxidants, and encourages digestibility. The slaw is high in folate, other B vitamins and vitamin K for cellular building and vitamin C for immune support.

Serving Note: Serve with Herbed Lemon White Fish (p. 243) or with some steamed broccoli tossed with Chermoula (p. 125). This slaw is also great alongside a bowl of Red Lentil Dal (p. 226) or the Spiced Tofu Scramble (p. 72).

In a large salad bowl, combine the cabbage, kale, red peppers, and beets. Add the oil, vinegar, and salt and massage for 1 minute.

Combine all the dressing ingredients in a food processor or high-powered blender. Blend on high until smooth. Adjust the seasoning with salt to taste.

Toss the salad with the dressing. You can enjoy it right away, but I like to let it sit for at least 30 minutes and up to 4 hours first to let the vegetables marinate. Garnish with sunflower seeds just before serving.

Store in an airtight container in the fridge for up to 3 days.

Note: Shred the kale and cabbage as finely as possible. Use a mandoline for the cabbage.

Calories/serving: 278

Carbs/serving: 17 g

Protein/serving: 7 g

Fat/serving: 18 g

Fiber/serving: 10 g

Arugula & Roasted Squash Salad

DF/GF/GRF/V

Beauty + Anti-Aging, Cellular Building + Healing, Gut Health

Makes 4 servings

Squash

1 delicata squash

1 tbsp extra virgin olive oil

¼ tsp sea salt

¼ tsp fresh ground pepper

¼ tsp onion powder

¼ tsp smoked paprika

Dressing

2 cloves garlic, pressed

½ cup extra virgin olive oil

¼ cup nutritional yeast

¼ cup gluten-free tamari

¼ cup apple cider vinegar

Fresh ground pepper to taste

Salad

4 cups baby arugula

4 cups baby spinach

1 cup grated carrot (or beet, or a mix of half and half)

⅓ cup toasted pumpkin seeds (see p. 276)

Variation: I've given instructions here for roasting squash, but feel free to replace it with about 2 cups of your favorite leftover roasted veggies, such as sweet potato (see p. 280). Or you could use my Acorn Squash (p. 182).

This is one of the salads I prepare most often because it's my favorite way to eat leftover roasted veggies, and because the dressing tastes like home to me. When I was little my mom used to take me to a retreat center on Cortes Island called Hollyhock. They made a dressing you wanted to drink because it tasted that good! My mom's version of it became our staple recipe in our home for my whole childhood, and was the first dressing I ever made on my own. It is now also one of the dressings most requested by my clients! The salad has both raw and cooked veggies, allowing for a wider array of nutrients, as veggies offer different amounts of vitamins, enzymes, and fiber depending on how they are prepared. This recipe has a little bit of everything: a mix of greens, crunchy carrots and toasted seeds, the soft and sweet squash, and a dressing full of B vitamins.

Serving Note: This salad goes well with Creamy Cashew Mushroom Soup (p. 154), Cauliflower Leek Soup (p. 148), Garlicky Roasted Portobellos (p. 188), Smoky Maple Tempeh (p. 95), hard-boiled eggs, Herbed Butter Beans (p. 105), or Chard-Wrapped Miso Fish (p. 250).

Preheat the oven to 375°F. Line a rimmed baking sheet with parchment paper.

Cut the squash in half lengthwise and remove all the seeds. Cut into ¼-inch slices (you should have about 2½ cups squash).

Place the squash in a large bowl and toss with the oil, salt, pepper, onion powder, and paprika. Spread out in a single layer on the prepared pan.

Roast for 20 minutes, turning halfway through, until tender. Remove from the oven and let cool.

In a small bowl or jar, combine all the dressing ingredients.

In a large salad bowl, combine the cooled squash, arugula, and spinach. Using kitchen scissors, roughly chop through the greens and squash. Add the carrot and pumpkin seeds. Toss with the dressing and serve immediately.

Calories/serving: 450

Carbs/serving: 19 g

Protein/serving: 10 g

Fat/serving: 36 g

Fiber/serving: 9 g

Garden Salad with Creamy Tahini Dressing

DF/GF/GRF/V

Beauty + Anti-Aging, Cellular Building + Healing, Energy + Focus

Makes 4 servings

Salad

4 cups baby spinach

4 cups baby arugula

1½ cups grated carrots

1½ cups thinly sliced halved
English cucumbers

1 cup thinly sliced radishes

1 cup sunflower sprouts

¾ cup very thinly sliced purple
cabbage

½ cup grated peeled beet

¼ cup toasted pumpkin seeds
(see p. 276)

¼ cup chopped fresh dill
(optional)

1 avocado, sliced (optional)

A handful of chopped sauerkraut
(optional)

Tahini Dressing

½ cup extra virgin olive oil

¼ cup tahini

¼ cup apple cider vinegar

3 tbsp gluten-free tamari

2 tbsp water

1 tsp micrograted peeled fresh
ginger (optional)

This is a giant, beautiful salad where everything and anything goes—which is how I want all salads to be! It's about maximizing texture and nutritional benefits in one bowl. I use a mix of bright greens, crunchy roots, hydrating cucumbers, decadent avocado, lively sunflower sprouts, and mineral-packed pumpkin seeds. But it can be made with whatever veg you have around—just look for a balance of green, crunchy, fresh, rooty, nutty, and sweet. The dressing makes it into a meal: it is dense with protein and essential fatty acids, and super high in vitamins and minerals, in particular vitamins K and E, iron, and magnesium—all the elements you need to support, beautify, and energize. Creamy with a hint of ginger and a blast of apple cider vinegar to help you digest all those veggies, it will complement any mix you throw together.

When I leave a client for a night or a weekend, I prep one of these salads for the fridge and a protein add-on or two so they can easily put together a satisfying meal. It's a great thing to do for yourself on a Sunday: get all the veg ready and store them separately in the fridge, and whip up the dressing. During the week, you can toss the salad together when you need a meal to go or a quick bite at home.

Serving Note: Add 1 cup cooked quinoa or a scoop of the Summer Pesto Quinoa Bowl (p. 224) if you want a more filling version, or serve it with hard-boiled eggs, Dill Dijon Salmon Bites (p. 97), or Smoky Maple Tempeh (p. 95). My favorite way to eat it, though, is with a scoop of Edamame Cilantro Hummus (p. 142) or the Marinated Mediterranean Tofu (p. 93).

In a large salad bowl, toss together the spinach, arugula, carrots, cucumbers, radishes, sunflower sprouts, cabbage, and beet.

Combine all the dressing ingredients in a high-powered blender. Blend on high until smooth.

To serve, add the pumpkin seeds and, if desired, the dill, avocado, and sauerkraut to the bowl. Pour in the dressing, and mix well until everything is coated.

Calories/serving: 407

Carbs/serving: 10 g

Protein/serving: 8 g

Fat/serving: 37 g

Fiber/serving: 6 g

sides

Sweet Potatoes: 2 Ways

Sweet Potato Fries
Buttered Sweet Potato Ribbons

Deep-orange sweet potatoes are loaded with beta-carotene, an especially important antioxidant to help keep your skin healthy, eyes sharp, and immune system strong. Nutrient-rich and full of flavor, they are also high in dietary fiber. I use them to bulk up a salad or create a satisfyingly starchy side. I make them into noodles, roll them in sushi, and blend them into soups. These are two of my favorite recipes to show off the natural sweet chewiness of this versatile vegetable.

Sweet Potato Fries

DF/GF/GRF/V

Beauty + Anti-Aging, Gut Health, Mood Balancing

Makes 4 servings

2 lb (900 g) sweet potatoes, cut into even ½ × ½-inch strips

2 tbsp extra virgin olive oil

2 tsp chili powder and/or onion powder (optional)

1 tsp sea salt + more to taste

Variation: For a crispier fry, cut the potatoes to ¼ × ¼-inch strips—just make sure they are uniform in size. This recipe is extra special with Japanese sweet potatoes subbed in, or you can use a mix of the two sweet potatoes.

I love fries, and this sweet potato version, alongside my Chipotle Cashew Aioli, is to die for! They are fun to eat and go with just about anything. I like to season them with chili or onion powder, but they are also delicious with just a bit of salt to bring out their natural sweetness. I recommend sharing them with friends, or you will eat them all yourself.

Serving Note: Serve these with Chipotle Cashew Aioli (p. 141). Make a plate by combining them with Ginger Cilantro Turkey Meatballs (p. 104) and Tzatziki (p. 240), or try them rolled in sushi, wraps, or salad rolls (see Wraps & Rolls, p. 202).

Preheat the oven to 425°F, with the racks placed in the upper and lower thirds. Line two rimmed baking sheets with parchment paper.

In a large bowl, toss the sweet potatoes with the oil, chili powder (if using), and salt. Arrange on the prepared pans so they aren't touching.

Place one pan on the upper rack and the other on the lower rack. Roast for 15 minutes, then flip the sweet potatoes and swap the positions of the pans in the oven. Roast for 10 to 12 minutes, until fork-tender. Adjust the seasoning with salt to taste.

Store the cooled fries in an airtight container in the fridge for up to 3 days. Enjoy cold in a sushi roll, or reheat in a single layer on a rimmed baking sheet in the oven at 400°F for 5 to 7 minutes, until warmed through.

Calories/serving: 329
Carbs/serving: 54 g
Protein/serving: 4 g
Fat/serving: 7 g
Fiber/serving: 10 g

Buttered Sweet Potato Ribbons

GF/GRF

Cellular Building + Healing, Immune Support

Makes 4 servings

¼ cup butter

1 to 2 large sweet potatoes
(1½ lb/680 g total),
skin off + peeled into wide
ribbons (see p. 277)

¼ cup chopped fresh thyme
+ more to taste

¾ to 1 tsp sea salt + more to
taste (see note)

½ to 1 tsp fresh ground pepper
+ more to taste (see note)

These sweet potato ribbons are one of my favorite comfort foods, and they are so easy to make! A simple vegetable peeler will create beautiful, decadent ribbons. And you can flavor them with anything. Here I keep the seasoning simple to showcase the sweet, tender, beta-carotene-rich potato, but you could also top these with Cilantro Sunflower Pesto (p. 123) or Chimichurri (p. 125) for something different.

Serving Note: These go great next to a salad with Dijon Vinaigrette (p. 128) or the Kale Pine Nut Caesar (p. 168). Or serve them with Garlicy Roasted Portobellos (p. 188) and Salsa Verde (p. 126), or with the Lentil Bolognese (p. 214) and a little Lemon Garlic Spinach (p. 184) on top! They're perfect to serve with Thyme Scallops (see variation, p. 187) and some roasted asparagus or next to any fish roasted and topped with one of the green sauces (p. 124)!

In a large sauté pan, melt the butter over medium-high heat. Add the sweet potato ribbons and sauté for 4 to 5 minutes, tossing frequently, until they begin to turn a brilliant orange and are tender and sweet. Add the thyme, salt, and pepper and gently toss together for 1 minute. Remove from the heat and season with more fresh thyme and salt and pepper to taste.

Store in an airtight container in the fridge for up to 3 days. Reheat in a sauté pan over medium heat for a few minutes until warm.

Note: If your butter is salted, start with ¾ tsp sea salt and add more to taste. If you don't love the spicy kick from the pepper, start with ½ tsp and add more as desired.

Calories/serving: 259
Carbs/serving: 29 g
Protein/serving: 2 g
Fat/serving: 12 g
Fiber/serving: 5 g

Acorn Squash
with Ginger & Shallot

DF/GF/GRF

Beauty + Anti-Aging, Cellular Building + Healing, Immune Support

Makes 4 servings

1 medium acorn or delicata squash or small kabocha squash

2 inches fresh ginger, peeled and micrograted

2½ tbsp extra virgin olive oil or avocado oil

½ tsp sea salt + more to taste

1 shallot, very thinly sliced

1½ tbsp fresh lime juice

1 tbsp fish sauce + ½ tbsp more if you love fish sauce (as I do!)

¼ cup fresh cilantro leaves and/or finely sliced green onions to garnish

Note: This is a very tasty and tender side, so make a double batch and keep it ready in the fridge for snacking and salads.

I love eating jewel-toned veggies because they are packed with antioxidants. Golden acorn squash is high in vitamins A and C, which are helpful for cell protection and support the immune system. This fiber-rich dish is seasoned with lime, fish sauce, and ginger, creating a delicate flavor combo that you won't be able to stop eating.

Serving Note: Serve with the Herbed Butter Beans (p. 105) or Ginger Cilantro Turkey Meatballs (p. 104), with Cucumber Herb Salad (p. 159) on the side. Use a few pieces to garnish Shiitake Ginger Mung Bean Noodles (p. 218), or make it part of a big spread next to the Salt & Pepper Veggies (p. 194), Sesame Gomae (p. 169), and some Citrus & Sesame Cabbage (p. 190).

Preheat the oven to 375°F. Line a rimmed baking sheet with parchment paper.

Cut the squash in half and remove the seeds. Slice each half into ½-inch crescents.

In a medium bowl, combine the ginger and 2 tablespoons of the oil. Add the squash, sprinkle with the salt, and toss to coat.

Place the squash on the prepared pan, making sure all the ginger and oil are transferred from the bowl. Roast for 15 minutes.

Meanwhile, in a small bowl, toss the shallots with the remaining ½ tablespoon of oil.

Flip the squash and sprinkle the shallots evenly over top. Roast for 15 minutes, until the squash is soft and golden brown.

In a small bowl, stir together the lime juice and fish sauce. Transfer the squash (and all the ginger, shallots, and oil) while hot to a serving bowl or plate and sprinkle with the lime vinaigrette. Serve garnished with cilantro.

Store the cooled squash in an airtight container in the fridge for up to 3 days. Leftovers can be enjoyed cold.

Calories/serving: 186
Carbs/serving: 20 g
Protein/serving: 3 g
Fat/serving: 9 g
Fiber/serving: 8 g

Lemon Garlic Spinach

DF/GF/GRF/V

Makes 4 servings

2 tbsp extra virgin olive oil
  + more to serve

Zest of 2 lemons

1 tbsp pressed garlic

½ tsp sea salt + more to serve

1 lb (454 g) baby spinach

1 tbsp fresh lemon juice

Chili flakes or fresh ground
  pepper to serve

Variation: My favorite way to eat this is with ½ cup goat feta crumbled over top (in which case, use ¼ tsp less salt), served on top of warm Broccoli Parmesan Mini Flatbreads (p. 83) with Tzatziki (p. 240).

For as long as I can remember, I've loved spinach made this way–simply sautéed with garlic and lemon. It is surprising that a little bowl of spinach packs this much protein, fiber, vitamins, and minerals! It builds the body from the inside out and is especially high in folate and magnesium, which are great for nervous system support. This recipe is nutritious, delicious, and easy to make!

Serving Note: I can always find a way to put this on any plate or table spread; it's a lovely green addition to mix and match with any other vegetable side.

In a large sauté pan, warm the oil over medium heat. Add the lemon zest, garlic, and salt and cook, stirring, for 1 minute, until the garlic is fragrant but not browned.

Reduce the heat slightly and add a couple handfuls of spinach, turning and tossing so that the spinach on the bottom gets coated in oil and wilts. Keep tossing and adding more spinach until all the spinach has been added and is bright green and just wilted. Add the lemon juice and give everything one final toss.

Serve immediately with a drizzle of olive oil and a sprinkle of salt and chili flakes.

Store cooled leftovers in an airtight container in the fridge for up to 2 days. Try adding leftovers to another dish, like an omelet or a soup, or reheat in a sauté pan over low heat.

Calories/serving: 92
Carbs/serving: 3 g
Protein/serving: 3 g
Fat/serving: 7 g
Fiber/serving: 3 g

Sautéed Greens with Toasted Spices

DF/GF/GRF/V

Anti-Inflammatory, Cellular Building + Healing, Gut Health

Makes 4 servings

1 tbsp black mustard seeds

1 tsp ground cumin

½ tsp ground coriander

2 tbsp virgin coconut oil or extra virgin olive oil

¼ tsp fresh ground pepper

¼ tsp cayenne

1 bunch curly or dinosaur kale, deveined and roughly chopped

1 bunch Swiss chard, deveined and roughly chopped

1 tbsp fresh lemon juice + more to taste

½ tsp sea salt + more to taste

Variation: To make a spicier, creamier version, increase the amount of spices you use and cook them in 3 to 4 tbsp ghee instead of oil. Then serve the greens over Lemon Cumin Yogurt (p. 236).

I'm always trying out different flavors and methods to make a side of greens more intriguing and delicious. For this recipe, I sauté Swiss chard and kale—which are full of vitamins A, C, and K—with a mix of warming, antioxidant-rich, anti-inflammatory spices that enhance the flavor and health benefits of the dish.

Serving Note: These are amazing as part of a benny for brunch (p. 76) or added to a breakfast bowl with scrambled eggs. They are also perfect with the Roasted Carrots (p. 236), the Shiitake Ginger Mung Bean Noodles (p. 218), or a piece of Almond-Crusted White Fish (p. 248) with some Chermoula (p. 125) They can even be chopped and added to the Rainbow Miso Soup (p. 156).

In a large sauté pan over medium heat, combine the mustard seeds, cumin, and coriander and toast, stirring, until fragrant and starting to brown, about 2 minutes. Add the oil and stir into the spices for 1 minute. Add the pepper and cayenne and let the mixture sizzle for a few seconds, then reduce the heat to medium-low.

Add the kale and Swiss chard and toss them in the spices. Add the lemon juice and salt, cover, and cook for 1 minute. Stir the greens, cover, and continue to cook, stirring every 2 minutes, until the greens are cooked to your desired tenderness. Season with lemon juice and salt to taste.

Store the cooled greens in an airtight container in the fridge for up to 3 days. Enjoy cold or reheat leftovers in a sauté pan over low heat.

Calories/serving: 80
Carbs/serving: 2 g
Protein/serving: 1 g
Fat/serving: 8 g
Fiber/serving: 2 g

Thyme Oyster Mushrooms

DFO/GF/GRF/VO

Anti-Inflammatory, Cellular Building + Healing, Immune Support

Makes 4 servings

1 lb (454 g) oyster mushrooms,
 or a mix of wild mushrooms

2 tbsp extra virgin olive oil or
 avocado oil

2 tbsp butter, ghee, or vegan
 butter

2 tbsp chopped fresh thyme
 + more to garnish

Sea salt and fresh ground pepper
 to taste

Lemon wedges to serve (optional)

Variation: Pat dry 1 lb (454 g) scallops, sprinkle with ½ tsp salt and some fresh ground pepper, and follow the same cooking method. Serve warm with pasta or salad.

Oyster mushrooms are full of antioxidants and provide anti-inflammatory support. I love them for their delicate texture and subtle savory flavor, but you can use any healing mushrooms, like lion's mane, shiitake, maitake, or king. This recipe seasons them perfectly with chopped thyme, which offers beautiful flavor and phytonutrients. If you eat seafood, try the variation: protein-rich scallops are similar to mushrooms in their texture and health-supporting benefits.

Serving Note: These go with so many other dishes as a topping, garnish, or side. Try them on the Creamy Cashew Mushroom Soup (p. 154) or Cauliflower Benny (p. 76). Serve them with the Kale Pine Nut Caesar (p. 168), Caper Feta Broccoli (p. 192), and Sweet Potato Fries (p. 178). Or arrange a few mushrooms (or scallops) over roasted spaghetti squash smothered in Cashew Cacio e Pepe (p. 211), Basil Pesto (p. 123), or Cilantro Sunflower Pesto (p. 123).

Remove and discard the stems from the mushrooms (or save them in the freezer to make stock). Tear the mushrooms into evenly sized pieces.

Heat a large skillet over medium-high heat. When the pan is hot, heat half of the oil until shimmering, then add half of the mushrooms in a single layer; avoid crowding them, so they cook evenly. Sear, without stirring, for 2 to 3 minutes, until one side is golden brown. Stir the mushrooms, then turn them golden side down and add half each of the butter and thyme. Reduce the heat to medium and cook for 2 to 3 minutes, until golden on the other side. Season to taste with salt and pepper, then transfer to a bowl and keep warm. Repeat with the remaining oil, mushrooms, butter, and thyme.

Serve immediately, garnished with more thyme, and, if desired, with lemon wedges to squeeze over top.

Calories/serving: 154
Carbs/serving: 4 g
Protein/serving: 4 g
Fat/serving: 14 g
Fiber/serving: 3 g

Garlicky Roasted Portobellos

DF/GF/GRF/V

Cellular Building + Healing, Gut Health, Immune Support

Makes 4 servings

4 portobello mushrooms

¼ cup extra virgin olive oil
  + more to serve

¼ cup balsamic vinegar

4 tsp pressed garlic

½ tsp sea salt + more to serve

¼ tsp fresh ground pepper

⅛ tsp chili flakes + more to serve

Note: The thickness of each mushroom will affect its cooking time; one or two may finish cooking before the others.

Portobello mushrooms have a wonderful meaty texture and the ability to absorb any flavor you throw at them. That makes them a great option for roasting, but I especially love them grilled. The simple marinade adds a light spice and tangy sweetness that perfectly complements the earthy flavor of the mushrooms. Portobellos contain vitamins (especially B), which are helpful for energy production, and minerals, which, alongside the garlic, provide strong support for your immune system!

Serving Note: After cooking the mushrooms, cut them into thin strips and serve warm over an arugula salad (or any salad, really), or leave them whole and stuff them with Lemon Garlic Spinach (p. 184) and goat cheese for a spectacular side. They go well with Cashew Cacio e Pepe (p. 211) or a pasta tossed with Basil Pesto (p. 123), or Lentil Bolognese (p. 214).

Wipe the mushrooms clean with a damp cloth or paper towel and discard the stems.

In a small bowl, whisk together the oil, vinegar, garlic, salt, pepper, and chili flakes.

Place the mushrooms gill side up in a flat-bottomed container or on a plate. Divide the marinade equally between them, pouring it so it rests in the gills. Let marinate at room temperature for at least 2 hours, or cover and refrigerate overnight, making sure the mushrooms stay upright so the marinade doesn't spill.

Preheat the oven to 400°F or the barbecue to medium-high.

If roasting, line a rimmed baking sheet with parchment paper. Place the mushrooms on the pan, gill side up, and roast for 13 to 18 minutes, until tender all the way through (the marinade may begin to bubble when they're close). If grilling, carefully place the mushrooms on the barbecue, gill side up, and grill for 6 to 10 minutes, until tender all the way through.

Let rest for 1 to 2 minutes, then serve sprinkled with a little more oil, salt, and chili flakes, if desired.

Store the cooled mushrooms in an airtight container in the fridge for up to 3 days. To reheat, cut into ½-inch-thick slices and heat in a sauté pan with a little olive oil over medium heat.

Calories/serving: 145
Carbs/serving: 4 g
Protein/serving: 1 g
Fat/serving: 14 g
Fiber/serving: 1 g

Citrus & Sesame Cabbage

DF/GF/GRF/V

Makes 4 servings

2 tbsp gluten-free tamari

1½ tbsp fresh lemon juice
+ more to serve

2¼ tsp toasted sesame oil

2 tbsp extra virgin olive oil

¼ cup finely chopped green
onions

1 tbsp pressed garlic

6 cups finely shredded purple
cabbage (see note)

¼ cup finely chopped fresh
cilantro + more to serve

¼ tsp fresh ground pepper

Sambal oelek to serve (optional)

1½ tbsp toasted black sesame
seeds to serve

Note: I highly recommend
using a mandoline to shred the
cabbage—it gives the best
results.

I love this one. I originally intended it to be a topping for salads or bowls, but every time I cooked it, I found myself eating it on its own. Purple cabbage is such an underrated vegetable. Fiber-rich and versatile, it contains beneficial compounds that help reduce inflammation, which can lead to accelerated aging and disease. This amethyst-colored dish seasoned with lemon, sesame, garlic, and herbs is easy to make, rich with nutrients, and can be incorporated into almost any meal!

Serving Note: I love to make a wrap with this cabbage plus chicken smothered with Chermoula (p. 125) or Avocado Cumin Dressing (p. 170). Or I serve it in a nutritious bowl with Shiitake Ginger Mung Bean Noodles (p. 218) and Lemon Garlic Spinach (p. 184). It is also great with Miso Maple Salmon Bites (p. 98) and Salt & Pepper Veggies (p. 194), or under Herbed Lemon White Fish (p. 243), topped with a drizzle of Salsa Verde (p. 126).

In a small bowl, combine the tamari, lemon juice, and sesame oil.

In a large sauté pan, heat the olive oil over medium-low heat. Add the green onions and garlic and cook for 1 minute, stirring constantly to ensure the garlic does not burn.

Add the cabbage and increase the heat to medium-high. Cook for 2 to 3 minutes, until the cabbage has started to soften but is still tender-crisp and evenly coated in the garlic oil. Use tongs to continuously mix the cabbage through the garlic oil, ensuring the cabbage gets even heat and the garlic never sticks to the pan for long. Pour in the tamari mixture and cook, stirring, for 2 minutes. Reduce the heat to low and add the cilantro and pepper. Cook for 1 to 2 minutes, until the cabbage is done to your liking.

Serve warm or cooled with sambal oelek, if desired, and sprinkled with lemon juice, sesame seeds, and cilantro.

Store the cooled cabbage in an airtight container in the fridge for up to 4 days. Leftovers can be enjoyed cold or reheated in a sauté pan over medium heat with a drizzle of olive oil for 2 to 3 minutes.

Calories/serving: 186
Carbs/serving: 7 g
Protein/serving: 2 g
Fat/serving: 16 g
Fiber/serving: 3 g

Caper Feta Broccoli

DFO/GF/GRF/VO

Cellular Building + Healing, Gut Health

Makes 4 servings

2 crowns broccoli

⅓ cup minced drained capers

3 tbsp extra virgin olive oil

¼ cup red wine vinegar

1 tsp pressed garlic

1 tsp lemon zest + more to serve

½ tsp sea salt

½ tsp fresh ground pepper

¼ tsp chili flakes + more to serve

¾ cup crumbled goat, sheep, or vegan feta

2 tbsp toasted pumpkin seeds to garnish (optional)

Chopped fresh parsley to garnish (optional)

This recipe makes its way into so many of my meals. It's packed with nutrients and full of flavor, turning one of my favorite vegetables into one of my favorite dishes. The broccoli is seasoned with capers, red wine vinegar, lemon zest, and garlic, then tossed warm with crumbled feta for a bright, salty, savory, and exceptionally satisfying experience.

Serving Note: I highly recommend serving this with Marinated Mediterranean Tofu (p. 93); it is the perfect flavor combination and increases the protein of the dish. Or try it with Cashew Cacio e Pepe (p. 211). It would also work with scrambled eggs, the Spiced Tofu Scramble (p. 72), or as part of a veggie platter beside the Mung Bean Falafel (p. 240), or the Almond-Crusted White Fish (p. 248) with Salsa Verde (p. 126).

Preheat the oven to 400°F. Line a rimmed baking sheet with parchment paper.

Using a mandoline (see note), cut the broccoli into slices about ¼ inch thick and 3 inches long (you should have about 8 cups).

Using your hands, toss the broccoli with the capers and 2 tablespoons of the oil. Spread out on the prepared pan. Roast for 15 minutes, until browned and tender.

Meanwhile, in a small bowl, whisk the remaining tablespoon of olive oil with the vinegar, garlic, lemon zest, salt, pepper, and chili flakes.

As soon as the broccoli comes out of the oven, toss it with the dressing and feta. Serve topped with more chili flakes and lemon zest. If desired, garnish with pumpkin seeds and parsley.

Store the cooled broccoli in an airtight container in the fridge for up to 4 days.

Note: Because broccoli is oddly shaped, you can cut thin slices by hand. You can also try this recipe with cauliflower, just cut the pieces even thinner.

Calories/serving: 219

Carbs/serving: 7 g

Protein/serving: 8 g

Fat/serving: 17 g

Fiber/serving: 5 g

Salt & Pepper Veggies

DF/GF/GRF/V

Anti-Inflammatory, Energy + Focus, Gut Health

Makes 4 servings

3 tbsp ume plum vinegar

2 tbsp extra virgin olive oil

1 tbsp toasted sesame oil

1 tsp fresh ground pepper
+ more to serve

2 cups bite-sized cauliflower
florets

2 cups bite-sized broccoli florets

2 cups sliced asparagus (2-inch
slices)

2 cups sliced halved zucchini
(¼-inch slices)

Variation: Try subbing in
chopped bok choy for the
cauliflower or broccoli.

I am always shocked by how fast these disappear—often before I even get a chance to put them on the table! The subtle combo of salty vinegar and ground pepper is amazing tossed with some of my favorite veggies: cauliflower, broccoli, asparagus, and zucchini. Full of fiber and nutrient-rich, they are all non-starchy vegetables that don't have a negative impact on your blood sugar, so they are on my "eat as much as you want!" list of foods. They are especially great for gut health, with pre-biotics from the asparagus, hydration from the zucchini, and fiber from the broccoli and cauliflower. You can read more about the health benefits of these veggies in the Glossary of Ingredients on p. 283.

Serving Note: These are a perfect pairing with the Chard-Wrapped Miso Fish (p. 250) or Mung Bean Falafel (p. 240). Serve them next to Shiitake Ginger Mung Bean Noodles (p. 218), Cashew Cacio e Pepe (p. 211), or Rainbow Miso Soup (p. 156). Keep them in the fridge to add to salads, or serve them warm on any veggie platter.

Preheat the oven to 375°F. Line a rimmed baking sheet with parchment paper.

In a large bowl, whisk together the vinegar, olive oil, sesame oil, and pepper until smooth. Add all the veggies and toss to coat. Arrange the veggies in a single layer on the prepared pan.

Roast for 15 minutes, then check their doneness. If they're not tender enough for your liking, stir the veggies and roast for another 2 to 3 minutes, to the desired tenderness. Season with pepper to taste.

Store the cooled veggies in an airtight container in the fridge for up to 3 days.

Calories/serving: 148

Carbs/serving: 7 g

Protein/serving: 5 g

Fat/serving: 11 g

Fiber/serving: 5 g

Wilted Swiss Chard with White Beans & Capers

DF/GF/GRF/V

Makes 4 servings

3 tbsp extra virgin olive oil

1 cup finely chopped green onions

3 tbsp minced drained capers

2 tbsp pressed garlic

1 tbsp finely minced jalapeños

¼ cup water

2 tbsp fresh lemon juice
+ more to taste

1 tbsp Dijon mustard

1 tsp sea salt + more to serve

3 cups cooked or canned, drained and rinsed white beans (I like cannellini or butter beans; let canned beans dry in the colander after rinsing)

8 cups roughly chopped deveined Swiss chard (about 2 large bunches)

Fresh ground pepper to serve

Lemon zest to garnish (optional)

4 to 6 tbsp Cilantro Sunflower Pesto (p. 123) to serve (optional)

Variation: Try topping this with pecorino or crumbled feta! Or replace the beans with 1 lb (454 g) fish, cut into four pieces, and add to the wilted greens and cover the pot. The fish will steam in the juices. Cook for about 10 minutes, until the fish can be flaked with a fork. Serve topped with pesto and more lemon juice.

This savory dish is an excellent source of both fiber and protein, making it a delightful way to incorporate luscious greens and buttery beans into your diet. You'll be pleasantly surprised by the rich and complex flavors created by the blend of capers, Dijon, jalapeño, and lemon. Notably, this recipe is rich in magnesium and vitamin K, which are crucial for supporting the body's muscle and connective tissues. In addition, it boasts high levels of vitamins A, C, and E, which promote immune health, reduce the risk of disease, and support healthy skin and vision.

Serving Note: Serve this with the Everyday Detox Salad (p. 166) or Caper Feta Broccoli (p. 192). Try it for breakfast with a scoop of Marinated Mediterranean Tofu (p. 93); on toast with lots of olive oil and chili flakes; or topped with a poached egg, avocado, and hot sauce (the best way).

In a large pot, heat 3 tablespoons of the oil over medium heat. Add the green onions, capers, garlic, and jalapeños and cook, stirring well, for 2 minutes. Add the water, lemon juice, Dijon, and salt, stirring for 30 seconds or until the liquid is thoroughly mixed. Add the beans and cook for 2 minutes, stirring to coat the beans with sauce. Add the Swiss chard and cook, stirring well, for 3 to 4 minutes, until wilted.

Remove from the heat and season with salt and pepper to taste, and garnish with lemon zest, if desired. Let sit in the warm pot for 3 to 5 minutes before serving so the flavors settle together. If using pesto, gently fold it in, 1 tablespoon at a time. (I like 4 tablespoons stirred in, with another 2 tablespoons as garnish).

Calories/serving: 287

Carbs/serving: 25 g

Protein/serving: 13 g

Fat/serving: 13 g

Fiber/serving: 11 g

Lemongrass Cauliflower & Sweet Potato with Turmeric

DF/GF/GRF/V

Anti-Inflammatory, Beauty + Anti-Aging, Immune Support

Makes 4 servings

Infused Coconut Oil

2 stalks lemongrass

1 small shallot

2 inches fresh ginger,
    peeled and minced

8 fresh lime leaves
    (about one ½ oz package)

Zest of 1 lime

½ cup virgin coconut oil

Vegetables

1 head cauliflower
    (about 2 lb/900 g)

2 medium sweet potatoes
    (about 1 lb/454 g)

½ tsp fine sea salt

½ tbsp ground turmeric

Flaky sea salt to taste

½ cup pomegranate seeds
    to garnish (see note)

Variation: If you don't want to use sweet potato, swap it out for another head of cauliflower. If you can't find pomegranate seeds, try chopped dried cranberries instead.

Perfect for a dinner party, this is an impressive and elevated side dish, rich in flavor and nutrition. It is light, bright, and packed with beautifying antioxidants from the brilliant gold-stained cauliflower, deep-orange sweet potatoes, and jewel-red pomegranate. Coconut oil infused with aromatic lemongrass and lime leaves complements the earthy turmeric and sweet pomegranate, creating a beautiful and unique flavor profile full of immune and anti-inflammatory support.

Serving Note: Serve alongside Chard-Wrapped Miso Fish (p. 250) or Ginger Cilantro Turkey Meatballs (p. 104). Or combine it with other sides—like Lemon Garlic Spinach (p. 184) and Citrus & Sesame Cabbage (p. 190) to make a beautiful spread!

Peel off the outside stalks of the lemongrass. Pound or press the insides with a wooden spoon to help release aromas, then chop them into ½-inch pieces. Peel the shallot and slice it lengthwise into quarters.

In a small pot, combine the lemongrass, shallots, ginger, lime leaves, lime zest, and coconut oil. Warm over medium-low heat, stirring constantly, until the coconut oil is melted. Reduce the heat to low and cook for 5 minutes, constantly spooning the oil over the spices, until the shallots are translucent and the oil is fragrant. Remove from the heat and let the spices infuse in the warm oil for 20 minutes.

Meanwhile, preheat the oven to 450°F. Line a large rimmed baking sheet with parchment paper.

Transfer the oil mixture to a blender and blend on high until smooth, about 30 to 60 seconds. Strain the oil through a fine-mesh sieve back into the pot, pressing the solids to get all the oil out. Reserve the oil (you should have about ¼ cup) and discard the solids.

Cut the florets off the cauliflower head, chop them into 1- to 2-inch pieces, and place in a large bowl. Peel the sweet potatoes, cut them into lengthwise quarters, then cut each quarter into small quarter-moons, about ¼ inch thick.

If your infused oil has solidified, gently warm it over low heat. Massage 2 tablespoons of the oil into the cauliflower and sweet potatoes, then toss with the fine sea salt. Spread the vegetables evenly over the prepared pan.

Roast for 20 to 25 minutes, stirring halfway through, until the vegetables are soft and starting to get brown and crispy.

Transfer to a large serving bowl and add the remaining infused oil and the turmeric, tossing until everything is a brilliant golden color. Season with flaky sea salt to taste. Serve garnished with pomegranate seeds. Store leftovers in an airtight container in the fridge for up to 3 days. Reheat (minus the pomegranate seeds) on a parchment-lined baking sheet in the oven at 400°F for about 8 minutes.

Calories/serving: 290
Carbs/serving: 30 g
Protein/serving: 5 g
Fat/serving: 14 g
Fiber/serving: 8 g

Large Plates

wraps & rolls

Sweet Potato & Avo Sushi with Cauliflower Rice

DF/GF/GRF/V

Beauty + Anti-Aging, Cellular Building + Healing, Mood Balancing

Makes 8 rolls (4 servings)

Cauliflower Sushi Rice

6 cups riced cauliflower (see p. 277) (about 2 lb/900 g cauliflower)

3 tbsp rice vinegar

2 tbsp toasted sesame oil

1 tsp sea salt

Sushi

8 toasted nori sheets

½ recipe Sweet Potato Fries (p. 178), cooled

2 avocados, thinly sliced

4 green onions, thinly sliced lengthwise

1 English cucumber, ends trimmed, seeds scraped out, and julienned

Pickled ginger (optional) + more to garnish

Dipping Sauce

2 tbsp gluten-free tamari

1 tsp finely grated peeled fresh ginger (optional)

Variation: To switch things up, feel free to substitute 4 cups of cooked sushi rice for the cauliflower rice! Or you can try changing up your fillings—add mango or your favorite canned fish with spicy mayo and something crunchy.

Nori is such a great way to include iodine and other beneficial minerals in your diet. Here, nori is wrapped around roasted sweet potatoes, creamy avocado, and cauliflower rice–an excellent grain-free, low-carbohydrate option–to create a delightful blend of flavors. Full of cell-supporting nutrients and mood-boosting B vitamins, these rolls are fresh, delicious, vibrant, and fun to make with friends.

Serving Note: Host a sushi-making night, with some Rainbow Miso Soup (p. 156) on hand for people to sip while they roll. I highly recommend serving these with the Sesame Gomae (p. 169) or a few different veggie dishes on a platter–try the Salt & Pepper Veggies (p. 194) or Citrus & Sesame Cabbage (p. 190)!

Preheat the oven to 350°F. Line a baking sheet with parchment paper.

Spread the cauliflower rice out evenly on the prepared pan. Bake for 25 minutes, stirring halfway through, until the cauliflower is tender.

Meanwhile, in a small bowl, whisk together the vinegar, oil, and salt.

Stir the vinegar mixture into the hot rice (still on the pan). Spread the rice back out into an even layer and let cool completely.

Place a nori sheet, bumpy side up and with a long edge facing you, on a bamboo sushi roller (this helps you form the sushi, but you can also roll without one). Spread ½ cup rice over the nori, leaving about 2 inches exposed at the edge farthest from you. Try to spread the rice so it is just one grain thick and thoroughly covers the area, then press it down with your hands to pack the rice into the nori.

Place a few sweet potato fries horizontally near the edge closest to you, then a few slices of avocado, some green onion, a few strips of cucumber, and some pickled ginger (if using), all side by side, layering them evenly so that each bite is similar.

Recipe continues

Fill a small bowl with water and dampen the exposed edge of the nori by dipping your fingertips in the water and brushing them across the nori. Begin gently rolling the bamboo mat away from you, tucking in the ingredients and lifting the mat as you go. Go slowly to ensure everything stays in place. When it is all rolled up, gently roll the sushi back and forth under the mat to create an even shape; this will also help everything stick together. Let the roll rest for a minute before slicing.

Using a very sharp knife, gently slice the rolls into 1-inch pieces, wiping the knife with a damp cloth in between cuts so it doesn't stick and tear the nori. Repeat with the remaining nori sheets to make 8 rolls total.

In a small bowl, mix the tamari and, if desired, ginger for the dipping sauce.

Serve the sushi with the dipping sauce and some more pickled ginger, if you like.

Calories/serving: 458
Carbs/serving: 37 g
Protein/serving: 11 g
Fat/serving: 25 g
Fiber/serving: 17 g

Rainbow Salad Rolls

DF/GF/VO
Beauty + Anti-Aging, Cellular Building + Healing

Makes 8 rolls (4 servings)

Marinated Red Peppers & Cucumber

1 cup finely sliced red peppers

2 cups julienned English cucumber or ribbons (see p. 277)

3 tbsp rice vinegar

Marinated Carrots

1 cup packed carrot ribbons

1 tbsp toasted sesame oil

1 tsp fish sauce or ume plum vinegar

To Assemble

8 rice paper wraps

1 cup loosely packed fresh basil, mint, or Thai basil leaves, or a mix

1 cup loosely packed fresh cilantro leaves

2 medium Alphonso mangoes, peeled and thinly sliced into 1½-inch-long strips

½ recipe Sweet Potato Fries (p. 178) or 2 medium avocados, sliced

4 green onions, thinly sliced lengthwise

Sesame Ginger Dipping Sauce

1 tbsp toasted sesame oil

1 tbsp fish sauce or ume plum vinegar

1 tsp micrograted peeled fresh ginger

Variation: Other filling options are Citrus & Sesame Cabbage (p. 190) or Smoky Maple Tempeh (p. 95). Add some finely chopped romaine lettuce if you want more crunch.

My rainbow salad rolls have become a favorite among my clients, and for good reason. The vegetables are marinated to enhance their natural flavors, with juicy mango added for a tropical twist. To further elevate the dish, I incorporate a ton of vibrant herbs, for both their fresh flavor and healing properties. These rolls are a creative and nutritious way to incorporate more vegetables into your diet, offering a wonderful blend of beautifying antioxidants and vitamins. (Keep extra rice papers on hand—I always ruin my first couple while assembling.)

Serving Note: Instead of the sesame ginger dipping sauce, try serving these with Coconut Almond Sauce (p. 132). For a more substantial meal, serve these with the Cucumber Herb Salad (p. 159) or the Sesame Gomae (p. 169).

In a small bowl, mix the red peppers and cucumbers with the rice vinegar. Let soak for 15 minutes, then squeeze the vegetables to remove excess liquid.

In another small bowl, mix the carrot ribbons with the oil and fish sauce. Let soak for 15 minutes—no need to squeeze at the end of the soaking time.

On a large work surface, lay out the marinated vegetables and the other fillings so everything is easy to grab as you start rolling.

Place a little room-temperature water in a plate, shallow pan, or large bowl, and add one rice paper wrap, laying it flat in the water for a few seconds; it should soften right away but still be slightly firm. Lay the wrap in front of you on a slightly damp lint-free towel or a cutting board.

On the bottom third of the wrap, add a layer of herbs, then a small handful of carrots, a small handful of the red pepper mixture, some mango, and about 4 pieces of sweet potato, spreading the ingredients evenly. Finish with a few slivers of green onion. Gently roll the wrapper away from you, tucking in the corners as you go so the contents are tightly rolled.

Repeat with the remaining rice paper wraps to make 8 rolls.

In a small bowl, mix the ingredients for the dipping sauce. Serve with the rolls.

Calories/serving: 292
Carbs/serving: 41 g
Protein/serving: 3 g
Fat/serving: 11 g
Fiber/serving: 6 g

Raw Walnut Lettuce Tacos

DF/GF/GRF/OF/V

Beauty + Anti-Aging, Cellular Building + Healing, Gut Health

Makes 4 servings

3 cups raw walnut halves

3 tbsp gluten-free tamari
+ more if needed

2 tbsp fresh lemon juice
+ more if needed

1½ tbsp ground cumin

1 tbsp chili powder

2 tsp ground coriander

1 head butter lettuce

4 medium tomatoes, diced

2 avocados, diced

½ cup finely sliced red onions
or Quick Pickled Onions
(p. 112)

Fresh cilantro leaves to garnish

Pickled Jalapeños (p. 112) to
garnish (optional)

½ recipe Hemp Chili Crema
(p. 121) to serve (optional
but highly recommended)

Lime or lemon wedges to serve

Variation: Instead of making
tacos, simply tear up the lettuce
leaves, toss them with the filling,
tomatoes, avocados, red onions,
and garnishes, and serve as a
salad dressed with the hemp
chili crema!

I cannot recommend this dish enough! Walnuts are a nutritional powerhouse, providing a range of benefits for our skin, cells, and overall health. They are an excellent source of energy and are packed with essential vitamins and minerals. However, it can be challenging to find creative ways to incorporate them into meals. This recipe is a game-changer. It transforms walnuts into a deliciously salty and spicy taco filling, full of flavor from antioxidant-packed cumin and coriander, both of which support digestion. Paired with classic taco toppings like vitamin-rich tomatoes and avocados, this is an incredibly nutrient-dense dish that my clients love. Make sure to store walnuts in an airtight container in the fridge to keep them fresh!

Serving Note: Serve these tacos with Sweet Potato Fries (p. 178) or lemon-spritzed cucumber slices. Stuff some thinly sliced Garlicky Roasted Portobellos (p. 188) in the tacos for a lovely chewiness. You can also use the walnut mixture as a filling for collard wraps or sprinkle it over a salad!

In a bowl, soak the walnuts in water for 4 hours, then rinse well and pat dry.

In a food processor, combine the walnuts, tamari, lemon juice, cumin, chili powder, and coriander. Pulse until chopped and crumbly, but not a paste (do not overprocess). Adjust the seasoning with more tamari or lemon juice if needed. The filling will keep in an airtight container in the fridge for up to 4 days.

To create lettuce "tacos," spoon the walnut filling onto a lettuce leaf and top with tomatoes, avocados, and red onions. Garnish with cilantro and, if desired, pickled jalapeños and a drizzle of hemp chili crema (if using). Serve with lime wedges to squeeze over top.

Calories/serving: 681
Carbs/serving: 16 g
Protein/serving: 17 g
Fat/serving: 61 g
Fiber/serving: 13 g

Lentil Lettuce Cups
with Tahini Ginger Sauce

DF/GF/GRF/V

Cellular Building + Healing, Gut Health, Immune Support

Makes 4 servings

1 cup dry brown lentils, rinsed (see note)

3 cups water

2 tbsp toasted sesame oil + more to taste

2 tbsp micrograted peeled fresh ginger

1½ cups finely chopped green onions + more to garnish

1½ cups finely chopped fresh cilantro + more leaves to garnish

¼ cup finely chopped seeded jalapeños (optional)

3 cups finely diced celery

2 cups julienned carrots

3 tbsp gluten-free tamari

2 tbsp fresh lime juice

Sea salt and fresh ground pepper to taste

About 16 butter lettuce leaves or 2 romaine hearts

1 cup Tahini Ginger Sauce (p. 130) + more if desired

Hot sauce to serve (optional)

Quick Pickled Onions (p. 112) or Caramelized Balsamic Onions (p. 110) to garnish (optional)

4 lime wedges to serve

Note: Instead of cooking dry lentils, you can use 2½ cups of canned lentils. Drain and rinse them in a colander, then let them dry as much as possible before using.

These delicious, nutrient-packed lettuce cups are filled with seasoned brown lentils infused with immune-boosting ginger and detoxifying cilantro. Packed with fiber and a whopping 22 grams of protein per serving, along with antioxidants from the herbs and vegetables, they can support the body at a cellular level. A creamy tahini sauce perfectly complements the earthy flavor of the lentils and provides a healthy dose of essential fats, which are especially important when you're consuming plant-based protein. I love adding jalapeño for an extra kick of spice, texture, and pop! This dish is well-balanced, filling, and fun to eat.

Serving Note: These lettuce cups make a perfect lunch as is, or chop the lettuce into bite-sized pieces and toss it all together as a salad with some cucumber and avocado! To build an even bigger meal, serve with a bowl of Salt & Pepper Veggies (p. 194) or add Sweet Potato Fries (p. 178) to the plate for a delicious, chewy side—never the wrong move.

In a small pot, combine the lentils and water. Bring to a boil, then reduce the heat, cover, and simmer for 17 to 18 minutes, until tender. Drain in a colander (it's important that the lentils are as dry as possible) and set aside.

In a large sauté pan, heat the oil over medium heat. Add the ginger and sauté for 10 seconds, then add the green onions, cilantro, and, if desired, jalapeños and sauté for 2 minutes. Add the celery, carrots, and tamari and sauté for 4 to 5 minutes, until the vegetables are just starting to soften but still have a little crunch.

Reduce the heat to medium-low and stir in the cooked lentils, then the lime juice. Cook for 5 to 6 minutes, until the liquid is absorbed. Taste and adjust with sesame oil or salt and pepper if necessary. Remove from the heat and let cool slightly. (Or let cool completely and store in an airtight container in the fridge for up to 3 days.)

Arrange the lettuce leaves on a platter. Spoon the lentils (warm or cold) onto the leaves and drizzle with the tahini ginger sauce and hot sauce (if using). Garnish with green onions, cilantro, and pickled onions (if using), and serve with lime wedges to squeeze over top.

Calories/serving: 452

Carbs/serving: 34 g

Protein/serving: 22 g

Fat/serving: 22 g

Fiber/serving: 16 g

noodles & bowls

Cashew Cacio e Pepe over Spaghetti Squash

DF/GF/V

Cellular Building + Healing, Energy + Focus, Mood Balancing

Makes 4 servings

Cashew Cacio e Pepe

1 cup raw cashews

½ cup nutritional yeast

¼ cup chopped green onions

¼ cup fresh lemon juice

2 tbsp extra virgin olive oil

3 tsp whole black peppercorns
+ more to taste (see note)

2 tsp shiro miso

½ tsp onion powder

½ tsp sea salt + more to taste

1 to 2 tbsp water (if needed)

Spaghetti Squash

3 lb (1.4 kg) spaghetti squash

1 tbsp extra virgin olive oil
or avocado oil

¼ tsp sea salt + more to taste

Fresh ground pepper to taste

Fresh basil and/or chives
to garnish

This plant-based version of cacio e pepe is a delicious and healthy alternative that emulates the cheesy richness of the original recipe wonderfully. The creamy cashews provide an abundance of plant-based protein, with over 10 grams per serving, and are a great source of healthy fats. The sauce is packed with B vitamins (providing over 100% of your daily B12), as well as copper, magnesium, and a range of minerals that support connective tissue health and overall longevity. Combining it with fiber-rich spaghetti squash creates a luxurious and nourishing meal that your taste buds and body will love.

Serving Note: I love this topped with Caramelized Balsamic Onions (p. 110), and grated pecorino, for added depth and sweetness! Try it with Garlicky Roasted Portobellos (p. 188) or some Thyme Oyster Mushrooms or the scallops variation (p. 187). You can also use the sauce with any kind of pasta or veggie noodle, or serve it with steamed broccoli in place of a creamy cheese sauce. Serve this dish with a salad starter of leafy greens, grated carrot, and cucumber all tossed with the Dijon Vinaigrette (p. 128).

In a bowl, soak the cashews in water overnight or for at least 4 hours. Drain and rinse well.

Preheat the oven to 375°F. Line a baking sheet with parchment paper.

Cut the squash in half lengthwise and scrape out the seeds. Rub the flesh with the oil and salt. Place the squash cut side down on the prepared pan.

Roast until the skin can be pierced with a fork and the strands are cooked but firm enough to hold their shape, more al dente. This should be 25 to 35 minutes but can take up to 40 minutes, depending on the size of the squash. Let the squash cool enough to handle.

Meanwhile, in a high-powered blender, combine the cashews, nutritional yeast, green onions, lemon juice, olive oil, peppercorns, miso, onion powder, and salt. Blend on high until smooth and creamy. If the sauce seems too thick and you want to thin it out, add water, 1 tablespoon at a time. Season with more salt if needed.

Recipe continues

Using a fork, pull the spaghetti squash from the skin to create noodle-like strands. Season with salt and pepper to taste.

In a saucepan over medium heat, gently heat the sauce until just warmed, about 1 minute. Serve over the warm squash noodles, garnished with basil. (If you need to reheat the squash, this can be done in the pan with the sauce, or on a parchment-lined baking sheet in a 425°F oven for a few minutes.)

Store extra sauce in an airtight container in the fridge for up to 4 days. Reheat before serving.

Note: The peppercorns are very spicy; start with 2 tsp if you are sensitive to spice and add more if you like—I go up to 4 tsp myself.

Calories/serving: 401
Carbs/serving: 28 g
Protein/serving: 14 g
Fat/serving: 25 g
Fiber/serving: 8 g

HP **SF** ♥

Lentil Bolognese over Zucchini Noodles

DF/GF/GRF/V

Cellular Building + Healing, Energy + Focus, Mood Balancing

Makes 4 servings

Lentil Bolognese

1 tbsp extra virgin olive oil + more to serve

1½ cups diced red onions

1¼ tsp sea salt + more to taste

1½ cups thinly sliced celery

1 cup dry red lentils, rinsed

1 cup water

2 (14 oz/398 ml) cans diced tomatoes

1 cup roughly chopped fresh basil + more to garnish

2 tbsp minced drained capers

1 tbsp pressed garlic (or more if you love garlic)

1½ tbsp balsamic vinegar

1 tbsp fresh lemon juice

½ tsp chili flakes + more to taste (optional)

Zucchini Noodles

8 cups zucchini noodles (see p. 277) (about 4 medium zucchini) (see note)

1 tbsp extra virgin olive oil

Fresh ground pepper and sea salt to taste

Note: You can cut the noodles to your desired length with kitchen scissors. Instead of spiralized noodles, you can make 8 cups of zucchini ribbons (see p. 277).

My clients and I absolutely love this sauce. I originally developed it to enhance a tomato sauce with more fiber and protein. The lentils give it a wonderful chewy texture and makes it both nourishing and deeply satisfying. The delicious blend of salty capers, garlic, tomatoes, and basil is perfect over delicate zucchini noodles. This recipe boasts an impressive 18 grams of plant-based protein and 13 grams of fiber per serving, and is rich in folate, potassium, and iron, making it an excellent choice for supporting gut health and overall radiance.

Serving Note: Serve with the Kale Pine Nut Caesar (p. 168) or the Everyday Detox Salad (p. 166). Try it with a poached egg or some warmed Marinated Mediterranean Tofu (p. 93). Sprinkle with Pistachio Dukkah (p. 116) or Caramelized Balsamic Onions (p. 110) for a little more texture!

Preheat the oven to 400°F. Line two large rimmed baking sheets with parchment paper.

In a medium pot, heat the oil over medium heat. Add the red onions and 1 teaspoon of the salt and sauté for 3 minutes. Add the celery and sauté for 3 minutes, until the onions and celery are soft and translucent. Add the lentils and water and bring to a simmer. Stir well, then reduce the heat to low, cover, and simmer for 10 minutes, stirring occasionally.

Stir in the tomatoes, basil, capers, garlic, vinegar, lemon juice, chili flakes, and remaining ¼ teaspoon of salt. Simmer, uncovered and stirring often, for 15 minutes, until the lentils are tender. Season with more salt or chili flakes to taste. (Store cooled sauce in an airtight container in the fridge for up to 4 days.)

Meanwhile, in a large bowl, toss the zucchini noodles with the olive oil and salt and pepper to taste. Arrange the noodles on the prepared pans so that they are lying flat (overlapping is okay). Place both pans in the oven and roast for 5 minutes, until the zucchini noodles are steaming and softening.

Serve the zucchini noodles topped with the lentil Bolognese, sprinkled with salt and, if using, chili flakes, and garnished with olive oil and basil.

Calories/serving: 363

Carbs/serving: 43 g

Protein/serving: 18 g

Fat/serving: 9 g

Fiber/serving: 13 g

Green Curry with Zucchini Noodles

DF/GF/GRF/V

Makes 4 servings

Green Curry Sauce

1 (4 oz/112 ml) jar Thai green curry paste

1 (14 oz/400 ml) can coconut milk

2 cups small broccoli florets

1 tbsp micrograted peeled fresh ginger

1 cup packed baby spinach

Zucchini Noodles

1 tbsp avocado oil or extra virgin olive oil

1½ cups chopped trimmed green beans (1-inch pieces)

3 cups roughly chopped finely shredded purple cabbage

8 cups spiralized zucchini ribbons (see p. 277) (about 4 medium zucchini)

2 tbsp Bragg Liquid Aminos

1 tbsp toasted sesame oil

Sea salt to taste

To Serve

Black sesame seeds

¼ to ½ cup fresh cilantro leaves

Lime wedges

The nutritious, fiber-rich broccoli and spinach–based green coconut curry is the standout feature of this dish, not only because of its vibrant color but also due to the innovative way it incorporates vegetables to thicken the sauce and provide additional nourishment. It is a remarkable way to sneak more vegetables into a meal. The sauce can be used in so many ways, making it a versatile addition to your recipe repertoire. Paired here with savory zucchini noodles, it creates a dish that's super supportive of glowing beauty, gut health, and detoxification.

Serving Note: Top the curry with a few Ginger Cilantro Turkey Meatballs (p. 104) or serve it with a more filling Chicken Satay (p. 102). Or keep it light with some Acorn Squash (p. 182), Salt & Pepper Veggies (p. 194), or cubed tofu.

In a 12-inch sauté pan over medium-high heat, toast the green curry paste for about 3 minutes, stirring constantly, until sizzling and fragrant. Stir in the coconut milk until combined, then bring to a simmer. Reduce the heat to medium-low, add the broccoli and ginger, and simmer until the broccoli is tender, about 3 minutes. Add the spinach and stir until wilted.

Transfer the sauce to a high-powered blender and blend on high until it becomes very smooth and a beautiful green. Set aside.

In a large sauté pan, heat the avocado oil over medium-high heat. Add the green beans and sauté for 2 minutes, until vibrant green. Add the cabbage and sauté for about 4 to 5 minutes, until tender. Stir in the zucchini, liquid aminos, and sesame oil and toss everything together. Reduce the heat to low and cook for 4 to 5 minutes, stirring often, until the noodles are tender.

The zucchini will have released some water, so transfer the veggies to a colander and press them gently to remove as much liquid as possible. Return them to the pan over low heat and mix in the green curry sauce. Using kitchen scissors, make a few rough chops through the pan to shorten the noodles, then season with salt to taste. Garnish with sesame seeds, cilantro, and lime wedges.

Store the cooled curry in an airtight container in the fridge for up to 3 days. Reheat over low heat.

Calories/serving: 323

Carbs/serving: 18 g

Protein/serving: 8 g

Fat/serving: 23 g

Fiber/serving: 6 g

Shiitake Ginger Mung Bean Noodles

DF/GF/GRF/VO

Anti-Inflammatory, Beauty + Anti-Aging

Makes 4 servings

6 oz (170 g) mung bean noodles

¼ cup gluten-free tamari

3 tbsp fish sauce or gluten-free vegan fish sauce

2 tbsp toasted sesame oil + more to serve

2 tbsp fresh lime juice

2 tbsp extra virgin olive oil

1 cup finely sliced red onions

2 cups peeled and julienned carrots

1 cup diced red pepper

½ cup sliced green onions

1½ tbsp minced peeled fresh ginger

6 oz (170 g) finely sliced stemmed shiitake mushrooms

2 cups finely sliced asparagus

½ cup roughly chopped fresh Thai basil + more to serve

Chopped fresh mint or cilantro, or a mix, to serve

¼ cup Quick Pickled Jalapeños (p. 112) or chili crunch to serve (optional)

Chopped toasted cashews (see p. 276) or crushed Spiced Mixed Nuts & Seeds (p. 109) to serve (optional)

Lime wedges to serve

Variation: I love mung bean noodles, but feel free to substitute your favorite noodles, like sweet potato or shirataki!

This dish offers a perfect balance of vibrant vegetables, savory and salty flavors, fresh herbs, and delicate noodles. The tender shiitake mushrooms, subtle crunch of julienned carrots, and crisp asparagus create a delightful texture, while providing a nice dose of vitamins A and C, which help protect the body. This recipe is a wonderful addition to any dinner party!

Serving Note: Serve with the Cucumber Herb Salad (p. 159), Salt & Pepper Veggies (p. 194), Sesame Gomae (p. 169), or Citrus & Sesame Cabbage (p. 190). Add a boost of protein with some Smoky Maple Tempeh (p. 95), Miso Maple Salmon Bites (p. 98), or Chicken Satay (p. 102), or serve as part of a big spread with the Sesame Orange Salmon (p. 244).

Cook the noodles according to the package directions, drain, rinse with cold water, then let them drip dry. Using kitchen scissors, cut the noodles into 4- to 5-inch lengths and set aside.

In a small bowl, mix the tamari, fish sauce, sesame oil, and 1 tablespoon of the lime juice. Set aside.

In a large sauté pan or wok, heat the olive oil over medium-high heat. Add the red onions and sauté for 2 minutes. Add the carrots, red peppers, green onions, and ginger and cook, stirring often, for 4 minutes, until tender-crisp, being careful not to overcook. Transfer to a large bowl and set aside.

In the same sauté pan or wok over medium heat, combine 3 tablespoons of the tamari mixture and the mushrooms and asparagus. Cook, stirring, until tender, about 2 to 3 minutes. If the mushrooms aren't cooking quickly, turn the heat up to medium-high. Transfer to the bowl.

Give the sauté pan or wok a quick wipe. Add the noodles, remaining tamari mixture and lime juice, and basil, stirring well. Cook over medium heat, stirring, for 2 to 3 minutes, until heated through. Transfer to the bowl.

Toss everything together and let sit for 2 minutes. Serve topped with a drizzle of sesame oil, more Thai basil, mint, pickled jalapeños, and cashews, with lime wedges to squeeze over top.

Calories/serving: 356
Carbs/serving: 49 g
Protein/serving: 7 g
Fat/serving: 14 g
Fiber/serving: 5 g

Roasted Rainbow Veggie Noodle Bowl

DF/GF/GRF/V

Anti-Inflammatory, Beauty + Anti-Aging, Gut Health

Makes 4 servings

3 cups cubed peeled butternut squash (½-inch cubes)

2½ cups chopped red peppers (½-inch squares)

2 cups broccoli florets (½-inch pieces)

2 cups cubed or sliced halved zucchinis (½-inch cubes or slices)

1½ cups thinly sliced halved carrots

1 cup diced red onions

2 tbsp extra virgin olive oil or avocado oil

1 tsp sea salt

1 tsp curry powder

1 tsp garlic powder

1 tbsp toasted sesame oil

3 cups cooked shirataki or mung bean noodles

½ cup roughly chopped fresh Thai basil

1 recipe Tahini Ginger Sauce (p. 130)

½ recipe Quick Pickled Onions (p. 112) to serve (optional)

½ cup finely chopped green onions or fresh herbs to serve (optional)

½ red beet, grated, to serve (optional)

Variation: Try 3 cups cooked quinoa in place of the noodles, for a quinoa bowl!

This bowl features a rainbow of roasted vegetables that complement each other beautifully in both texture and flavor. From the soft squash to the crunchy broccoli, the earthy carrots to the sweet red peppers, this dish offers an array of antioxidants. The creamy tahini sauce brings everything together while providing exceptional health benefits and flavor. This noodle bowl is filling and keeps well, making it an ideal meal prep option for a busy week.

Serving Note: I like to bring this dish to a dinner party and set it out next to a little topping station for people to make their own bowls. To boost the nutrition even more, add a scoop of the Marinated Mediterranean Tofu (p. 93) or a Chicken Satay (p. 102).

Preheat the oven to 375°F, with the racks placed in the upper and lower thirds. Line two rimmed baking sheets with parchment paper or aluminum foil.

In a large bowl, combine all the veggies. Add the olive oil, salt, curry powder, and garlic powder and toss well. Spread the veggies evenly on the prepared pans.

Place one pan on the upper rack and the other on the lower rack. Roast for 10 minutes. Stir the veggies, rotate the pans, and swap their positions on the racks. Roast for 5 to 10 minutes, until the squash is tender.

In a sauté pan, heat the sesame oil over medium heat. Make sure to drain excess water from the cooked noodles, then add with the Thai basil and toss for about 3 minutes, until the noodles are warmed through.

Transfer the warm noodles and vegetables to a large bowl. (I like to use kitchen scissors to cut the noodles shorter.) Toss everything together with the tahini ginger sauce. If needed, bring back to heat in a large pan over low heat. Serve topped with pickled onions, green onions, and grated beet as desired for a pop of color.

Store the cooled noodle bowl in an airtight container in the fridge for up to 4 days. Reheat over low heat before serving.

Calories/serving: 581

Carbs/serving: 35 g

Protein/serving: 15 g

Fat/serving: 39 g

Fiber/serving: 19 g

Cauliflower Fried Rice

DF/GF/GRF

Beauty + Anti-Aging, Cellular Building + Healing, Gut Health

Makes 4 servings

Eggs

3 eggs

2 tsp gluten-free tamari

2 tsp toasted sesame oil

½ tsp fresh ground pepper

¼ tsp chili flakes

Vegetables

1 tbsp extra virgin olive oil

1 cup finely chopped white onions

½ cup finely chopped green onions

2 tbsp minced peeled fresh ginger

1 tbsp minced garlic

6 cups riced cauliflower (see p. 277) (about 2 lb/900 g cauliflower)

1½ tbsp toasted sesame oil

½ tsp fresh ground pepper

1 cup very thinly sliced snow peas (see variation)

1 cup frozen peas

2½ tbsp gluten-free tamari

1 tbsp rice wine vinegar

Garnishes

½ cup chopped kimchi

½ cup Spiced Mixed Nuts & Seeds (p. 109), roughly chopped (optional)

¼ cup chopped green onions or other fresh herbs

¼ cup toasted sesame seeds

Variation: This also works with 4 cups cooked, cooled jasmine rice! Can't find snow peas? Increase the frozen peas to 1½ cups. For a vegan version, omit eggs, and use vegan kimchi and more seasoning to taste.

Fried rice is undeniably delicious, so I wanted to try seasoning cauliflower to create a grain-free alternative to one of my all-time favorite dishes. This cauliflower version is high in fiber, protein, vitamins, and minerals, making it an excellent choice for supporting gut health, cellular function, and overall radiance. I find this meal to be incredibly delicious and a testament to the versatility of cauliflower. It's great served cold the next day too!

Serving Note: To add more protein, try the Miso Maple Salmon Bites (p. 98), Ginger Cilantro Turkey Meatballs (p. 104), or top with a poached egg and some sliced avocado! Or serve with the Cucumber Herb Salad (p. 159) or Citrus & Sesame Cabbage (p. 190) for a perfect veggie pairing.

In a medium bowl, beat the eggs with the tamari, sesame oil, pepper, and chili flakes. Set aside.

In a large sauté pan or wok, heat the olive oil over medium heat. Add the white onions and cook, stirring often, for 3 to 4 minutes, until translucent. Add the green onions, ginger, and garlic and cook, stirring, for 3 minutes.

Increase the heat to medium-high and stir in the cauliflower, sesame oil, and pepper. Cook, stirring often, for 3 minutes. Add the snow peas, frozen peas, tamari, and vinegar and sauté for 2 minutes, until the peas and cauliflower are tender but still have a little bite.

Reduce the heat to medium and make a hole in the center of the rice mixture. Pour in the egg mixture, let sit for 1 minute, then gently scramble. As the eggs begin to set, fold them into the rice and cook for 1 to 3 minutes, stirring often, until the eggs are fully cooked and mixed well. Remove from the heat and let sit for 2 minutes before serving.

Garnish with kimchi, chopped nuts and seeds (if using), green onions, and sesame seeds.

Store the cooled rice in an airtight container in the fridge for up to 2 days. Serve cold or reheat in a pan with a touch of oil until warm.

Calories/serving: 358

Carbs/serving: 21 g

Protein/serving: 15 g

Fat/serving: 22 g

Fiber/serving: 10 g

Summer Pesto Quinoa Bowl

DFO/GF/GRF/VO

Beauty + Anti-Aging, Energy + Focus, Mood Balancing

Makes 4 servings

Zucchini

4 cups sliced zucchini or yellow summer squash (¼-inch rounds)

1 tbsp extra virgin olive oil

¼ tsp sea salt

¼ tsp fresh ground pepper

¼ tsp dried basil

Quinoa

2 tbsp extra virgin olive oil

1½ cups finely chopped red onions

1 cup finely chopped red pepper

½ tsp sea salt + more to taste

2 tsp gluten-free tamari

3 cups cooked quinoa

1 recipe Basil Pesto (p. 123)

Fresh ground pepper to taste

To Serve

A few handfuls of arugula

½ cup crumbled goat, sheep, or vegan feta

¼ cup toasted pine nuts (see p. 276) (optional)

Lemon zest to garnish (optional)

This recipe is a perfect ode to summertime, especially when gardens are brimming with zucchini and basil. Basil pesto and warm sautéed vegetables season the quinoa, resulting in a delicious, satisfying, and nutritionally balanced bowl. It is abundant in supportive minerals, fiber, and protein (15 grams per serving), along with B vitamins, magnesium, antioxidants, and healthy fats. And did you know that basil can enhance mental focus and memory?

Serving Note: This is an energizing and uplifting addition to any spread at a dinner party, garden party, or brunch. You could top it with a poached egg, a Mung Bean Falafel (p. 240) or two, or some Marinated Mediterranean Tofu (p. 93). It is also great with a light green salad with Dijon Vinaigrette (p. 128) or with the Everyday Detox Salad (p. 166).

Preheat the oven to 375°F. Line a rimmed baking sheet with parchment paper.

In a large bowl, toss the zucchini with the oil, salt, pepper, and basil. Spread in a single layer on the prepared pan. Roast for 8 minutes, until tender-crisp.

For the quinoa, in a large sauté pan, heat the oil over medium heat. Add the onions and cook for about 5 minutes, until softened and tender. Add the red peppers and cook, stirring often, for 5 minutes. Stir in the salt and tamari. Add the cooked quinoa and toss to combine and warm through. Season with more salt and pepper to taste.

Transfer the quinoa mixture to a large bowl and stir in the pesto. Add the zucchini and toss to coat.

Just before serving, add the arugula and feta and toss to coat. (Only add the arugula if you are serving right away, or if the dish has cooled, as it will wilt otherwise.) Divide evenly among four bowls and garnish with pine nuts and lemon zest to taste (if using).

Calories/serving: 679

Carbs/serving: 39 g

Protein/serving: 15 g

Fat/serving: 50 g

Fiber/serving: 9 g

Red Lentil Dal

DF/GF/GRF/V

Anti-Inflammatory, Energy + Focus, Gut Health

Makes 4 servings

1 tbsp extra virgin olive oil

1¼ cups diced celery

1 cup diced white onions

1 tbsp micrograted peeled fresh ginger

1 tsp pressed garlic

2 tsp curry powder

1 tsp coriander seeds (or 2 tsp if you love the taste!)

½ tsp onion powder

¼ tsp black mustard seeds (optional)

3½ cups water

2 cups cubed peeled sweet potato (½-inch cubes)

1 cup dry red lentils, rinsed

4 cups packed baby spinach, roughly chopped

2 tbsp fresh lemon juice

Sea salt to taste

Chopped fresh herbs (cilantro, chives, mint) to garnish (optional)

The first dish I ever cooked with my dad was a traditional dal. He had spent a great deal of time in India, where he developed a profound appreciation for the country's culture and cuisine. The vibrant colors, rich flavors, and captivating aroma of the spices we cooked with left a lasting impression on me. Later, I would learn that these spices not only enhance the depth and complexity of a dish but also provide an array of amazing health benefits, like helping to reduce inflammation, support digestion, and strengthen the immune system. Among the many variations of this dish, the one closest to my heart is this sweet potato and spinach dal. In addition to being incredibly delicious, it is packed with nutrients: the spinach provides a boost of iron, the sweet potatoes are a rich source of vitamin A, and the red lentils offer a generous serving of protein.

Serving Note: Serve with a salad, like the Everyday Detox Salad (p. 166) or Creamy Avo Cumin Coleslaw (p. 170), next to the Sautéed Greens (p. 186) and some warm Curried Socca (p. 86). Or top with some fresh avocado slices or a poached egg.

In a medium pot, heat the oil over medium heat. Add the celery, onions, ginger, garlic, curry powder, coriander seeds, onion powder, and, if desired, mustard seeds and sauté for 5 to 8 minutes, until the onions are soft.

Stir in the water, sweet potatoes, and lentils. Bring to a boil, then cover, reduce the heat to low, and simmer for 30 minutes, stirring occasionally. Add the spinach and stir until wilted. Stir in the lemon juice and salt to taste. Serve garnished with herbs.

Store the cooled dal in an airtight container in the fridge for up to 4 days. Reheat in a pot over low heat until it reaches your desired temperature.

Calories/serving: 293
Carbs/serving: 40 g
Protein/serving: 15 g
Fat/serving: 5 g
Fiber/serving: 10 g

HP **HF** **LC** (turkey);
HP **SF** (tempeh)

Bean-Free Butternut Chili

DF/GF/GRF/VO

Makes 4 servings

2 tbsp extra virgin olive oil

1 cup diced red onions

1 tbsp pressed garlic

1 lb (454 g) ground turkey or
    2 (6 oz/170 g) packages grain-
    free tempeh (3 cups crumbled)

2 tsp sea salt + more to taste

2 tsp ground cumin

2 tsp onion powder

2 tsp chili powder

1 tsp ground coriander

1 tsp chipotle powder, only half
    if sensitive to spice

½ tsp smoked paprika

2 cups diced zucchinis (½-inch
    thick triangles)

2 cups sliced celery

2 cups small-cubed butternut
    squash

2 (14 oz/398 ml) cans diced
    tomatoes

½ jalapeño, seeded and diced
    (optional)

½ cup fresh cilantro leaves to
    garnish (optional)

I love this bean-free chili recipe. It's delicious, energy-stabilizing, nutrient-dense, packed with protein, and high in fiber! I focused on hydrating veggies, like celery and zucchini, cooking them down into a luscious, melt-in-your-mouth sauce. I designed the recipe to work perfectly with either turkey or tempeh–both are easy to cook with and are high in protein. Either way, you won't be disappointed.

Serving Note: Top this chili with some avocado and a drizzle of olive oil. I also love it with the Creamy Avo Cumin Coleslaw (p. 170)–they're perfect together! If I'm building a larger meal for a few people, I will serve the Kale Pine Nut Caesar (p. 168) on the side.

In a large pot, heat the oil over medium heat. Add the onions and sauté for 5 minutes, until translucent. Add the garlic and sauté for 1 minute. Add the turkey or tempeh and cook, stirring often to break up any large clumps, until starting to brown, about 5 to 6 minutes. Add the salt and other spices, stirring well, and a splash of water or olive oil if the pan seems too dry.

Add the zucchini, celery, squash, tomatoes, and jalapeños. Bring to a simmer, stirring frequently. Reduce the heat to medium-low, cover, and cook, stirring occasionally, for 25 to 30 minutes, until the chili is thickened and the squash and zucchini are tender. Feel free to add a little more spice to taste while cooking.

Remove from the heat and let stand, covered, for 15 minutes to allow the flavors to release and meld. Season with salt to taste and serve garnished with cilantro.

Store the cooled chili in an airtight container in the fridge for up to 4 days. Reheat over medium-low to your desired temperature.

Note: Some of my clients don't eat beans (for a myriad of reasons), and this recipe is such a nice solution—just know that if you choose the tempeh option, it will not be bean-free, as tempeh is fermented soybean.

Calories/serving: 373	Calories/serving: 366
Carbs/serving: 21 g	Carbs/serving: 23 g
Protein/serving: 26 g	Protein/serving: 22 g
Fat/serving: 17 g	Fat/serving: 17 g
Fiber/serving: 10 g	Fiber/serving: 13 g
(for turkey)	(for tempeh)

plates

Zucchini Enchiladas

DF/GF/GRF/V

Makes 8 enchiladas (4 servings)

Zucchini Enchilada Wrappers

3 to 4 medium zucchinis

Spinach & Leek Filling

2 tbsp extra virgin olive oil

2 cups thinly sliced halved leeks, white parts only

1 tsp sea salt

2 tbsp fresh lemon juice

2 tsp pressed garlic

10 cups packed baby spinach

Mushroom Enchilada Sauce

2 cups vegetable broth

3 tbsp hemp hearts

1 tbsp + ½ tsp chili powder

1½ tsp ground cumin

1½ tsp sea salt + more to taste

1 tsp dried oregano

5 tbsp extra virgin olive oil

2 tbsp tomato paste

2 tsp apple cider vinegar

4 cups finely chopped portobello mushrooms

½ cup finely chopped tomato

Fresh ground pepper to serve

This beautiful plant-based dish is full of protein and fiber. Delicate zucchini wraps a tender spinach and leek filling that's topped with a mushroom tomato sauce (thickened with nutrient-dense hemp hearts) to create delicious vegetable enchiladas. With its abundance of beautiful flavor and supportive minerals, this dish is a treat to eat and will help your body thrive.

Serving Note: Plate these enchiladas alongside a simple green salad with grated carrot, beet, lettuce, and Dijon Vinaigrette (p. 128) or with some warm basmati or cauliflower rice. Or serve next to a Chicken Satay (p. 102) with Chunky Guacamole (p. 137), Caper Feta Broccoli (p. 192), Wilted Swiss Chard (p. 196), or, for a colorful crunch, the Creamy Avo Cumin Coleslaw (p. 170).

To make the zucchini enchilada wrappers, use a mandoline to slice the zucchinis into very thin lengthwise strips, about ⅛ inch thick, stopping when you reach the core. You need about 40 slices in total. Set aside.

To make the spinach and leek filling, heat the oil in a large sauté pan over medium heat. Add the leeks and salt and cook, stirring well, for 6 minutes, until soft and browned. Add the lemon juice and garlic and cook, stirring well and reducing the heat if the garlic seems to be burning, for 1 minute, until the garlic is fragrant. Add the spinach, reduce the heat to low, and cook, turning the spinach often, for 1 to 2 minutes, until wilted. Remove from the heat and set aside.

To make the mushroom enchilada sauce, in a high-powered blender, combine the broth, hemp hearts, 1 tablespoon of the chili powder, cumin, ½ teaspoon of the salt, oregano, 3 tablespoons of the oil, tomato paste, and vinegar. Blend on high until smooth. Set aside.

In another large sauté pan, heat the remaining 2 tablespoons of oil over high heat. Add the mushrooms and remaining ½ teaspoon of chili powder, and remaining 1 teaspoon of salt and cook, stirring often, for 4 minutes. Add the tomato, reduce the heat to medium, and cook for 1 to 2 minutes, until the mushrooms are fully cooked. Reduce the heat to medium-low, add the blended sauce, and cook, stirring occasionally, for 15 to 20 minutes, until it starts to thicken into a cream-like consistency (reduce the heat more if it spatters). Remove from the heat and set aside.

Recipe continues

Preheat the oven to 350°F.

Lay some of the zucchini slices overlapping to form a 5- to 6-inch square (this will be about 5 slices, or maybe less, depending on their size). Top the square with about ¼ cup of the filling and roll it up as tightly as you can. Place the enchilada in a baking dish or a cast-iron pan. Repeat with the remaining zucchini slices and filling to make 8 enchiladas in total.

Bake for 11 to 12 minutes, until the zucchini is al dente and the filling is heated through. Pour the sauce over the enchiladas and bake for 2 minutes or until warm again. Serve sprinkled with pepper.

Calories/serving: 373
Carbs/serving: 17 g
Protein/serving: 10 g
Fat/serving: 30 g
Fiber/serving: 7 g

Wild Mushrooms with Pine Nut Cream on Sweet Potato Toasts

DFO/GF/GRF/VO

Cellular Building + Healing, Energy + Focus, Immune Support

Makes 4 servings

2 medium or 1 very large sweet potato (1½ lb/680 g total), skin on + washed

1 tbsp extra virgin olive oil

Sea salt

Pine Nut Cream

¾ cup pine nuts, lightly toasted (see p. 277)

¾ cup water

1 tsp lemon zest + more taste and to garnish

¾ tsp sea salt + more to taste

¾ tsp fresh ground pepper + more to taste

2 tbsp extra virgin olive oil

½ cup finely chopped shallots

1 tbsp pressed garlic

1 tbsp chopped fresh thyme + leaves to garnish

To Serve

1 recipe Thyme Oyster Mushrooms or scallops variation (p. 187)

2 tbsp toasted pine nuts to garnish (optional)

Variation: Combine the mushrooms and pine nut cream to serve as a sauce over veggie noodles or pasta.

I adore this recipe—a delightful combination of wild thyme mushrooms atop a garlic-infused pine nut cream sauce, served on slices of roasted sweet potato. It perfectly showcases how exquisite flavors and nutritionally dense food can coexist. The delicious mushrooms contribute to optimal cellular functioning, while the aromatic garlic and shallots provide a rich source of antioxidants. The decadent pine nut cream offers a wealth of minerals, and the tender sweet potatoes are packed with fiber and beta-carotene.

Serving Note: Serve with the Everyday Detox Salad (p. 166) or Herby Greek Salad (p. 164). Wilted Swiss Chard (p. 196) or Marinated Mediterranean Tofu (p. 93), would be a great add for more protein too!

Preheat the oven to 400°F. Line a rimmed baking sheet with parchment paper.

Cut the sweet potatoes into ½-inch angled rounds. In a large bowl, toss the rounds with the oil, ensuring all sides are equally greased. Spread them evenly on the prepared pan and sprinkle with salt.

Roast the sweet potatoes for about 30 minutes, flipping them halfway through, until cooked through and slightly browned.

Meanwhile, make the pine nut cream. In a high-powered blender, combine the pine nuts, water, lemon zest, salt, and pepper. Blend on high until smooth and set aside.

In a sauté pan, heat the oil over medium heat. Add the shallots and sauté for 3 minutes, until translucent. Add the garlic and thyme and cook, stirring well so the garlic doesn't burn, for 1 minute, until the garlic is fragrant.

Add the shallot mixture, including all the oil, to the blender and blend until smooth. Adjust the seasoning with more salt, pepper, or lemon zest, if desired. Transfer the pine nut cream to the sauté pan and warm over low heat for a few seconds, stirring constantly, until just heated (skip this step if the cream is still warm after blending).

Serve the warm sweet potato slices topped with the pine nut cream and the mushrooms. Garnish with lemon zest, thyme, and the pine nuts (if using).

Calories/serving: 570
Carbs/serving: 40 g
Protein/serving: 10 g
Fat/serving: 39 g
Fiber/serving: 12 g

Roasted Carrots over Lentils & Lemon Cumin Yogurt

DFO/GRF/GF/VO

Beauty + Anti-Aging, Energy + Focus, Gut Health

Makes 4 servings

Seasoned Lentils

1 tbsp extra virgin olive oil

1 cup finely chopped shallots

3 tbsp red wine vinegar

Sea salt to taste

¾ cup dry green or brown lentils, rinsed (see note)

2½ cups water

Roasted Carrots

1½ lb (680 g) rainbow or orange carrots

2 tbsp extra virgin olive oil

1½ tbsp maple syrup

½ tsp sea salt + more to taste

¼ tsp fresh ground pepper

Lemon Cumin Yogurt

1½ cups plain coconut, goat, or Greek yogurt

1½ to 2 tbsp fresh lemon juice (see note)

1 tsp ground cumin

1 tsp curry powder

½ tsp sea salt + more to taste

Garnish

½ cup chopped fresh mint, cilantro leaves, and/or green onions

2 tsp black mustard seeds, toasted (see p. 277) (optional)

Fresh ground pepper

With sweet roasted carrots, seasoned lentils, and zesty cumin yogurt, this dish is a work of art, both beautiful and delicious! Roasting carrots is so simple and really concentrates their flavor as they become sweet and caramelized–plus they're loaded with beta-carotene, promoting radiant skin, healthy eyes, and a resilient immune system! I first developed this recipe for a client who was a vegan athlete. I needed to ensure that every dish I served them included plant-based protein. A generous handful of lentils provides that protein and also adds fiber and essential minerals.

Serving Note: Bring this stunning dish to share at a dinner party. It goes well alongside Thyme Oyster Mushrooms or the scallops variation (p. 187), Wilted Swiss Chard (p. 196), Mung Bean Falafel (p. 240), or Chicken Satay (p. 102). Or make it the star with a side of the Creamy Avo Cumin Coleslaw (p. 170), Everyday Detox Salad (p. 166), or Sautéed Greens (p. 186).

In a small pot, heat the oil over medium heat. Add the shallots and sauté for 2 minutes. Add the vinegar and cook, stirring, for 4 to 5 minutes, until the liquid has cooked off and the shallots are translucent. Transfer to a bowl, sprinkle with salt to taste, and set aside.

In the same pot, combine the lentils and water. Bring to a boil, then reduce the heat to low, cover, and simmer for about 17 to 20 minutes, until the lentils are tender but not mushy. Drain any excess water and set aside to cool and dry, then add to the shallot mixture and toss to coat.

Preheat the oven to 400°F. Line a rimmed baking sheet with parchment paper.

Trim off the tops of the carrots. Cut the carrots into sticks about 4 inches long and no more than ½ inch thick. Place them in a large bowl, drizzle with the oil and maple syrup, and sprinkle with the salt and pepper. Rub the carrots so they are well coated in the seasoning. Arrange the carrots in a single layer on the prepared baking sheet.

Roast the carrots for 30 minutes, turning halfway through, until nicely caramelized and tender. Adjust the seasoning with salt to taste.

In a small bowl, combine all of the lemon cumin yogurt ingredients. Adjust the seasoning with salt to taste.

Divide the yogurt between four plates. Place a scoop of the lentils on top of the yogurt and then some roasted carrots. (Or plate on one big, beautiful platter to share.) Garnish with herbs, mustard seeds, and pepper.

Store leftovers in an airtight container in the fridge for up to 4 days.

Note: Instead of cooking dry lentils, you can use 1½ cups of green or brown canned lentils. Drain and rinse them in a colander, then let them dry as much as possible before tossing them with the shallot mixture. If using coconut yogurt, use 2 tbsp lemon juice; if using Greek or goat yogurt, use just 1½ tbsp lemon juice, as those types of yogurt are more tart.

Calories/serving: 428
Carbs/serving: 56 g
Protein/serving: 12 g
Fat/serving: 14 g
Fiber/serving: 12 g

**Roasted Carrots
over Lentils & Lemon
Cumin Yogurt**

(p. 236)

**Everyday
Detox Salad**
(p. 166)

**Mung Bean Falafel
with Tzatziki
& Greek Salad**
(p. 240)

Mung Bean Falafel with Tzatziki & Greek Salad

DFO/GF/GRF/VO

Cellular Building + Healing, Energy + Focus, Gut Health

Makes 4 servings + extra falafel

Falafel

1 cup dried mung beans

8 cups water

2 cups roughly chopped fresh cilantro

1½ cups roughly chopped fresh flat-leaf parsley

1½ cups roughly chopped white onions

1 cup finely grated carrots

1 large jalapeño, chopped and seeded

1 tbsp gluten-free tamari

1 tbsp ground cumin

1½ tsp ground coriander

1½ tsp sea salt

1 tsp garlic powder

½ cup packed almond meal or chickpea flour

½ tsp baking soda

¼ cup extra virgin olive oil

Tzatziki

1 cup plain coconut, goat, Greek, or cashew yogurt

3 cloves garlic

2 tbsp fresh lemon juice

2 tsp apple cider vinegar

½ tsp sea salt + more to taste

½ English cucumber, grated

2 tbsp finely chopped fresh dill + more to garnish

Fresh ground pepper to taste

To Serve

1 recipe Herby Greek Salad (p. 164)

Mung beans may be tiny, but they have mighty health benefits: they're high in fiber, protein, antioxidants, and minerals. I use them to replace chickpeas in this recipe while staying faithful to all the flavors typical of a falafel, such as cumin, coriander, and tons of fresh, detoxifying herbs—and one serving of falafel provides 12 g of protein! Do not fret if your falafel is not perfectly round; this is because they are slow-baked instead of flash-fried. I've also included recipes for a Greek salad and a refreshing tzatziki to make a bright and seriously supportive meal. Though straightforward, this recipe is a bit time-consuming, so I designed it to make a few extra falafel. Not only are they fabulous straight out of the oven, but they also make a great grab-and-go snack throughout the week.

Serving Note: Best served warm; bring a platter of these falafel, along with the tzatziki and Greek salad, to add to any dinner spread. They go well with the Everyday Detox Salad (p. 166) too!

In a large bowl, soak the mung beans in the water for 12 hours. Drain and rinse.

Meanwhile, prepare the tzatziki. In a high-powered blender, combine the yogurt, garlic, lemon juice, vinegar, and salt. Blend on high until smooth.

Wrap the grated cucumber in a dish towel and squeeze out the excess water until mostly dry. Add to the blender and pulse a few times to incorporate.

Transfer the tzatziki to a bowl and stir in the dill. Adjust the seasoning with salt and pepper to taste. Cover and chill in the fridge until set, at least 30 minutes and up to 2 hours (the longer, the better).

Preheat the oven to 400°F, with the racks placed in the upper and lower thirds. Line two baking sheets with oiled parchment paper.

In a food processor, combine the mung beans, cilantro, parsley, onions, carrots, jalapeño, tamari, cumin, coriander, salt, and garlic powder. Pulse, stopping to scrape down the sides once or twice, until finely chopped–you want all the beans to be broken down, but the mixture should not be completely smooth.

Transfer the bean mixture to a large bowl and stir in the almond meal, baking soda, and oil. Chill in the fridge for at least 30 minutes and up to 2 hours.

Scoop up 2 tablespoons of the falafel mixture and form it into a round in the palm of your hand, about 2 inches in diameter and 1 inch thick. Don't worry if it's wet; it will firm up when baked. Repeat to shape about 28 falafels total of the same size. Place on the prepared baking sheets.

Place one baking sheet on the upper rack and the other on the lower rack. Bake for 15 minutes. Flip the falafel, rotate the baking sheets, and swap their positions on the racks. Bake for 13 to 15 minutes, until golden. Let sit for 5 minutes before serving.

Arrange 5 warm falafel on each plate, along with a quarter of the tzatziki and a helping of Greek salad. Garnish with dill.

Store the extra falafel in an airtight container in the fridge for up to 5 days, and the tzatziki in an airtight container in the fridge for up to 3 days. Reheat the falafel wrapped in aluminum foil in the oven at 400°F for 5 to 8 minutes.

Calories/serving: 669
Carbs/serving: 41 g
Protein/serving: 22 g
Fat/serving: 42 g
Fiber/serving: 15 g

Fish in Parchment Parcels: 2 Ways

Herbed Lemon White Fish over Vegetables
Sesame Orange Salmon with Broccoli & Bok Choy

These parcels have been a staple of my dinner party repertoire since I started cooking–there's something special about wrapping up little meals in parchment. They add a touch of sophistication, are an almost foolproof way to get beautifully moist and flavorful fish, and make it easier to prep dinner in advance. Each of these parcels is high in antioxidants, fiber, and skin-healthy A and C vitamins from the veggies. Meanwhile, the fish provides not only a substantial amount of protein but also omega-3 fatty acids to combat inflammation.

Herbed Lemon White Fish over Vegetables

GF/GRF
Beauty + Anti-Aging, Cellular Building + Healing, Mood Balancing

Makes 4 servings

2 cups carrot ribbons (see p. 277)

2 cups thinly sliced red peppers

2 cups trimmed asparagus ribbons (or sliced in half lengthwise if spears are thin)

1 cup roughly chopped fresh herbs (cilantro, basil, Thai basil, tarragon, dill, parsley, or a mix!)

4 cloves garlic, thinly sliced

½ cup finely chopped shallots

1 tbsp extra virgin olive oil

1 tsp sea salt + more to taste

½ tsp fresh ground pepper + more to sprinkle

1 to 1¼ lb (454 to 567 g) white fish (such as halibut, trout, or cod), skin and bones removed, cut into 4 equal pieces

2 tsp chopped jalapeños

Zest of 1 lemon

4 tbsp fresh lemon juice

4 tbsp salted butter

½ large lemon, cut into 8 thin rounds

These parchment parcels feature a medley of vibrant vegetables that are steamed alongside the fish and delicately seasoned with lemon, butter, and shallots. Subtle and simple, this dish highlights the natural flavors of all the ingredients. Swap in seasonal vegetables as you like.

Serving Note: These are great served with something green, like a salad or Lemon Garlic Spinach (p. 184), and something a bit starchier, like Buttered Sweet Potato Ribbons (p. 179)–or perhaps a mix of the two, such as the Arugula & Roasted Squash Salad (p. 172).

Preheat the oven to 400°F. Cut four 12- to 14-inch squares of parchment paper, fold each perfectly in half to make a crease, then unfold.

In a large bowl, combine the carrots, red peppers, asparagus, herbs, garlic, shallots, oil, ½ teaspoon of the salt, and pepper, mixing well. Divide evenly between the four parchment squares, placing the vegetables on one side of the center crease.

Place a piece of fish on top of each nest of veggies. Evenly season the fish with the remaining ½ teaspoon of salt and a sprinkle of pepper, then top with the jalapeños and lemon zest. Add 1 tablespoon each of the lemon juice and butter to each bundle, over the fish, and finish with 2 lemon rounds.

To close each packet, fold the opposite side over so that the edges meet and the paper is folded in half over the fish. Seal the package by crimping the edges: starting from the bottom folded corner, make overlapping folds, almost like pleats, all the way around until the package is sealed and looks like a half moon. Twist or tuck the end to secure it, or use a paper clip to hold the packet closed. You want it sealed, so air can't get in and flavor can't get out. Place the packets on a baking sheet.

Bake for 13 to 16 minutes, until the fish is opaque and flakes easily with a fork. (The time may vary depending on the thickness of the fish.) Season with more salt and pepper to taste.

Calories/serving: 340
Carbs/serving: 13 g
Protein/serving: 27 g
Fat/serving: 18 g
Fiber/serving: 6 g

 F LC

Sesame Orange Salmon with Broccoli & Bok Choy

DF/GF/GRF

Anti-Inflammatory, Beauty + Anti-Aging, Mood Balancing

Makes 4 servings

Sauce

½ cup chopped sweet onions

½ cup chopped fresh cilantro

2 tbsp finely grated peeled fresh ginger

1 tsp pressed garlic

2 tsp orange zest

¼ cup fresh orange juice

3 tbsp gluten-free tamari

3 tbsp toasted sesame oil

2 tbsp rice vinegar

Salmon Packets

1 lb (454 g) wild salmon, skin and bones removed, cut into 4 equal pieces

½ tsp sea salt + more to serve

½ tsp fresh ground pepper + more to serve

4 cups chopped bok choy or baby bok choy

4 cups small broccoli florets

1 tbsp extra virgin olive oil

¼ cup chopped fresh cilantro + more to garnish

2 tsp finely chopped jalapeños or 1 tsp red Thai chili (see note)

Note: Zest the orange before you juice it. Use a jalapeño if you would like a little heat, and a Thai chili if you want a real kick! Thai chilies are much spicier.

These steamy packets combine salmon with a delicious ginger, orange, cilantro, and sesame sauce to create a sweet and spicy dish, the flavors melding as they cook. They are delicately seasoned, fun to make, and versatile enough to go with any side, salad, or soup.

Serving Note: Serve these with the Cucumber Herb Salad (p. 159), Citrus & Sesame Cabbage (p. 190), or a small side of Shiitake Ginger Mung Bean Noodles (p. 218). A simple side of rice or quinoa will also do nicely!

Preheat the oven to 400°F. Cut four 12- to 14-inch square pieces of parchment, fold each perfectly in half to make a crease, then unfold.

In a high-powered blender, blend all the sauce ingredients on high until smooth.

Season both sides of the salmon with the salt and pepper (about ¼ teaspoon of each).

In a large bowl, toss the broccoli and bok choy with the oil and remaining ¼ teaspoon each of salt and pepper. Divide evenly between the four parchment squares, placing the vegetables on one side of the center crease.

Place a piece of salmon on top of each nest of veggies. Evenly spoon the sauce over top, then sprinkle with the cilantro and jalapeños.

To close each packet, fold the opposite side over so that the edges meet and the paper is folded in half over the fish. Seal the package by crimping the edges: starting from the bottom folded corner, make overlapping folds, almost like pleats, all the way around until the package is sealed and looks like a half moon. Twist or tuck the end to secure it, or use a paper clip to hold the packet closed. You want it sealed, so air can't get in and flavor can't get out. Place the packets on a baking sheet.

Bake for 14 to 16 minutes, until the fish reaches an internal temperature of 165°F, is almost opaque, and flakes easily with a fork, and the broccoli and bok choy are tender. (The time may vary depending on the thickness of the fish.) Garnish with cilantro and salt to taste.

Calories/serving: 320

Carbs/serving: 12 g

Protein/serving: 31 g

Fat/serving: 16 g

Fiber/serving: 4 g

Almond-Crusted White Fish in Savory Tomato Sauce

DF/GF/GRF

Beauty + Anti-Aging, Cellular Building + Healing, Mood Balancing

Makes 4 servings

2 tsp extra virgin olive oil

1 egg

¾ cup raw almonds (see variation)

1 tsp garlic powder

1 tsp onion powder

1 tsp lemon zest

½ tsp chopped fresh thyme or dried

¾ tsp sea salt

¾ tsp fresh ground pepper

1 lb (454 g) white fish (such as ling cod, halibut, or wild cod), skin and bones removed, cut into 4 equal pieces

Sauce

3 cups small broccoli florets

1 recipe Savory Tomato Sauce (p. 248)

5 cups baby spinach

Fresh basil leaves to garnish

Grated parmesan or hard sheep cheese to garnish (optional)

Variation: If you don't want almonds, try raw pistachios instead! You can add an extra 1 to 2 cups of veggies to this sauce to make it a super-dense veggie dish; try sliced asparagus, green beans, and/or zucchini ribbons.

This recipe has it all: it's loaded with vitamins, minerals, fiber, omega-3s, and lovely flavors. The delicate white fish, coated in a crunchy almond crust, provides cell-supportive minerals. It's plated over an antioxidant-packed tomato sauce full of green vegetables, which provide all the skin-nourishing vitamins (A, C, and E), to create a beautifully balanced dish: mood boosting, healing, and delicious. Enjoy!

Serving Note: This fish would be lovely next to the Kale Pine Nut Caesar (p. 168) or Everyday Detox Salad (p. 166), or with a beautiful starter of the Roasted Beet Carpaccio (p. 160).

Preheat the oven to 425°F. Line a rimmed baking sheet with parchment paper and brush it with the oil.

In a shallow dish, beat the egg.

In a high-powered blender or food processor, pulse the almonds into chunky, coarse crumbs. Transfer to a shallow bowl and add the garlic powder, onion powder, lemon zest, thyme, and ½ teaspoon each of the salt and pepper.

Pat the fish dry and season both sides with ¼ teaspoon each of the salt and pepper. One by one, dip each piece in the egg, then press into the bowl of crumbs, coating the fish entirely on all sides. Arrange the fish on the prepared pan.

Roast for 12 to 14 minutes, until the fish is opaque and flakes easily with a fork and the almonds are toasted. (The time may vary depending on the thickness of the fish.)

Meanwhile, in a pot, combine the broccoli and tomato sauce and bring to a low simmer. Simmer, uncovered, for 5 to 7 minutes, until the broccoli is tender. Add the spinach and stir just to wilt.

Ladle the sauce into shallow bowls and top with the fish. Serve garnished with basil and cheese, if desired.

Calories/serving: 582

Carbs/serving: 23 g

Protein/serving: 34 g

Fat/serving: 34 g

Fiber/serving: 14 g

Chard-Wrapped Miso Fish with Acorn Squash

Cellular Building + Healing, Immune Support, Mood Balancing

Makes 4 servings

¼ cup aka or shiro miso

2 tbsp fresh lemon juice

½ cup butter

1½ cups finely chopped leeks, white and light green parts only, or ¾ cup grated white onions

2 tsp micrograted peeled fresh ginger

1 tsp pressed garlic

4 large Swiss chard leaves, halved lengthwise and deveined (center stems cut out)

1 lb (454 g) white fish (such as cod or halibut), skin and bones removed, cut into 4 equal pieces

4 thinly sliced lemon rounds

1 recipe Acorn Squash with Ginger & Shallot (p. 182)

This is such a beautiful way to eat fish: miso butter and tender leeks combine for a luscious topping that melds into the fish as it steams within the edible chard leaf wrap; the hints of citrus and ginger infuse for a divine flavor perfectly complemented by the bright acorn squash. White fish is a great source of omega-3s, the chard adds color, fiber, and antioxidants, while the onion, ginger, and garlic give both a spicy kick and immune-supporting properties.

Serving Note: Serve with a side of Lemon Garlic Spinach (p. 184) or at a dinner party with Lemongrass Cauliflower & Sweet Potato (p. 198).

Preheat the oven to 400°F. Line a rimmed baking sheet with parchment.

In a small bowl, mix the miso and lemon juice until smooth.

In a medium pan, melt the butter over medium-low heat. Add the leeks, reduce the heat to low, and cook for about 10 minutes, until the leeks start to soften and brown. Add the ginger and cook, stirring, for 1 minute. Add the garlic and the miso mixture and cook, stirring, for 1 to 2 minutes, until the garlic is cooked and the miso is mixed through evenly. Remove from the heat and let cool for 5 minutes.

Lay out the chard leaves, shiny side down, overlapping the halves of each leaf lengthwise. Place one piece of fish at the bottom of each overlapping leaf set. Spread each piece of fish with about one-quarter of the leek mixture, leaving about 1 teaspoon of miso butter in the pan. Wrap the leaf around the fish to create a sealed parcel, ensuring the leek mixture ends up on top. (Depending on how big your leaf is, you might not be able to cover the fish completely, but do your best! You can even try wrapping it like a burrito.) Use the reserved miso butter to lightly coat the outside of the parcels, to prevent from drying out while baking. Place a lemon round on top of each parcel, squeezing it to release some juice. Place the parcels on the prepared pan.

Bake for 12 to 15 minutes, until the fish is opaque and flakes easily with a fork. (The time may vary depending on the thickness of the fish.)

Plate the warm fish parcels next to the acorn squash.

Calories/serving: 557
Carbs/serving: 30 g
Protein/serving: 28 g
Fat/serving: 35 g
Fiber/serving: 10 g

Chimichurri Chicken with Lemon Garlic Veggie Ribbons

DF/GF/GRF

Beauty + Anti-Aging, Cellular Building + Healing, Energy + Focus

Makes 4 servings

Chicken

1 lb (454 g) brined boneless skinless chicken breasts or thighs (see p. 280)

1 tbsp extra virgin olive oil

¼ tsp sea salt + more to serve

¼ tsp fresh ground pepper

1 recipe Chimichurri (p. 125)

Veggie Ribbons

3 tbsp extra virgin olive oil

4 cloves garlic, minced

2 cups carrot ribbons (see p. 277)

2 cups parsnip or sweet potato ribbons

2 cups broccoli stalk or zucchini ribbons

Zest of 2 lemons

2 tbsp gluten-free tamari

4 lemon wedges

Variation: This recipe also works with 1 lb (454 g) white fish, such as halibut or cod, instead of chicken; bake for about 12 to 13 minutes, until the fish is opaque and flakes easily with a fork.

I love this Argentinian chimichurri over chicken, especially when paired with lightly lemon-seasoned veggie ribbons. The vegetable medley is a delicate mix of colors, textures, and nutrients. Zucchini is a classic choice, or try broccoli stalk ribbons, which are a hidden gem full of vitamins A and C–and a fantastic use of leftover broccoli stalks! I like using parsnips for their lovely earthiness, but sweet potatoes are another starchy option to bring the ribbon medley together. And carrots offer a sweet chew and pop of color. This herb-rich dish supports the immune system, promotes healthy skin, and is full of energy-balancing fat and protein.

Serving Note: Serve with the Cucumber Herb Salad (p. 159) or Citrus & Sesame Cabbage (p. 190), or add even more parsley to the meal by serving with the Everyday Detox Salad (p. 166)!

Preheat the oven to 425°F. Line a rimmed baking sheet with parchment paper.

In a bowl, mix the brined chicken with the oil, salt, and pepper. Transfer the chicken to the prepared pan.

Bake for 17 to 20 minutes, turning halfway through, until the chicken reaches an internal temperature of 165°F and is no longer pink inside. Let rest for 5 minutes.

Meanwhile, make the veggie ribbons. In a large sauté pan, heat the oil over medium-high heat. Add the garlic and sauté for 30 seconds, until fragrant. Add the carrot and parsnip ribbons and sauté for 2 minutes, stirring constantly. Add the broccoli ribbons and toss to combine. Add the lemon zest and tamari and cook for 3 to 4 minutes, stirring occasionally, until the ribbons are tender but still al dente.

To serve, slice the chicken and top with the chimichurri. Place the veggie ribbons alongside, with the lemon wedges to squeeze over top. Season with salt, if desired

Store cooled leftovers in an airtight container in the fridge for up to 3 days.

Calories/serving: 673

Carbs/serving: 18 g

Protein/serving: 40 g

Fat/serving: 46 g

Fiber/serving: 7 g

Sweets

sweets

Muffins: 3 Ways

Apple Maple Millet Muffins
Raspberry Coconut Muffins
Banana Bread Muffins

These muffin recipes were designed to be simple and approachable, and the muffins themselves have less-refined sugar than most standard store-bought muffins. If you are a pastry lover or muffin person, make a batch to get you through the week. By making them yourself, you control the quality of the ingredients, and you know exactly which nutrients your body is getting!

Apple Maple Millet Muffins

Mood Balancing

Makes 12 muffins

⅓ cup water

2 tbsp flax meal

2 cups oat flour

¾ cup millet flour (see note)

¼ cup whole millet

1½ tsp ground cinnamon + more to top

1½ tsp grain-free baking powder

1 tsp baking soda

½ tsp ground nutmeg

½ tsp sea salt

⅓ cup virgin coconut oil, melted

½ cup plant-based milk of choice (see p. 275 or use store-bought)

½ cup maple syrup

½ cup unsweetened applesauce

2 tsp fresh lemon juice

1 tsp pure vanilla extract

1¼ cups grated peeled apples

½ cup finely chopped pitted Medjool dates

Spiced with warming cinnamon and nutmeg, these muffins have a comforting flavor reminiscent of apple pie. The addition of flax meal not only contributes fiber but also provides a little dose of omega-3s. With manganese and a little protein, these muffins are designed to support a healthy mind and good mood. They are a great option for a sweet treat.

Preheat the oven to 350°F. Line a 12-cup muffin tin with muffin cup liners.

In a medium bowl, whisk together the water and flax meal. Let sit for 10 minutes.

In a large bowl, combine the oat flour, millet flour, millet, cinnamon, baking powder, baking soda, nutmeg, and salt.

Whisk the coconut oil, milk, maple syrup, applesauce, lemon juice, and vanilla into the flax mixture. Add to the dry ingredients and stir until incorporated. Fold in 1 cup of the apples and all of the dates.

Divide the batter evenly between the prepared muffin cups. Top with the remaining apples, dividing evenly, and a sprinkle of cinnamon.

Bake for 25 to 30 minutes, until the edges are golden and the muffins seem set. These muffins are a bit dense, so they may seem slightly undercooked compared to regular gluten- and dairy-based muffins. Let cool on a wire rack for at least 15 minutes before serving.

Cooled muffins can be stored in an airtight container on the counter or in the fridge for up to 3 days, or in the freezer for up to 2 months.

Note: Millet flour may be hard to find, but you can make it yourself by grinding or blending whole millet in a high-powered blender, then sifting. One cup of seeds makes about 1¼ cups flour.

Calories/muffin: 234
Carbs/muffin: 33 g
Protein/muffin: 4 g
Fat/muffin: 8 g
Fiber/muffin: 3 g

Raspberry Coconut Muffins

DF/GF/GFR

Energy + Focus, Mood Balancing

Makes 12 muffins

2 eggs

⅔ cup coconut milk

½ cup + 2 tbsp maple syrup

⅓ cup melted virgin coconut oil

1 tsp pure vanilla extract

2 cups almond flour

⅓ cup coconut flour

1 tsp grain-free baking powder

1 tsp sea salt

½ tsp baking soda

1¼ cups fresh or frozen raspberries

2 tbsp unsweetened shredded coconut or flakes to garnish

These muffins are incredibly fluffy and delicious. Tart raspberries, sweet maple, and creamy coconut make for a most delightful cake-like treat that's full of flavor, berry goodness, and a little bit of protein too. I highly recommend them!

Preheat the oven to 350°F. Line a 12-cup muffin tin with muffin cup liners.

In a large bowl, whisk together the eggs, coconut milk, maple syrup, coconut oil, and vanilla.

In a separate bowl, combine the almond flour, coconut flour, baking powder, salt, and baking soda. Add to the wet ingredients and, using a spatula, stir until incorporated. Gently fold in the raspberries.

Divide the batter evenly between the prepared muffin cups. Sprinkle with the coconut, dividing evenly.

Bake for 25 to 30 minutes, until the muffins are golden brown and spring back when lightly touched in the center. Let rest for 10 to 15 minutes in the tin (to give them time to firm up before moving them), then transfer to a wire rack to let cool before serving.

Cooled muffins can be stored in an airtight container on the counter or in the fridge for up to 3 days, or in the freezer for up to 2 months.

Calories/muffin: 265
Carbs/muffin: 15 g
Protein/muffin: 6 g
Fat/muffin: 20 g
Fiber/muffin: 4 g

Banana Bread Muffins

DF/GF/GRF/V

Makes 10 muffins

2½ cups almond meal

½ cup arrowroot powder or tapioca starch

1 tsp baking soda

1 tsp grain-free baking powder

1 tsp ground cinnamon

½ tsp ground nutmeg

½ tsp sea salt

4 ripe medium bananas

⅓ cup maple syrup

¼ cup extra virgin olive or avocado oil

½ tsp pure vanilla extract

Handful of cacao nibs

Variation: You can use ½ cup applesauce to replace the maple syrup and oil.

These are one of my go-to treats. They are so moist and delicious, like mini banana breads. Packed with protein from the almond meal, plus fiber and potassium from the bananas, these muffins will boost your energy and lift your mood since bananas are thought to increase brain serotonin–but if not, I can guarantee the flavor alone will! I have a client who would request a batch every time I cooked for her! This is the muffin dreams are made of.

Preheat the oven to 350°F. Line 10 cups of a 12-cup muffin tin with muffin cup liners.

In a large bowl, whisk together the almond meal, arrowroot powder, baking soda, baking powder, cinnamon, nutmeg, and salt.

In a blender, combine 3 of the bananas with the maple syrup, oil, and vanilla. Purée on medium until smooth. (Alternatively, you can mix the ingredients by hand in a bowl.)

Stir the wet ingredients into the dry ingredients, mixing well.

Divide the batter evenly between the prepared muffin cups. Sprinkle the muffins with cacao nibs. Slice the remaining banana and place a slice of banana on top of each muffin.

Bake for 25 to 30 minutes, until risen and golden. Let cool on a wire rack for 15 minutes.

Cooled muffins can be stored in an airtight container on the counter or in the fridge for up to 3 days, or in the freezer for up to 2 months.

Calories/muffin: 320

Carbs/muffin: 25 g

Protein/muffin: 7 g

Fat/muffin: 21 g

Fiber/muffin: 5 g

Golden Dreamsicles

DF/GF/GRF/OF/V

Anti-Inflammatory, Immune Support

Makes 6 ice pops

1 (14 oz/400 ml) can coconut milk

2 medium fresh or frozen bananas

Zest of 1 navel orange

2 whole navel oranges, peeled

Juice of ½ lemon

1- to 2-inch piece fresh turmeric, peeled

2 tsp pure vanilla extract

1 to 2 tsp ginger juice (see p. 276), depending on how much you like ginger!

Pinch of fresh ground pepper

Variation: You can make this into a sorbet by freezing the mixture in a shallow dish or ice cube molds, then blending it until smooth and creamy. You could even drink the mixture as a smoothie if you can't wait to freeze it—it's that good!

These aren't your typical frozen treats. Made with fresh turmeric and ginger, they offer a spicy kick of anti-inflammatory and immune support. (For an even bigger boost, just add more!) The creamy coconut milk provides a rich base for the heart-healthy nutrients in the oranges and bananas. We are utilizing the fruit's fiber here by blending the whole orange, not just its juice. These ice pops are high in vitamin C and antioxidants to help protect the body. You can even sneak in some spirulina powder, for a green blast of protein and additional nutrients.

In a high-powered blender, combine the coconut milk, bananas, orange zest, oranges, and lemon juice. Blend on high until very smooth. Add the turmeric, vanilla, and ginger juice. Pulse until the turmeric has colored the mixture a bright orange.

Pour into six ice pop molds and freeze until firm. Store in the freezer for up to 3 weeks.

Calories/ice pop: 170
Carbs/ice pop: 16 g
Protein/ice pop: 2 g
Fat/ice pop: 10 g
Fiber/ice pop: 2 g

Hazelnut Goji Berry Freezer Fudge

DF/GF/GRF/V

Makes 16 pieces

½ cup maple syrup

¼ cup virgin coconut oil

1 cup hazelnut butter

¼ cup cacao powder

1 tsp pure vanilla extract

¼ cup + 1 tbsp cacao nibs

¼ cup + 1 tbsp unsweetened shredded coconut

¼ cup + 1 tbsp goji berries

This fudge is so good, you'll want to eat it all in one sitting! It's one of my favorite ways to make dessert: melt a bunch of beautiful flavors together, add some crunchy and chewy textures, then chill to firm. Here, I spike a hazelnut butter base with superfoods–crunchy antioxidant–packed cacao and chewy vitamin C–rich goji berries–for a great texture. The combo of ingredients makes it a dessert you can happily indulge in, knowing it can help your skin glow!

Line an 8-inch square baking pan with parchment paper.

In a small saucepan over low heat, heat the maple syrup and coconut oil until the coconut oil is fully melted. Add the hazelnut butter, cacao powder, and vanilla, stirring well. Turn the heat off and stir in ¼ cup each of the cacao nibs, coconut, and goji berries.

Scoop the mixture into the prepared pan and press it with the back of a spoon to make as even a layer as possible. Sprinkle with the remaining 1 tablespoon each of cacao nibs, coconut, and goji berries. Freeze for at least 4 hours, until firm.

Lift the parchment paper to remove the fudge from the pan. Cut the fudge into 16 small squares.

Store in an airtight container in the freezer for up to 1 month. Serve frozen or, if you prefer a more fudge-like texture, let soften at room temperature for 5 minutes before serving.

Calories/piece: 163
Carbs/piece: 12 g
Protein/piece: 3 g
Fat/piece: 11 g
Fiber/piece: 3 g

Salted Chocolate Cookies

DF/GF/GRF/OF/V

Energy + Focus, Mood Balancing

Makes 12 cookies

1 cup hazelnut butter

½ cup maple syrup

1½ tsp pure vanilla extract

1⅓ cups almond meal

1 tsp grain-free baking powder

½ tsp fine sea salt

½ cup vegan chocolate chips or chunks of your favorite chocolate bar

⅓ cup finely chopped raw hazelnuts

2 tbsp cacao nibs (optional)

Crumbled flaky sea salt to garnish

Variation: Try using chopped almonds instead of hazelnuts (as pictured here).

The combo of chocolate and hazelnut is my absolute favorite. If I am going to make cookies for a client, there are a couple of non-negotiables: first, they have to be delicious; second, I want them to be full of healthy fats, protein, and fiber to help balance the sugars. In these cookies, beautiful ingredients come together to make a chewy, crispy, almost buttery treat that offers lots of beneficial minerals. They are lower in carbs and higher in protein than many other cookies. So indulge!

Preheat the oven to 350°F. Line a baking sheet with parchment paper.

In a large bowl, cream together the hazelnut butter, maple syrup, and vanilla. Stir in the almond meal, baking powder, and fine salt. Fold in the chocolate, hazelnuts, and cacao nibs (if using).

Spoon 12 scoops of the cookie dough onto the prepared pan, or roll the dough into 12 balls and arrange on the pan, spacing them apart equally. Press down on each scoop or ball to flatten it to ½ inch thick. Sprinkle a touch of crumbled flaky salt evenly over the cookies.

Bake for 10 minutes, until the cookies look set. Let cool on the pan for 3 to 4 minutes or until they are cool enough to transfer without falling apart, then transfer to a wire rack to cool completely.

Store in an airtight container in the fridge for up to 1 week.

Calories/cookie: 282

Carbs/cookie: 15 g

Protein/cookie: 7 g

Fat/cookie: 21 g

Fiber/cookie: 5 g

Citrus Olive Oil Cake

DF/GF/GRF

Makes 9 servings

1½ cups almond meal

½ tsp grain-free baking powder

¼ tsp baking soda

¼ tsp sea salt

2 eggs

¼ cup honey

¼ cup extra virgin olive oil

1 tsp orange zest

2 tbsp fresh orange juice

1 tsp lemon zest

1 tbsp fresh lemon juice

½ tsp pure vanilla extract

Variation: You can also use a round cake pan, as pictured. For a sparkly garnish, sprinkle 1 tbsp coconut sugar over the top before baking.

I came across quite a few olive oil cakes while working in Italy, and I really appreciated their delicate, not-too-sweet nature. This one is a subtle, simple, and satisfying dessert, lightly flavored with a hint of citrus. High in skin-healthy vitamin E and stress-reducing magnesium, it's a treat that won't spike your blood sugar and will keep you feeling content. I picture eating a slice with a cup of coffee or tea in the sunshine.

Serving Note: This is wonderful topped with fresh fruit, Blueberry Compote (p. 272), or coconut cream!

Preheat the oven to 325°F. Line the bottom of a 9-inch square cake pan with parchment paper and lightly oil the sides.

In a large bowl, combine the almond meal, baking powder, baking soda, and salt.

In a medium bowl, whisk together the remaining ingredients until smooth. Add to the dry ingredients and stir until you have a smooth batter.

Pour the batter into the prepared pan.

Bake for 25 to 30 minutes, until golden and it springs back lightly when touched. Remove and let cool in the pan for 10 minutes, then turn out onto a wire rack to cool completely.

Store in an airtight container in the fridge for up to 4 days.

Calories/serving: 209

Carbs/serving: 10 g

Protein/serving: 5 g

Fat/serving: 17 g

Fiber/serving: 2 g

Raw Blackberry Cashew Cheesecake

DF/GF/GRF/V

Mood Balancing

Makes 12 servings

Filling

2 cups raw cashews

½ cup fresh lemon juice

½ cup maple syrup

½ cup melted virgin coconut oil

2 tsp pure vanilla extract

¼ tsp sea salt

2 cups ripe blackberries
(see note)

Zest of 1 lemon

Crust

1 cup pitted Medjool dates

2 cups boiling water

1 cup whole raw almonds

1 tbsp unsweetened coconut
flakes

2 tsp virgin coconut oil

1 tsp ground cinnamon

½ tsp sea salt

Lots of fresh berries or sliced fresh
fruit to garnish (see note)

Note: Fresh fruit is best, so use the sweetest berries you can find, or any fruit that is in season or local. In place of the blackberries, try raspberries, strawberries, blueberries, mangoes, peaches, or passionfruit. Your favorite frozen fruit will work too.

What I like most about cashew cheesecake is how easy it is to make it your own. Play around with local seasonal fruit or whatever you have on hand. When we created this cheesecake while on the west coast of Canada, wild blackberries were growing on the side of the road and the fig trees were full, so these became the flavors of ours. This is a fun, energizing raw cake, and the more fruit you put on top, the more vitamins and antioxidants you'll get!

In a bowl, soak the cashews for the filling in water overnight. Drain and rinse well.

In a heatproof bowl, cover the dates for the crust entirely with the boiling water. Let soak for 10 minutes, then drain.

Line a 9-inch springform pan with parchment paper.

In a food processor, combine all the crust ingredients, including the soaked and drained dates. Pulse until a rough dough forms.

Press the dough evenly into the prepared pan, using the back of a spoon to make sure it's nice and compact.

In a high-powered blender, combine the cashews, lemon juice, maple syrup, coconut oil, vanilla, and salt. Purée on high until very smooth. Transfer about one-third of the cashew mixture to a bowl and set aside.

To the remaining cashew mixture in the blender, add the blackberries and blend on high until uniformly dark purple and smooth. Pour over the crust. Freeze for 1 hour, until set.

Add the lemon zest to the reserved cashew mixture and stir to combine. Gently spread over the blackberry layer. Cover and return to the freezer for at least 6 hours or overnight.

Let the cake thaw at room temperature for 10 to 20 minutes (or in the fridge for 1 hour) before serving. Serve topped with fruit.

This cake will store well, covered with plastic wrap, in the freezer for up to 2 weeks. Thaw as directed above before serving.

Calories/serving: 368

Carbs/serving: 31 g

Protein/serving: 7 g

Fat/serving: 24 g

Fiber/serving: 5 g

Blueberry Squares

Anti-Inflammatory, Energy + Focus, Mood Balancing

Makes 8 squares

Crust & Topping

8 large Medjool dates, pitted

2 cups boiling water

¼ cup flax meal

¼ cup water

1 cup unsweetened shredded coconut

1 tsp sea salt

1 tsp ground cinnamon

1 tsp pure vanilla extract

1½ cups almond meal

⅓ cup warmed virgin coconut oil

Blueberry Compote

1 tbsp arrowroot powder

2 tsp cold water

3 cups frozen blueberries

¼ cup honey

2 tsp lemon zest

1 tbsp pure vanilla extract

½ tsp ground cinnamon

Blueberry desserts have a special place in my heart, so this is my favorite dessert in the book. Flavor truly meets health in these squares, with mood-lifting omega-3s from the flax, they are fiber-rich and antioxidant-packed, all while capturing the juicy flavor of a blueberry pie.

Place the dates in a heatproof bowl and cover entirely with the boiling water. Let soak for 10 minutes, then drain.

Meanwhile, in a small bowl, combine the flax meal and the ¼ cup water. Let sit for 10 to 20 minutes, until the mixture has a gel-like consistency.

Preheat the oven to 350°F. Line an 8-inch square baking pan with parchment paper.

To make the blueberry compote, combine the arrowroot and cold water in a small bowl, stirring to dissolve.

In a small pot, combine the blueberries, honey, and lemon zest. Bring to a simmer over medium heat. Simmer, stirring, for 2 minutes. Reduce the heat to medium-low and stir in the vanilla and cinnamon. Add the arrowroot mixture and cook, stirring well, for 2 minutes, until thick and jammy. Remove from the heat and let cool.

In a food processor, pulse the coconut once or twice, until small and grain-like. Add the dates, flax mixture, salt, cinnamon, and vanilla and pulse until it appears dough-like. Transfer to a large bowl and add the almond meal and coconut oil, mixing very well with your hands. Tightly pack ½ cup of the dough and set aside for the topping.

Transfer the remaining dough to the prepared pan and use your hands to pack it down so it is evenly spread and level.

Pour the cooled blueberry mixture over the prepared crust, spreading evenly with a spatula. Sprinkle with the reserved topping and press it into the blueberry filling.

Bake for 25 minutes, until golden. These are delicious warm, or let them cool then chill in the fridge for 2 hours to firm up.

Store in an airtight container in the fridge for up to 5 days.

Calories/square: 497

Carbs/square: 38 g

Protein/square: 7 g

Fat/square: 33 g

Fiber/square: 11 g

How-To
Techniques

How to Make Plant-Based Milks

Base Ingredients

1 cup raw almonds, walnuts, macadamia nuts, Brazil nuts, cashews, sunflower seeds, pumpkin seeds, or a mix!

4 cups filtered water

2 tsp pure vanilla extract (optional)

¼ tsp sea salt

Optional Flavorings

1 inch fresh ginger, peeled + 3 inches fresh turmeric, peeled

½ tsp ground cinnamon + ¼ tsp ground nutmeg

Optional Sweeteners

1 to 2 pitted Medjool dates, soaked in hot water for 10 minutes, then drained

1 to 2 tsp maple syrup

Optional Nutritional Additions

¼ cup hemp hearts (to boost any milk's protein and creaminess)

1 to 2 scoops collagen, protein powder, or glutathione

1 tbsp Udo's oil, MCT oil, virgin coconut oil, or hemp oil (for added fat and frothiness), or more if desired

Optional Superfood Additions

2 tsp mushroom powder, ashwagandha, maca, spirulina, or chlorella

Place the nuts or seeds in a bowl, cover with water, and soak overnight in the fridge. Drain and rinse well.

In a high-powered blender, combine the nuts or seeds, filtered water, vanilla, salt, and any optional flavorings or sweeteners. Blend on high until very well blended.

Place cheesecloth or a milk bag inside the mouth of a large wide-mouthed jar, letting some hang over the rim. Secure it with an elastic band or hold it tight with your hand. Slowly pour the mixture through the cloth, allowing the pulp to settle in the cloth as the liquid drips into the jar. Squeeze the cheesecloth firmly to press out any extra liquid.

If using any nutritional or superfood additions, return the strained milk to the blender, add the additions, and blend on high, just enough to mix everything together.

Store in an airtight container in the fridge for up to 3 days. Shake well before serving, as the contents can separate while at rest.

Note: Make the milk just with the base ingredients first, then play around with one or two of the additions to find your favorite combination. If you are using the milk for homemade smoothies, oatmeal, or chia pudding, you can choose to strain it or not; the nut solids will add extra fiber and nutrients (and make it a touch thicker)! But if you use ginger or turmeric, it's best to strain them out first.

How to Make Ginger Juice

Peel fresh ginger. (Two inches will give you about 1 tablespoon micrograted and ½ tablespoon juice.)

Using the smallest holes of a grater or a Microplane, grate the ginger. Squeeze the grated ginger over a small bowl, catching the pulp in your hands so your fingers act like a strainer as the juice drips through. Or press the grated ginger through cheesecloth, a fine-mesh sieve, or a garlic press.

Store in an airtight container in the fridge for up to 2 days.

Note: You can also use a juicer to make ginger juice: simply run the ginger through the juicer; no need to peel or grate!

How to Toast Seeds & Nuts

STOVETOP OPTION (PREFERRED FOR SEEDS)

Place a medium sauté pan over medium-low heat. Evenly sprinkle shelled seeds (or nuts) of choice into the pan. You want them all to be touching the bottom of the pan, so don't overcrowd them. Work in batches if necessary.

Toast, tossing frequently. You should start to smell them cooking and see that they are beginning to brown. Keep moving the seeds around to ensure they do not burn.

Remove from the heat once they are lightly browned and there is a toasted fragrance in the air. Some seeds will begin to make crackling sounds! They will be done in about 2 to 5 minutes (or 3 to 6 minutes for nuts), depending on the stovetop and seed size. Transfer to a plate and let cool completely before using.

Store in an airtight container in the fridge for up to 1 week.

OVEN OPTION (PREFERRED FOR NUTS)

Preheat the oven to 300°F. Line a baking sheet with parchment paper.

Arrange shelled nuts (or seeds) of choice on the pan in a single layer. Roast for 10 to 12 minutes (or 5 to 6 minutes for most seeds), until they have a toasty fragrance and are starting to take on a golden-brown hue. Transfer to a plate and let cool completely before using.

Store in an airtight container in the fridge for up to 1 week.

Note: I prefer to toast seeds on the stovetop (so I can keep them moving and watch that they don't burn) and roast nuts in the oven (so they receive even dry heat), but you can use either method for both. You can also toast shredded coconut or flakes using either method, but I prefer in the oven.

How to Rice Broccoli or Cauliflower

For broccoli, trim the florets from the stalk. Then either peel the stalk and reserve it to make broccoli noodles (see below) or add thinly sliced to any stir-fry or salad.

For cauliflower, remove the leaves and core from the cauliflower. Cut the head into florets.

FOOD PROCESSOR OPTION

Make sure the florets are not larger than 1 inch, or they won't process evenly. Add the florets to the food processor in batches, depending on how much you are making. The food processor should only be three-quarters full. Pulse each batch a few times into grain-sized pieces. Be careful not to pulse too long; you don't want to create a wet purée. I prefer this method for making sushi rice.

BOX GRATER OPTION

Grate the florets against the large holes of a grater, turning them into a fine veggie "rice." I prefer this method for stir-fries and bowls.

FINELY CHOP OPTION

Using a large chef's knife, finely chop each floret into grain-sized pieces.

Store in an airtight container in the fridge for up to 3 days.

How to Make Vegetable Ribbons or Noodles

VEGETABLE PEELER OPTION
(TO MAKE RIBBONS)

Remove the stalks or tough fibrous layer of harder vegetables, like broccoli stems, sweet potatoes, and carrots. Keep the peel on softer vegetables, like zucchinis and English cucumbers.

Run the peeler away from you along the length of the vegetable, creating long, wide ribbons. For harder veggies, keep peeling, rotating as necessary, until it's impossible to get any more ribbons. For zucchinis or cucumbers, continue peeling on one side until you see the seeded center. Once all sides have been peeled and only the seeded core is left, stop and set the core aside to use for something else.

A julienne peeler will work in some cases, but will give you finer and narrower ribbons that won't be suitable for recipes in this book.

MANDOLINE SLICER OPTION
(TO MAKE RIBBONS)

Use a veggie peeler to remove the outer skin of harder vegetables, then very carefully use the mandoline to create long, wide ribbons. It's best to avoid the mandoline option for very hard vegetables, like sweet potatoes or butternut squash, because it is easier to slip when making ribbons.

SPIRALIZER OPTION
(TO MAKE VEGGIE NOODLES)

You can use a spiralizer for many different vegetables. Peel off the outer skin of harder vegetables, then follow your spiralizer's set-up instructions to achieve your desired width.

Store veggie noodles and ribbons in an airtight container in the fridge for up to 3 days.

Note: My favorite method is the veggie peeler! But I've specified which technique best suits each recipe. You'll always be left with a bit of the veg after peeling; slice and roast, or add to a soup.

How to Blanch Vegetables

Cut the vegetables into uniform pieces. If you're blanching a variety of veggies, blanch each type separately, but use the same boiling water.

Bring a large pot of water to a boil. Prepare an ice bath (optional, see below).

Submerge the vegetables in the boiling water or place them in a wire basket and lower the basket into the water. Cook until tender; the time will vary depending on the type of vegetable and the size of the pieces (see note; leafy greens are much quicker). Check for desired doneness after 30 seconds by tasting or piercing with a small knife. Test again after another 30 seconds, and so on. Remove the veggies with a slotted spoon or remove the basket from the pot.

Plunge the vegetables into the ice bath (or run them under cold water) to stop cooking, just for a few seconds or until they're cool enough to touch. Squeeze out excess water (if using leafy greens),

then let them dry in a colander or pat them dry with a paper towel. (I skip the cooling step when I plan to eat them right away.)

Repeat as needed with other vegetables.

Store in an airtight container in the fridge for up to 3 days.

Blanching Time: Blanching times vary depending on how small you chop your veg, but here is a general guide for a few of my favorite veggies to blanch:

- **Asparagus:** 1 to 2 minutes
- **Bok choy, halved:** 1 to 2 minutes
- **Broccoli florets:** 1 to 2 minutes
- **Carrot, sliced:** 2 minutes
- **Collard greens:** 5 to 15 seconds
- **Green beans:** 1 to 2 minutes
- **Kale:** 15 to 30 seconds
- **Spinach:** 5 to 15 seconds

How to Sauté Greens

Gently wash dark leafy greens (such as kale, Swiss chard, spinach, or collard greens) to remove any dirt. If using tougher greens, remove and discard the stems, then either rip the leaves into bite-sized pieces or finely chop into thin strips; if using spinach, you can leave the leaves whole.

In a medium sauté pan, heat a drizzle of olive oil over medium heat. Add some minced garlic or ginger and a sprinkle of sea salt and cook, stirring, for about

30 seconds, until fragrant. Add the greens and toss well. Cook, stirring often, until the greens are tender and wilted, about 2 to 5 minutes.

Serve immediately, or let cool and store in an airtight container in the fridge for up to 3 days.

How to Prep Collard Greens for Wraps

Put the brighter side of a leaf face down on a cutting board. Trim off the hard stem at the bottom, then carefully shave back the main stem that runs along the length of the leaf so that it is flush with the softer part of the leaf.

Gently wash the collard leaves and use them raw, or follow the directions on p. 278 to blanch them for 5 to 15 seconds, then let them dry.

To store, line the bottom of an airtight container with a paper towel or dish towel. Place the collard leaves on top, then cover with another paper towel or dish towel. Store in the fridge for up to 3 days.

When ready to use, add your spreads or filling along the middle line of the leaf, then tuck the ends under and roll it up tightly so the fillings stay inside.

Note: Collard greens are a sturdy vegetable, perfect for making fajitas, breakfast burritos, or veggie wraps. Reheat leftover collard greens by dipping them in boiling water for just 1 to 2 seconds.

How to Roast Beets

Preheat the oven to 400°F. Line a baking sheet with parchment paper.

Scrub the beets to remove any dirt from the outside. Cut off any stems or long roots. Rub the beets with a little olive oil and sprinkle with sea salt. Wrap individually in aluminum foil and place on the prepared pan.

Roast until tender all the way through. The cooking time depends greatly on the size of the beets, anywhere from 45 minutes for smaller beets to 75 minutes or more for medium to large beets. Check after 45 minutes by piercing with a sharp knife–if they are tender all the way through, they are done. If they are still hard, continue to roast, checking every 15 minutes.

Remove from the oven and let cool. When they're cool enough to handle, rub the outer layer of the beets with your hands; the skin should come off easily. Remove the skin, or you're welcome to leave the skin on if you prefer! It's a great source of fiber.

Use a mandoline or sharp knife to slice thin rounds, or chop the beets into bite-sized pieces.

Store in an airtight container in the fridge for up to 4 days.

How to Roast Vegetables

1 lb (454 g) vegetables,
    a single type or a mix!

1 tbsp extra virgin olive oil

¼ tsp sea salt + more to taste

Fresh ground pepper

¼ tsp seasoning, like onion
    powder, garlic powder, Italian
    seasoning, dried thyme, or
    chili powder (optional)

Note: One pound (454 g)
of veggies will be enough for
one person for about 2 days.
Double or triple the recipe
if you are cooking for more
people.

Preheat the oven to 375°F or 400°F (roast at 400°F for a touch more caramelization). Line a rimmed baking sheet with parchment paper.

Chop the veggies into uniform bite-sized pieces. Veggies have different cooking times (see below), so group like veggies together, or add the faster-cooking ones partway through.

In a large bowl, toss the veggies with the oil, salt, a few grinds of pepper, and your seasoning of choice. Feel free to add more or a mix of a few! Add more oil and salt as needed for denser, starchier vegetables. Toss well to ensure they are evenly coated. Spread the veggies out evenly on the prepared pan.

Roast for 10 to 45 minutes, depending on the type of vegetables and the size of the pieces. Check at 10-minute intervals to monitor their tenderness and rotate the tray if needed, and toss the veggies halfway through the roasting time. If you are using small cuts or less dense vegetables, watch closely after the first 8 minutes to make sure they don't overcook.

Serve immediately, or let cool and store in an airtight container in the fridge for up to 4 days.

Roasting Time: The roasting time will vary depending on how small you chop your veg, but here is a general guide:

- **Asparagus, green beans, peppers, zucchinis:**
  8 to 20 minutes
- **Beets, carrots, potatoes, sweet potatoes, winter squash:**
  25 to 40 minutes
- **Broccoli, brussels sprouts, cauliflower, purple cabbage:**
  15 to 25 minutes

How to Brine Chicken Breasts or Thighs

4 cups water, at room temperature

¼ cup sea salt

1 lb (454 g) boneless skinless
    chicken breasts or thighs

Note: Add any spices you
desire for more flavor.

In a large bowl, mix the water and salt, stirring until the salt is dissolved. Add the chicken and let soak for 15 to 30 minutes.

Remove the chicken from the brine and discard the brine. Rinse the chicken with cold water and pat dry.

Glossary of Ingredients

*Look out for my flavor makers! See p. 24.

Fruits & Vegetables

APPLES, when eaten with the skin, are high in fiber and reasonably low in natural sugars. They are considered a low-glycemic food, and their vitamins support immune health. I like to keep them around to snack on, or bake grated into muffins to add sweetness and fiber. You can also bake apples with a touch of honey and some cinnamon to satisfy a dessert craving!

ASPARAGUS is rich in sulfur, a precursor for glutathione, which supports the body's ability to detoxify while mitigating potential damage from excessive free-radical production. Asparagus is both healthy and beautiful. Steam or blanch it for a bright addition to any plate.

AVOCADOS are an ideal source of good-for-you fats. They are rich in dietary fiber, magnesium, folate, and vitamins A, E, and K. They help to satiate hunger, support bone health, and provide beauty nutrients for the skin, hair, and nails. Use them in dips and wraps or on their own. They add a perfect texture and richness to a meal.

BANANAS are a great source of potassium, vitamins B6 and C, and fiber. They contain antioxidants that help protect the body from free radicals and offer a great boost of energy. I like to use them in smoothies, hemp milks, and desserts to get a boost of fiber alongside the sweetness.

BEETS are supportive of the liver and provide lots of antioxidant protection. They are high in fiber as well as folate, which helps protect and nourish the body. The nutrients in beets have been said to also help optimize oxygen delivery and utilization throughout the body, aiding in athletic performance and focus. I love them grated raw in bowls and salads, or roasted whole and marinated.

BLUEBERRIES contain large amounts of powerful antioxidants that work to encourage healthy aging and skin by combating free-radical damage. They support healthy connective tissues (particularly blood vessels), as well as eye, kidney, and cardiovascular health. They also help the digestive system by providing high amounts of insoluble and soluble fiber. Eat them anywhere! I especially love them in smoothies and desserts.

CARROTS contain an antioxidant called beta-carotene, which is a precursor to vitamin A. It supports a healthy complexion and protects the heart and lungs. Carrots are also high in fiber, helping to eliminate toxic buildup. I use them to bulk up savory baking or as colorful noodle curls in sautés. I also love adding them grated to salads to sweeten up the flavor and taste.

CELERY is an excellent source of vitamin C, fiber, and potassium. It adds crunch to salads, works wonders as a base that cooks down for soups, or can be eaten on its own next to a beautiful dip.

CRUCIFEROUS VEGETABLES are some of THE MOST important vegetables you can eat and should play a large part in your diet. They are extremely nutrient-dense and fiber-rich and contain sulfur compounds that help neutralize toxicity in the body. Across the board, they have detoxifying and disease-fighting abilities and are high in vitamins like K and C. **Broccoli** is packed with vitamin C, which supports the skin and collagen production. **Cabbage** is underrated, but is so versatile and packed with nutrients. I can't speak highly enough about cabbages of all kinds (**purple**, **green**, **bok choy**, **savoy**). They are high in glutamine and amino acids, which can help heal the gut lining. **Cauliflower** is high in protein and folate, and is easy to use in cooking, as it can take on so many flavors and shapes. **Collard greens** are full of calcium, protein, and fiber and are a wonderful addition to any meal. **Kale** is extremely high in vitamin K and offers a good dose of protein too.

CUCUMBERS are high in nutrients, low in calories, and packed with fiber. They help to care for a healthy complexion because they are rich with silica and hydration. My recipes generally call for English cucumbers, but you can use Persian cucumbers (skin on) or regular field cucumbers (peeled and seeded) in their place.

LEAFY GREENS are full of vitamins, minerals, and fiber, an abundance of beneficial properties to support overall health. They help clear out toxins and keep your body strong; they also support digestive health and the immune system. **Spinach** is packed full of iron, potassium, and vitamin K. It is unbelievably versatile and easy to incorporate into meals. **Swiss chard** is one of those impressive superfoods that often goes unnoticed, with high amounts of vitamins A, C, and K, magnesium, iron, and so much more. It supports healthy skin, hair,

and nails. **Arugula** is part of the cruciferous family but acts like a leafy green. It is packed with vitamins, offers detoxifying properties, and may also help protect against cancer. Its bitterness stimulates digestion. I like to think it primes the body to digest and absorb more nutrients when eaten before a meal. One of my main tips for clients is to start every meal with a salad of fresh greens, like arugula, **butter lettuce**, or **romaine**!

❋ **LEMONS** contain high amounts of vitamin C, essential for the health and support of the immune system and complexion. Lemons can protect the body, they provide anti-inflammatory support, and they are one of my favorite ways to add flavor to my cooking. Having a warm glass of water with lemon at the beginning of the day is often recommended to help reset and rehydrate the digestive tract and prepare an optimal environment for the day ahead.

❋ **LIMES** are packed with immune-supporting vitamin C. They also contain several distinctive phytochemicals that are high in antioxidant and anticancer properties, including flavonoids and limonene. I use limes in sauces and dressings, or to add bright acidity wherever I need it.

MANGOES are an excellent source of carotenoids and vitamin C. I like to use them inside salad rolls and sushi, or in desserts–or they can be eaten as is!

MUSHROOMS contain selenium and B vitamins, and have a little protein too. **Portobello** and **cremini** mushrooms help with energy production and protect the body from damage. **Shiitake** and **maitake**, examples of two of the more healing mushrooms, are known to support the immune system.

❋ **ONIONS** are the most wonderful flavor maker, and are also anti-inflammatory, full of minerals, and packed with antioxidants. They are very supportive of overall health and the immune system. **Leeks** are in the same family and offer important prebiotic fiber. **Shallots** are one of my favorite flavor makers!

ORANGES are high in vitamin C and rich in flavonoids. They support the immune system, are anti-inflammatory, and may encourage collagen production. I try to use the whole orange (not just the juice) as much as possible to sweeten my recipes, to gain all the benefits they may provide. Orange zest offers nutrients too and is a flavorful addition to sweets, smoothies, and drinks.

RASPBERRIES are a great source of dietary fiber. They are packed with immune-supporting antioxidants, working to support the brain and overall health by lowering oxidative stress, reducing inflammation, and supporting mood. Try adding raspberries to oatmeal, acai bowls, or granola, or eat them as a snack!

RED PEPPERS add a spark of color and texture to meals and are very high in vitamins A and C and other antioxidants. I like using red more than green, orange, or yellow peppers not just because they are richer in nutrients but also because I find my clients digest them better.

SPROUTS are remarkably high in protein, dietary fiber, and a wide range of vitamins and minerals. They are unbelievably supportive to the body and can be put on any plate or salad. **Broccoli sprouts** and **sunflower sprouts** are my favorites.

STRAWBERRIES are thought to help lower blood pressure and work to reduce the risk of heart disease, stroke, and cancer. They contain fiber and are lower in sugar compared with other fruits, making them a great snack or a gentle way to sweeten a smoothie or dessert.

SWEET POTATOES are rich in antioxidants, helping to protect the body against oxidative damage. They supply a great amount of dietary fiber and help to maintain healthy energy levels throughout the day.

TOMATOES are luscious, antioxidant-rich, and great for sauces and salads. You will see them speckled throughout the book to add flavor, texture, and a little splash of color to dishes. Fresh or canned, they contain many vitamins and minerals and are high in lycopene, which helps protect against cellular damage and cardiovascular disease.

WATERMELON is a hydrating fruit that is rich in antioxidants and flavor. It can take on the flavor profile of a marinade, which makes it a great addition to or the star of any salad.

WINTER SQUASHES provide vitamin A, potassium, and fiber, help curb hunger, and support healthy skin, hair, and nails. **Spaghetti squash** is a standout in that it is less starchy than the others. Some of my other favorites are **acorn**, **butternut**, and **kabocha**.

ZUCCHINIS are high in fiber and minerals and have a high water content. They are filling but very low in calories and extremely versatile to work with, so you can eat lots and in many different ways.

Herbs & Spices

BASIL is rich in antioxidants and vitamins and plays a large role in reducing inflammation and swelling. It helps to support and soothe the digestive tract, creating an optimal environment for nutrient absorption. Basil is a great addition to sauces, salads, dips, and main meals.

BLACK PEPPER increases nutrient absorption and supports optimal digestion. It's an easy way to add a kick to any meal.

CAYENNE, RED CHILIES, AND CHILI POWDER have been shown to increase metabolic rate and may act as a mild appetite suppressant. They also have anti-inflammatory properties, are high in vitamin C, and can stimulate detoxification.

❋ **CILANTRO** is often consumed as a garnish, but this powerful little herb may help detox heavy metals from the body. I add it to (almost) everything to provide depth of flavor and for its health benefits.

CINNAMON is a beneficial ingredient for regulating blood-sugar levels. Adding it to anything with sugar (from honey to bananas) helps to mitigate the sugar's effects on the body.

CUMIN stimulates digestion and helps with nutrient assimilation. I love to add it to warm veggie sides or soups.

DILL is rich in antioxidants and provides the body with powerful protection from damage. Dill is such a distinct and enjoyable way to flavor a dish, brightening up anything from salads to dips to fish.

❋ **GARLIC** is full of beneficial qualities for maintaining good health. It is anti-viral, antiseptic, anti-parasitic, anti-spasmodic, immune-enhancing, and blood-vessel strengthening, and contains many antioxidants. You will notice I use a lot of garlic! I love it for its flavor and its amazing full-body support.

❋ **GINGER** is one of the best foods for soothing a stomachache, aiding nausea, and reducing inflammation. Combining it with meals helps to stimulate and support digestion and provides a great boost of nutrients to the body.

❋ **JALAPEÑOS** are packed with immune- and beauty-supportive vitamins and antioxidants. They also help protect the cells from damage due to oxidative stress. I use them for flavor, texture, and nutrition.

MINT soothes digestion and eases bloating, offers a wonderful freshness to salads and sauces, makes a flavorful garnish, and can be infused into hot water as a tea.

OREGANO is rich in antioxidants and has high antimicrobial properties. It adds a nice seasoning to anything it is added to, from sautés to dressings to sauces.

PARSLEY is extremely high in many nutrients, including chlorophyll, carotenes, and fiber. It is a great source of vitamins A, C, and K and other essential nutrients, promoting optimal health while adding beautiful flavor to sauces and salads.

❋ **SMOKED PAPRIKA** is from the same family as cayenne pepper, but is much less spicy. It is high in vitamins A and C, supports healthy skin, and helps reduce inflammation. I love the smokiness and depth it gives to a recipe and will add it to just about anything.

❋ **THYME** is high in antioxidants and flavor. It helps protect the body from infection and supports the health of the lungs.

❋ **TURMERIC** offers significant antioxidant and anti-inflammatory activity. You can use it in the form of curry powder or ground turmeric, or fresh in juices and smoothies. I love its bright color and how it adds both nutrition and spicy flavor to my cooking.

Legumes & Whole Grains

BLACK BEANS, CHICKPEAS, AND WHITE BEANS are high in fiber and protein and help stabilize blood sugar. They are also high in antioxidants, folate, and molybdenum, which are essential for optimal functioning. Beans make great creamy dips and are a terrific way to bulk up a dish as a filling, protein-rich addition.

EDAMAME (young soybeans) are abundantly high in protein, making them an optimal choice for a plant-based protein source. They support healthy hormonal balance and have been known to help with depression and anxiety. Marinate and bake them; steam them and toss with oil, tamari, and fresh herbs; or mix them into a roasted veggie bowl or salad.

LENTILS are a great source of protein and are full of fiber and antioxidants. One cup of cooked lentils provides just over 15 grams of fiber, which helps keep you feeling full for longer and decreases the desire to snack between meals. The high protein and fiber content helps manage blood-sugar levels and regulate energy. They are my favorite legume! I like to use them in soups and curries.

QUINOA, while used as a grain, is technically a seed! Gluten-free and high in protein, quinoa is fiber-rich and mineral-packed. It promotes energy production, stabilizes appetite, and reduces cravings. The high fiber content provides a satisfyingly full feeling, which is why it is a great idea to add a scoop to a soup or salad, serve it with curry, or use it as the base of a bowl with roasted veggies and tahini sauce.

TEMPEH contains protein, some B vitamins, and some cell-supportive minerals. It is a cultured food with diverse cooking applications, such as sautéing or roasting, and can be flavored in many ways, like with a sweet and smoky marinade or dressed with a creamy almond sauce.

Nuts & Seeds

＊**ALMONDS** are an excellent source of important antioxidants, including vitamin E. Because of their high fat, fiber, and protein content, a small amount will help to curb hunger cravings. I use them to add crunch, flavor, and nutrition to all sorts of meals. **Almond meal** is one of my favorite ingredients for gluten-free baking. **Almond butter** (raw when possible) can be added to salad dressings or smoothies.

BRAZIL NUTS are loaded with healthy fats and are a rich and reliable source of selenium. I love to eat them as they are or pulse them into a dust with garlic and sea salt to sprinkle on salads.

CASHEWS are an excellent source of healthy fats and contain many minerals too. They have a lower fat content and higher protein and carbohydrate content than most other nuts, making them an excellent way to thicken sauces or creams or to build desserts.

CHIA SEEDS are a great source of essential fatty acids, plant-based protein, and dietary fiber. They

can be made into savory sauces or sweet puddings or simply added to smoothies. I often use them to help bind baked goods as well.

FLAX is fiber- and nutrient-rich and helps to pull toxins from the body. I use flax meal to add nutrients and fiber to smoothies, or a mix of flax and water to substitute for an egg in some of my baking.

HEMP HEARTS are rich in healthy fats and plant-based protein. Combined, these two macronutrients help to curb hunger cravings by regulating blood-sugar levels, thereby supporting energy management throughout the day. They are also a plentiful source of fiber and minerals. Whether in a savory sauce or sweet plant-based milk, they are one of my favorite ways to add creaminess and nutrition to a dish.

PINE NUTS are high in minerals and vitamins, rich in healthy fats, packed with protein, and full of flavor. They're heart-healthy and perfect for making creamy sauces or adding toasted texture to meals as a garnish. Make sure to store pine nuts in the fridge.

PSYLLIUM is very high in gut-supportive soluble fiber and can help induce a sense of satiety, making you less likely to overeat or have sugar cravings; be sure to drink plenty of water if consuming it as a fiber supplement. Incorporate psyllium into baking or a warm oatmeal, add to your favorite smoothie, or simply mix on its own into warm water.

PUMPKIN SEEDS, also known as pepitas, are rich in magnesium and tryptophan, an amino acid that supports sleep and acts as a "feel good" hormone. I like them toasted and tossed in salads or blended into sauces!

SUNFLOWER SEEDS contain selenium, a mineral involved in your antioxidant defense system that protects against cellular damage. They are also high in magnesium, which supports muscle function, a deep sleep, and a healthy nervous system. I love to use toasted sunflower seeds to garnish roasted veggies and salads.

TAHINI, a creamy butter made from ground sesame seeds, is high in healthy fats, copper, and iron. Its nutrients help to balance blood-sugar levels and promote skin health. I often use tahini to thicken and add flavor to dressings and sauces.

WALNUTS are high in omega-3 fatty acids, which can help the body manage stress! I like to incorporate them into desserts or use them as a taco stuffing. They also make great veggie pâtés and spreads.

Pantry & Fridge Essentials

APPLE CIDER VINEGAR is thought to aid digestion by raising acid levels in the stomach. It is an amazing way to add brightness to a soup, sauce, or salad dressing. You can also drink it on its own in warm water.

ASHWAGANDHA is an adaptogen thought to help the body manage and adapt to stress, and may also enhance performance. It is a root that is ground into a powder and can be added to smoothies and sweets.

BALSAMIC VINEGAR is a great way to add a tangy sweetness and more acid to a dish. It has trace minerals and antioxidants, but it is mostly just an amazing way to build depth of flavor.

CACAO, not to be confused with cocoa, is an amazing ingredient whether in the form of a powder or a nib. It is high in antioxidants and magnesium and is the best way to build chocolate flavor into desserts and smoothies. Make sure you purchase unsweetened so you can add your own sweetness as you like.

CANNED COLD-WATER FISH are high in omega-3s and are an excellent protein source. Keep **sardines**, **salmon**, **mackerel**, **anchovies**, and **herring** on hand to add to sauces, put in wraps, or make fish cakes.

CAPERS are, by far, one of the ingredients I most love to build flavor with. They can be used on any

meal or in any dressing–to me, they are the ultimate way to season. They are pickled flower buds that are chewy, salty, and briny!

CHLORELLA AND SPIRULINA are blue-green algae packed with protein, antioxidants, chlorophyll, and B vitamins. They can bind to harmful metals and toxins to help remove them from the body. Considered to be some of the most nutrient-dense ingredients you can eat, they are a great way to boost a smoothie or dessert!

CHLOROPHYLL is high in antioxidants and may help protect the body from disease. It is thought to work as a vasodilator, allowing for greater blood flow and therefore oxygen transport throughout the body, increasing energy and mental focus. It is a great way to add an extra dose of health to a mint tea or smoothie.

COCONUT FLAKES AND COCONUT MILK contain healthy fat and minerals. I love using **coconut milk** for sauces and soups because it adds a decadent texture and taste. **Coconut flakes** are great for texture and have all the same health benefits. Be sure to buy unsweetened.

COCONUT OIL (virgin), used in moderation, is a great fat for baking and cooking. It has a unique flavor and can help prolong energy when eaten in a sweet treat. Avoid hydrogenated coconut oil.

DIJON MUSTARD is made from mustard seeds, which are full of phytonutrients and antioxidants and are thought to provide an array of health benefits! I use Dijon, my favorite condiment, in sauces, salads, soups, and truly anything I can!

EGGS are a good source of protein, iodine, and vitamins B12 and D. Eating high-protein foods helps to support metabolic health, and eggs are a perfect way to incorporate more protein into your diet. I would add eggs to just about anything, but my favorite way to eat them is in a simple scramble.

* **FISH SAUCE**, made from fermented fish, is salty and very umami. It can be used in marinades or as a seasoning, and it gives sauces and dips a complex, rich saltiness.

GHEE AND BUTTER are very similar. Butter is made from milk fat. To make clarified butter or ghee, butter is melted to separate the milk solids from the fat. The reserved fat is the ghee. Ghee can withstand higher cooking temperatures than butter. Both are used for cooking and can provide a creamy taste.

HEMP OIL AND UDO'S OIL are my favorite oils that I like to blend in moderation into smoothies or coffees to make them frothier. Hemp oil is made from hemp seeds, and Udo's oil is a combo of flax, sunflower, and sesame oils. Both contain some omega-3s, which support healthy joints and skin. MCT oil from coconuts is another option to add to drinks and has been thought to help with energy management.

KIMCHI AND SAUERKRAUT are high in fiber and probiotics, and are a great way to support healthy gut flora and improve digestion, mood, and energy. Fermented cabbage may also aid with detoxification. Add chopped sauerkraut to collard wraps or salads, or use kimchi to top soups, sautés, and bowls.

MACA is a cruciferous root that is ground into a powder. It contains nutrients that support the endocrine system, and is a good source of iron and vitamin C. I add it unnoticed to desserts and smoothies!

* **MISO PASTE** (organic) is high in minerals, protein, and fiber. This salty, nutrition-boosting flavor maker is an amazing addition to sautés, soups, and sauces.

MUSHROOM POWDERS, like **reishi**, **lion's mane**, **cordyceps**, **chaga**, and more, have a range of benefits, supporting everything from the immune system to longevity to memory. Find the powder that serves you best. I like to keep these on hand to add to smoothies and hot drinks for an added boost of support.

NUTRITIONAL YEAST is abundant in B vitamins, vital for optimal carbohydrate, fat, and protein metabolism. It is also a source of plant-based protein! Mix it into sauces and dressings for added flavor and texture.

OLIVE OIL (organic extra virgin) is my favorite oil to cook with. It contains vitamin E and is high in monounsaturated fat.

OLIVES add healthy fats and a beautiful salty, buttery texture. They promote cellular health and are high in vitamin E, a potent antioxidant. I love cooking with green olives in particular.

RICE VINEGAR is a light vinegar made from fermented rice. It adds a beautiful subtle acid to stir-fries, marinades, and dressings. Purchase unseasoned versions to avoid added salt, sugar, and MSG.

SEAWEEDS offer a huge range of minerals. They are high in iodine, necessary for thyroid health, and are a good source of folate and magnesium. **Wakame** is a great addition to soups and salads. **Nori** is used for sushi or nori wraps, and I add **dulse** to smoothies and soups. Power-packed with nutrients, seaweeds add a lovely saltiness and texture to recipes.

* **TAMARI** (gluten-free, organic) is a fermented soy seasoning, and I love it. You will notice I use it to enhance flavor and depth throughout the book. It contains some minerals but is mostly sodium, so use it in moderation if you are on a low-sodium diet. It can be replaced with Bragg Liquid Aminos if avoiding tamari or coconut aminos if avoiding soy.

* **TOASTED SESAME OIL** is a super-nutty, aromatic finishing oil pressed from toasted sesame seeds. It is an amazing way to season a side dish or a sauce.

* **UME PLUM VINEGAR** is the briny liquid left after pickling umeboshi plums. It is tart and salty and provides a little acid when sprinkled on steamed or sautéed vegetables or used in a dressing.

Glossary of Vitamins & Minerals

For those of you who want to know a bit more about the vitamins and minerals I talk about in the book, here's an overview to guide you through the basics.

VITAMIN A promotes healthy eyes, supports the immune system, and maintains the integrity of blood cells and epithelial tissue, which lines the gut, lungs, and reproductive tract.

B VITAMINS boost mood; aid digestion; support cellular metabolism; enhance the metabolic, cardiovascular, immune, endocrine, musculoskeletal, hepatic, and nervous systems; promote healthy skin, nails, and hair; regulate gene expression and DNA repair; and help break down and release energy from food.

> **B1 (thiamine)** supports energy production and the nervous, cardiovascular, and immune systems.

> **B2 (riboflavin)** works as an antioxidant to help fight free radicals; is important for the production of red blood cells, which transport oxygen throughout the body; and supports the immune, cardiovascular, and nervous systems.

> **B3 (niacin)** promotes healthy skin, supports healthy brain functioning, helps maintain good blood circulation, and helps the digestive tract absorb sufficient proteins, carbohydrates, and fats.

B5 (pantothenic acid) helps maintain a healthy digestive tract and supports the endocrine and hepatic systems.

B6 (pyridoxine) promotes healthy brain function, supports the immune system, boosts mood, and enhances sleep patterns because it helps the body produce serotonin, melatonin, and norepinephrine (a stress hormone).

B7 (biotin) builds healthy skin, nails, and hair; helps metabolize proteins, fats, and carbohydrates; and supports the nervous, integumentary, and hepatic systems.

B9 (folate) is an essential element in the formation of red blood cells, a significant contributor to building and repairing skin cells in the human body. The cells found in the lining of the small intestine are also fabricated from this vitamin. Folate is extra important for pregnant women because it helps support the healthy growth of the baby.

B12 (cobalamin) promotes energy and DNA production, works with vitamin B9 to produce red blood cells and help iron do its job, and supports the metabolic, cardiovascular, immune, endocrine, musculoskeletal, and nervous systems.

VITAMIN C is required for the formation of collagen and connective tissue. It promotes healthy skin, as well as blood vessel, tooth, and bone integrity, and supports the immune system.

VITAMIN D is essential for bone health, promotes healthy blood pressure, and supports the maturation of white blood cells, insulin secretion, and the immune, cardiovascular, and endocrine systems.

VITAMIN E is immune-enhancing, supports proper nerve and muscle function, promotes healthy circulation and tissue regeneration, and is essential for maintaining healthy skin.

VITAMIN K supports healthy blood clotting and strengthens the skeletal system.

CALCIUM is essential for strong bone structure, teeth, muscle tissue, and nerve function, and helps balance blood pH.

COPPER is critical for building red blood cells, is required for the synthesis of collagen, and is the main structural protein in blood vessels, connective tissue, and bone.

IRON is essential for transporting and releasing oxygen and energy to the body (for less fatigue) and supports the metabolic, nervous, immune, and reproductive systems.

MAGNESIUM helps alleviate PMS symptoms, reduces inflammation, anxiety, and migraines, supports healthy blood pressure and a healthy heart, enhances sleep quality, and boosts physical performance.

MANGANESE supports normal bone and collagen formation and promotes brain health.

PHOSPHORUS supports energy production and cell growth and repair, regulates healthy pH, and promotes healthy kidney functions.

ZINC is essential for numerous enzyme functions and cellular processes. It plays a structural role in cell membranes and proteins, and supports the immune system.

Nutrition Chart

	Dairy-Free	Gluten-Free	Grain-Free	Oil-Free	Vegan	Protein	High Protein
TONICS, PLANT MILKS & SMOOTHIES							
Lemon Ginger Tonic	♥	♥	♥	♥	♥		
Turmeric Tonic	♥	♥			♥		
Electrolyte Chlorophyll Drink	♥	♥	♥	♥	♥		
Blended Morning Coffee	♥	♥	♥		♥	♥	
Brazil Nut Ginger Milk	♥	♥	♥		♥		
Almond Lavender Cardamom Milk	♥	♥	♥		♥		
Pumpkin Seed Coconut Milk	♥	♥	♥		♥		
Strawberry Hemp Milk	♥	♥	♥		♥	♥	
Cacao Cold Brew Smoothie	♥	♥	♥		♥	♥	
Turmeric Orange Strawberry Smoothie	♥	♥	♥		♥		
Mixed Berry Antioxidant Smoothie	♥	♥	♥		♥	♥	
Mint Chocolate Smoothie	♥	♥	♥		♥	♥	
Acai Bowl	♥	♥	♥		♥	♥	
BREAKFAST & BRUNCH							
Coconut Berry Chia Pudding	♥	♥	♥		♥		
Tahini Honey Parfait	♥	♥		♥		♥	
Blueberry Vanilla Overnight Oats	♥	♥		♥	♥	♥	
Tahini Orange Granola	♥	♥			♥		
Breakfast Scones	♥	♥			♥	♥	
Buckwheat Crepes	♥	♥	♥				♥
Zucchini Parmesan Egg Muffins		♥	♥	♥			♥
Spiced Tofu Scramble	♥	♥			♥	♥	♥
Spring Vegetable Frittata	♥	♥					♥
Cauliflower Benny with Spinach & Pesto	♥	♥	♥				
Eggplant Shakshuka	♥	♥	♥				♥
BREADS & CRACKERS							
Broccoli Parmesan Mini Flatbreads		♥	♥	♥			♥
Sesame Flax Crackers	♥	♥	♥		♥	♥	
Curried Socca	♥	♥	♥		♥	♥	
Seed Bread	♥	♥	♥	♥	♥	♥	
Rosemary Onion Skillet Bread	♥	♥	♥			♥	
PROTEIN ADD-ONS							
Marinated Mediterranean Tofu	♥	♥			♥		♥
Smoky Maple Tempeh	♥	♥	♥		♥		♥
Dill Dijon Salmon Bites	♥	♥	♥				♥
Miso Maple Salmon Bites	♥	♥	♥				♥
White Fish & Potato Cakes	♥	♥	♥				♥
Chicken Satay	♥	♥	♥				♥
Ginger Cilantro Turkey Meatballs	♥	♥	♥				♥
Herbed Butter Beans	♥	♥	♥		♥	♥	
OTHER ESSENTIALS							
Spiced Mixed Nuts & Seeds	♥	♥	♥	♥	♥	♥	
Caramelized Balsamic Onions	♥	♥	♥		♥		

Fiber	High Fiber	Super Fiber	Low Carbohydrate	Recommended Recipe	Anti-Inflammatory	Beauty + Anti-Aging	Cellular Building + Healing	Detoxifying	Energy + Focus	Gut Health	Immune Support	Mood Balancing
						♥				♥	♥	
			♥		♥	♥					♥	
						♥	♥					♥
♥			♥						♥			♥
			♥		♥						♥	
			♥			♥						♥
♥			♥		♥	♥			♥			
		♥					♥		♥			♥
		♥		♥		♥		♥				
		♥			♥		♥			♥		♥
	♥					♥		♥				
	♥				♥				♥	♥		
	♥					♥					♥	♥
♥						♥				♥	♥	
♥									♥			♥
♥							♥		♥	♥		
♥			♥						♥			♥
♥			♥		♥					♥		♥
	♥		♥	♥		♥	♥		♥			
	♥		♥		♥	♥				♥		
	♥		♥		♥	♥						♥
♥			♥				♥					
	♥		♥						♥	♥		
♥			♥		♥				♥			
♥			♥	♥		♥				♥		♥
♥										♥		♥
			♥			♥	♥					♥
			♥				♥			♥		
			♥		♥		♥					
♥									♥		♥	♥
			♥			♥						♥
			♥						♥		♥	
		♥					♥				♥	♥
♥			♥				♥		♥			♥
								♥		♥		

	Dairy-Free	Gluten-Free	Grain-Free	Oil-Free	Vegan	Protein	High Protein
Quick Pickled Jalapeños or Onions	♥	♥	♥	♥	♥		
Rainbow Escabeche	♥	♥	♥	♥	♥		
Pistachio Dukkah	♥	♥	♥	♥	♥	♥	
SAUCES							
Hemp Chili Crema	♥	♥	♥	♥	♥	♥	
Basil Pesto	♥	♥	♥		♥		
Cilantro Sunflower Pesto	♥	♥	♥		♥		
Chermoula	♥	♥	♥		♥		
Chimichurri	♥	♥	♥		♥		
Salsa Verde	♥	♥	♥		♥		
Dijon Vinaigrette	♥	♥	♥		♥		
Tahini Ginger Sauce	♥	♥	♥		♥	♥	
Coconut Almond Sauce	♥	♥	♥	♥	♥	♥	
Savory Tomato Sauce	♥	♥	♥		♥		
SPREADS							
Chunky Guacamole	♥	♥	♥		♥		
Beet Thyme Cashew Dip	♥	♥	♥		♥	♥	
Roasted Carrot Tahini Dip	♥	♥	♥		♥	♥	
Chipotle Cashew Aioli	♥	♥	♥		♥	♥	
Edamame Cilantro Hummus	♥	♥	♥		♥	♥	
SOUPS							
Lemon Lentil Soup	♥	♥	♥		♥	♥	
Cauliflower Leek Soup	♥	♥	♥		♥	♥	
Green Detox Soup	♥	♥	♥		♥		
Butternut Squash Soup	♥	♥	♥		♥		
Creamy Cashew Mushroom Soup	♥	♥	♥		♥	♥	
Rainbow Miso Soup	♥	♥	♥		♥	♥	
SALADS							
Cucumber Herb Salad	♥	♥	♥			♥	
Roasted Beet Carpaccio with Herb Salad	♥	♥	♥		♥		
Watermelon Feta Salad	♥	♥	♥		♥	♥	
Herby Greek Salad	♥	♥	♥		♥	♥	
Everyday Detox Salad	♥	♥	♥		♥	♥	
Kale Pine Nut Caesar	♥	♥	♥		♥		
Sesame Gomae	♥	♥	♥		♥		♥
Creamy Avo Cumin Coleslaw	♥	♥	♥		♥	♥	
Arugula & Roasted Squash Salad	♥	♥	♥		♥		
Garden Salad with Creamy Tahini Dressing	♥	♥	♥		♥		
SIDES							
Sweet Potato Fries	♥	♥	♥		♥		
Buttered Sweet Potato Ribbons		♥	♥				
Acorn Squash with Ginger & Shallot	♥	♥	♥				
Lemon Garlic Spinach	♥	♥	♥		♥	♥	
Sautéed Greens with Toasted Spices	♥	♥	♥		♥		

Fiber	High Fiber	Super Fiber	Low Carbohydrate	Recommended Recipe	Anti-Inflammatory	Beauty + Anti-Aging	Cellular Building + Healing	Detoxifying	Energy + Focus	Gut Health	Immune Support	Mood Balancing
			♥							♥	♥	
										♥	♥	
			♥	♥	♥	♥						♥
			♥	♥		♥	♥				♥	
			♥		♥	♥	♥				♥	
			♥			♥		♥	♥			
			♥		♥	♥		♥				
			♥			♥				♥	♥	
			♥			♥			♥	♥		
			♥			♥	♥					
♥			♥			♥	♥					
	♥					♥	♥					
	♥		♥			♥			♥			
			♥				♥		♥			
			♥			♥		♥		♥	♥	
♥			♥	♥			♥		♥	♥		
	♥				♥			♥		♥		
♥			♥		♥	♥		♥		♥	♥	
♥			♥			♥	♥				♥	
		♥		♥		♥			♥			♥
♥						♥		♥		♥		
	♥				♥		♥	♥				♥
			♥			♥				♥		♥
♥			♥	♥		♥		♥			♥	
♥			♥				♥				♥	
	♥		♥	♥		♥				♥	♥	
	♥		♥	♥		♥				♥		
	♥		♥			♥	♥		♥			
	♥					♥				♥		♥
♥						♥					♥	
	♥					♥	♥				♥	
♥			♥			♥	♥				♥	♥
			♥		♥		♥			♥		

	Dairy-Free	Gluten-Free	Grain-Free	Oil-Free	Vegan	Protein	High Protein
Thyme Oysters Mushrooms	♥	♥			♥	♥	
Garlicky Roasted Portobellos	♥	♥	♥		♥		
Citrus & Sesame Cabbage	♥	♥	♥		♥		
Caper Feta Broccoli	♥	♥	♥		♥	♥	
Salt & Pepper Veggies	♥	♥	♥		♥	♥	
Wilted Swiss Chard with White Beans & Capers	♥	♥			♥	♥	
Lemongrass Cauliflower & Sweet Potato with Turmeric	♥	♥	♥		♥		
WRAPS & ROLLS							
Sweet Potato & Avo Sushi with Cauliflower Rice	♥	♥			♥	♥	
Rainbow Salad Rolls	♥	♥			♥		
Raw Walnut Lettuce Tacos	♥	♥	♥	♥	♥		
Lentil Lettuce Cups with Tahini Ginger Sauce	♥	♥	♥		♥		♥
NOODLES & BOWLS							
Cashew Cacio e Pepe over Spaghetti Squash	♥	♥			♥	♥	
Lentil Bolognese over Zucchini Noodles	♥	♥	♥		♥		♥
Green Curry with Zucchini Noodles	♥	♥	♥		♥	♥	
Shiitake Ginger Mung Bean Noodles	♥	♥	♥		♥		
Roasted Rainbow Veggie Noodle Bowl	♥	♥			♥	♥	
Cauliflower Fried Rice	♥	♥	♥		♥		
Summer Pesto Quinoa Bowl	♥	♥			♥		
Red Lentil Dal	♥	♥			♥		♥
Bean-Free Butternut Chili	♥	♥	♥		♥		♥
PLATES							
Zucchini Enchiladas	♥	♥	♥		♥	♥	
Wild Mushrooms with Pine Nut Cream on Sweet Potato Toasts	♥	♥	♥		♥		
Roasted Carrots over Lentils & Lemon Cumin Yogurt	♥	♥	♥		♥	♥	
Mung Bean Falafel with Tzatziki & Greek Salad	♥	♥	♥		♥	♥	
Herbed Lemon White Fish over Vegetables		♥	♥				♥
Sesame Orange Salmon with Broccoli & Bok Choy	♥	♥	♥				♥
Almond-Crusted White Fish in Savory Tomato Sauce	♥	♥	♥				♥
Chard-Wrapped Miso Fish with Acorn Squash		♥					♥
Chimichurri Chicken with Lemon Garlic Veggie Ribbons	♥	♥	♥				♥
SWEETS							
Apple Maple Millet Muffins	♥	♥			♥		
Raspberry Coconut Muffins	♥	♥	♥				
Banana Bread Muffins	♥	♥	♥		♥		
Golden Dreamsicles	♥	♥	♥	♥	♥		
Hazelnut Goji Berry Freezer Fudge	♥	♥	♥		♥		
Salted Chocolate Cookies	♥	♥	♥	♥	♥	♥	
Citrus Olive Oil Cake	♥	♥	♥				
Raw Blackberry Cashew Cheesecake	♥	♥	♥		♥		
Blueberry Squares	♥	♥	♥				

Fiber	High Fiber	Super Fiber	Low Carbohydrate	Recommended Recipe	Anti-Inflammatory	Beauty + Anti-Aging	Cellular Building + Healing	Detoxifying	Energy + Focus	Gut Health	Immune Support	Mood Balancing
♥			♥		♥		♥				♥	
			♥				♥				♥	
♥			♥			♥	♥	♥				
♥			♥				♥			♥		
♥			♥		♥					♥	♥	
	♥				♥	♥					♥	
		♥		♥		♥	♥					♥
	♥					♥	♥					
		♥					♥			♥	♥	
	♥						♥		♥			♥
		♥		♥			♥		♥			♥
	♥		♥			♥		♥		♥		
♥					♥	♥						
		♥	♥		♥	♥				♥		
	♥		♥	♥		♥	♥			♥		
	♥								♥			♥
	♥		♥		♥		♥		♥			♥
		♥	♥		♥				♥			
	♥		♥				♥				♥	♥
		♥					♥		♥		♥	
		♥			♥				♥	♥		
		♥		♥			♥		♥	♥		
	♥		♥			♥	♥					♥
♥			♥		♥	♥	♥					♥
		♥	♥	♥		♥						
	♥		♥				♥				♥	♥
	♥		♥			♥	♥		♥			
♥												♥
♥			♥						♥			♥
♥												♥
					♥						♥	
♥						♥						♥
♥			♥						♥			♥
			♥						♥			♥
♥												♥
		♥			♥				♥			♥

Acknowledgments

Thank you to everyone who played a part in creating this book–for every house we stayed in, and every kitchen and garden we cooked from–I couldn't have done it without your endless support.

To Lindsay, Whitney, and the team at Appetite, thank you for being eternally patient with my ever-changing vision!

I want to thank the people who contributed to this book. Sophie, for being the glue of our traveling photo shoot, and for all the extra moments of support. Robyn, for being the original muse and inspiration, and for all your beautiful photos. Tara, for hair, makeup, and wardrobe styling, and for bringing your generous spirit to this project. Thank you to Clea, for helping put together the first *giant* draft. To Callum and Hank, for being part of the adventure. To Steve, for motivating me to just do it–this literally wouldn't have happened without your encouragement. To Penni, for pushing me to finish the original proposal, and pulling the creativity out of me when it was stuck. To Azita, for your support through some of the hardest moments, and for helping me get some of the first words on paper!

There are more people I'd like to thank for pushing this over the finish line. Michael, you showed up like a brother and helped me with the writing and look of the book from front to back (twice) when I was too sick to take it on myself. I will be forever grateful. Thank you to Marissa, for reviewing my nutrition queries and questions (even when I sent them last minute). To Colette, for reading through (and endlessly listening to me as I questioned) my every thought and word. To Lexy, for the late night proofreading and pep talks, and for taking care of my sister. To Winona, for helping with the styling and photo shoot on Kauai. Zack, thank you for your endless support, even when I was on the 2,000th round of book edits.

To the people who are always in my corner: Deena, Thuy, Dave, and Ben–thank you for being my ultimate cheerleaders. Rach, for not letting me quit. Dustin, for facilitating so many adventures. Ariel, Serinda, Kristin, and Alandra, for helping me stay balanced. Danielle and Babs, for believing in me and for giving enthusiastic and loving feedback. Erica and Claire, for always treating me like family. Vienna, for inspiring me to keep going as we both wrote our books. Ash, for encouraging me to embrace my artistry. And Dr. Hyman, for keeping me healthy.

Lastly, to my family: Mom, thank you for having my back throughout everything, for the goddess dips, and for always driving me forward. To Tom and Gail, for keeping the family together! To Dad, for inspiring me to always push the boundaries, to reimagine the world, and to flavor it however I want. To Gabby, for being my heart and the ultimate taste tester. To Auntie Margie, for testing so many recipes. And to Annamarie, for always helping; your support means the world.

Index

C

Mikaela Reuben is a nutritional chef who brings a sprinkling of magic to everything she does. For the past 15 years she has cooked for private celebrity clients and athletes including Ryan Reynolds and Blake Lively, Karlie Kloss, Maya Gabeira, Owen Wilson, Hugh Jackman, Woody Harrelson, Ben Stiller, and Brie Larson. Mikaela also consults in different culinary capacities for wellness retreats, lifestyle brands, and doctors, including Dr. Mark Hyman, The Class, Lululemon, Summit Series, and Free People. Mikaela has been featured in *Vogue*, *Self*, *Forbes*, and *Well+Good*. @mikaelareuben

Photography by Robyn Penn

appetite
by RANDOM HOUSE

www.penguinrandomhouse.ca